Mr Lewisham

A LIFE OF LES STANNARD

Mr Lewisham

A LIFE OF LES STANNARD

HELEN TOMKINS

Lewisham Pensioners' Forum
LONDON

First published in Great Britain 2001
by Lewisham Pensioners' Forum
120 Rushey Green
London SE6 4HQ

ISBN 0-9540989-0-0

Set in Linotype Sabon by
Rowland Phototypesetting Ltd
Printed in Great Britain by
St Edmundsbury Press Ltd
both of Bury St Edmunds, Suffolk

A CIP catalogue record for this book
is available from the British Library

For
Gladys, Lesley, Matthew and Owen

'Never trust biographies.
Too many events in a man's life are invisible'

Fugitive Pieces, Anne Michaels, Bloomsbury, 1997

'His work endures and will endure'

Richard Balfe MEP

Ethics for Everyman

Throwing a bomb is bad,
Dropping a bomb is good:
Terror, no need to add,
Depends on who's wearing the hood.

Kangaroo courts are wrong,
Specialist courts are right;
Discipline by the strong
Is fair if your collar is white.

Company output 'soars',
Wages of course 'explode';
Profits deserve applause,
Pay-claims the criminal code.

Daily the Church declares
Betting-shops are a curse;
Gambling with stocks and shares
Enlarges the national purse.

Workers are 'absentees',
Businessmen 'relax',
Different as chalk and cheese;
Social morality
Has a duality —
One for each side of the tracks.

Roger Woddis, 1978

CONTENTS

FOREWORD
by Jack Jones

'Pensioners unite and organise' was the theme of much of Les Stannard's activities over many years, up to his passing. In this setting he drew inspiration and ideas from his trade union days and his political associations.

His extensive efforts for pensioners in Lewisham are detailed in this record of his life. In this connection I got to know him best, following my own first links with Lewisham Borough Council leaders to whom I conveyed information about consultation with pensioners in the Southwark borough.

Les Stannard was like a fiery rocket, moving fast and gaining momentum as it progressed. To say I was impressed by his enthusiasm and commitment would be an understatement. His contribution to the advance of pensioners' interests in Lewisham was absolutely outstanding. It is to the credit of so many of his friends and supporters in the borough that this story of his life should be published.

In the wider field of the pensioners' movement Les rendered great work as a Vice-President of the British Pensioners and Trade Union Action Association and also the National Pensioners' Convention. His clarity and commitment endeared him to masses of people whom he encountered in many areas of the country.

Although the groundwork for pensioners' travel concessions in London was laid as far back as 1969, they were speeded up and greatly extended with the inception of the Greater London Council. What is known as the 'Freedom Pass' for pensioners in Greater London today owes a lot to the efforts of Les. For me and so many others he was a splendid and reliable colleague who played well in the leading team of pensioner activists.

Many facets of his life are covered in this volume. His deep feelings about events in the Electrical Trade Union and his consistent loyalty to his political ideals were matched by his enthusiastic support for Millwall Football Club. Usually when I met him, our conversation would include much banter about Millwall FC and I soon learnt that I had to exercise caution in any criticism I was inclined to offer!

Helen Tomkins, who has discharged the onerous task of bringing this book together with remarkable efficiency, has included personal statements and material bringing to light the varied aspects of Les Stannard's life. She deserves the warmest thanks and deep appreciation from all who knew Les. Her work as the author of this volume is based upon her close contact with his work for pensioners in Lewisham.

Les Stannard was an all round and honest fighter, clear-minded and firm in his approach. He will long be remembered. I am sure his great hope would be that the example he set in fighting for pensioner justice will be followed by increasing numbers of younger people in the future. It is a worthy record and I hope it will be widely read.

INTRODUCTION

When I was growing up in a predominantly Catholic country after the end of World War II the Catholic Church was engaged in a powerful underground war against Communism. This was in the aftermath of the war against Hitler's Germany but also of the Spanish Civil War in which the Catholic Church stood firmly on the side of General Franco.

In my country the majority of adults attended church at least once a day and some took an active part in the organisation called Catholic Action which at that time was working to confront the evils of Communism. Paradoxically, another Catholic organisation, with a similar name (Catholic Social Action), was based on quite different principles and worked exclusively towards creating a social conscience about post-war poverty on the islands and, in time, formed the model for social work training.

This was a traditional society in which women were the mothers and home-makers, rarely taking part in the male-oriented world of politics and work; the Pope nevertheless urged women into public life because he wanted to warn them not to be tempted by so-called 'totalitarian' regimes which promised them equality with men, relief from domestic burdens, public crèches, free education and health – all aimed at taking women outside the home![1] I recollect that women played a prominent part in Catholic Action, attending frequent meetings on Church premises. The priests actively encouraged women's involvement and their husbands (who would not have wanted their wives to leave the home for anything other than domestic reasons) did not seem to object to the frequency and the length of the Catholic Action meetings, even if this meant that someone had to be found to look after the children! Through this organisation the faithful were issued with small cards (similar to, and the same size as, the devotional holy pictures featuring images of saints, which they were accustomed to placing between the leaves of their missals or prayer books). These particular cards were different. Blank on one side, the other side showed a black silhouette of a man's face and shoulders. Beneath this icon were the words:

THIS MAN IS A COMMUNIST
HE HAS A SOUL
PRAY FOR HIM

I had no political education at all; our religion was so deeply embedded in our daily lives that whatever political message the Church wanted its adherents to follow was automatically woven into its teachings, sermons and Church newspapers and thus absorbed without question by most people. That was the intention: the Church knew what was best for us and good Catholics were not supposed to hold any opinions of their own on political issues but simply to accept the Church's stance. No wonder it supported Fascism in the thirties. In fact it would be true to say that politics and religion were interchangeable. Growing children are not, usually, very concerned about politics so I was not greatly affected by what was going on. Yet, the black silhouette

[1] 'Women's Duties in Social and Political Life' 21.10.45 from *Selected Letters and Addresses of Pius XII 1949*.

troubled me. The image was sinister and seemed to contradict the message 'pray for him'. I think I came to the conclusion that the message was deceitful and hypocritical – after all, praying for someone meant that you cared about them, yet the featureless face did not inspire one to warmth or affection. It inspired fear and mistrust. The Church's response, then as now, was that Catholics should love the sinner but hate the sin but there was little evidence that anyone followed this maxim. Communists, then, were to be both feared and detested.

In Britain a 'cell' movement had been established in the fifties by an eminent Jesuit, with the aim of organising people by emulating Communist Party methods and infiltrating the Communist Party of Great Britain and the trade unions. Catholic Social Action in Britain encouraged Catholics to join trade unions, to rise through the ranks and to persuade Communists to leave the Party.

Many years later, in south-east London, I came to know Les Stannard, then Honorary Secretary of Lewisham Pensioners' Forum, when he offered me the job of co-ordinator. This was 1988 – right in the middle of the Thatcher reign. The Vietnam War had been fought and lost with far-reaching consequences and obscene loss of life. Communism was still despised by the amassed right-wing forces all over the world, though in the USSR strong forces were working which a few years later resulted in the fall of Soviet Communism, the demolition of the Berlin Wall and the downfall of Communist governments throughout Eastern Europe, the outcome of which has been further and continuing tragedy. Cruise missiles were growing instead of wild flowers on Greenham Common.

The Catholic Church itself was undergoing change, particularly in South America where the priests who came to be known as Liberation Theologists bravely fought and died on the side of poor and landless people, causing not a little disquiet to the reactionary Vatican forces. Archbishop Camara of Brazil put this moral dilemma into words when he said, 'When I give food to the poor they call me a saint; when I ask why the poor have no food they call me a Communist'.

As this work will show, Les Stannard rarely, if ever, spoke about what his Communism meant to him. It was clear to me, as I worked closely with him, that he was 'left-wing', but it was a very long time before I realised that the man I was getting to know so well and with whom I worked closely for the greater part of three years was a Communist and had been a member of the Communist Party of Great Britain for about 50 years – since the beginning of the Spanish Civil War, in fact, when his first political action was in support of Aid for Spain.

Les Stannard was the only Communist I have ever known as a colleague and friend. Had he not made such a lasting impression on me I would never have come to write about his life. Unlike the black icon I grew up with, Les inspired only warmth, affection and enormous respect amongst all who knew him. He epitomised incorruptibility, goodness, love for humanity and – exceptionally – respect for those who did not share his views and those who hated what he stood for. He had experienced the antagonism of Catholic Social Action adherents in the 1950s but had never once allowed himself to be lowered into any display of animosity towards those whose political views could not have been more different from his own. Moreover, he would have been the first to admit that some Communist governments tortured, persecuted and murdered Catholics.

While working on the account of his life over two years I have come to learn a great deal more about his character. All that has been written about him in the final section of this work might sound so easy. Of course we would all like to empathise with fellow committee members, and to be diplomatic in our liaisons with colleagues. In theory we do respect our opponents; we do try to make sure that we are well informed before we speak. We think our emotions and our thinking processes work together. We say we wish our enemies well but find it difficult not to speak against them behind their backs. In examining myself in all these respects I began to realise just how difficult it is to do what Les did – not just occasionally but over time, even when he was discouraged and angered, when everything seemed to be going against what he and his colleagues were striving for.

Les Stannard was an exceptional person. Some who knew him have said that he was a most unusual kind of Communist but that may only mean that he did not fit the public image of what a Communist is. The account of his life which follows is, no doubt, flawed and incomplete. I experienced difficulty in obtaining crucial information from some sources and the one person who could correct its errors and omissions is not here to do so.

For all those errors and omissions I must take full responsibility.

ACKNOWLEDGEMENTS

I started to work on this biography in July 1998 and have received help, advice and support from a number of friends, former colleagues and institutions as well as Les Stannard's own family, friends and former colleagues.

I would first like to express my greatest debt of thanks to the person who helped me most of all by her willingness to read and comment critically on numerous drafts and on most of the final, complete, draft. My friend and former colleague, Dr Pam Percy, worked speedily to return my work to me (fitting it into her own punishing work schedule), and her insights were always sensitive and perceptive, her remarks constructive and sharp yet always encouraging and enlightening. Her generosity and willingness to support and advise me were unlimited.

I thank Les's widow Mrs Gladys Stannard, his daughter and son-in-law Lesley and John Griffiths, his brother Stanley Stannard, his nephews Dr Kevin Stannard (Head of the Geography Department at Eton College) and Michael Stannard and their mother Mrs Daphne Stannard, as well as Les's mother-in-law Mrs Vera Croot, his aunt, Mrs Nell Bryett, and his cousin, John Hoadley. Michael Stannard supplied me with much of the material on the Stannard grandparents and ancestors and was always generous and responsive to my many telephone calls and questions. Mary Williams, another descendant of the Bryett family, generously passed on the results of her researches into that family tree.

I thank the London Borough of Lewisham, the Barry Amiel and Norman Melburn Trust, South East Co-op, the Millwall Community Sports Scheme/the BPTUAA and the GLPA for their generous grants.

I am grateful to the University of Michigan Press for permission to reprint *Mourn Not the Dead* by Ralph Chaplin from *Rebel Voices* (*Industrial Workers of the World Anthology*) edited by J. L. Kornbluh 1964. Extracts from *Ethel and Ernest* by Raymond Briggs, originally published by Jonathan Cape are reprinted by permission of the Random House Group Limited, copyright Raymond Briggs 1998. Although the illustrations are here printed in black and white, they are originally in colour. The poem *Ethics for Everyman* by Roger Woddis, from the *Roger Woddis Collection*, originally published by Barrie and Jenkins, is reprinted by permission of the Random House Group Limited, copyright Roger Woddis 1978.

Many thanks are due also to Andy Hawkins (Leader of Lewisham Council 1971–84), for reading and commenting on drafts, and to Dr Nina Fishman and Dr Glyn Powell who were both immensely generous and supportive, giving me time to discuss specific issues and directing me to particular sources. Dr Powell also commented on and made valuable suggestions on specific drafts. Dr Gary Kitchen, former National Organiser and Neil Duncan-Jordan, Press Officer at the National Pensioners' Convention, also commented on some of my drafts. The late Simon Purcell, Information Officer at the National Pensioners' Convention gave me much useful information and guidance. I extend thanks to Jackie Roberts who read and commented on a number of early drafts.

I would like to pay tribute to five people who granted me interviews shortly before their own deaths: Margaret Witham, former President of the Greater London Pensioners'

Association, Jim Cronin and Rosalia Mooney, both Vice-Chairs and outstandingly active members of Lewisham Pensioners' Forum Management Committee, Alfred Stockwell and Wally Barnes, also, until recently, active members of the Forum's Management Committee. I would also like to record the names of other members of the Forum's first Management Committee and other active members of the Forum who have died in recent years: Eileen Ashman, Pat Burke, Lily Burns, Bob Carter, Kenneth Clark, Belle Esterson, Rose Kerrigan, founder member and first Chair of the Forum, Kay Hall, Bill Prestage and Marjorie Tully.

I thank Alison Purshouse, former Co-ordinator of Lewisham Pensioners' Forum, and Beverley Ammon (Administrator) for their constant support throughout the preparation of this work, and the following officers and members of the Forum: Harry Bacon (Chair), Doris Smith (Secretary), Trudi Coutinho, Peggy Cronin, John Esterson, Fred Ferris, Mary Holland, Moya McKay, John Rampling and former Forum Vice-President Stan Tulloch. Thanks must go also to a number of members of the Lewisham Pensioners' Action Group, including Doug Smith and Betty Cayzer. John Esterson and John Rampling also kindly commented on some drafts.

I received helpful comment and support from Jack Jones, President of the National Pensioners' Convention, and also from Jack Thain (General Secretary), Cyril Marshall (Treasurer), Helen Grew and Joan Hall (Vice-Presidents).

I also thank Carole Newman, Director of the Greater London Forum for the Elderly.

I received help and guidance from Kevin Halpin, Martin Levy and Sian Price of the British Communist Party.

The list of individuals who helped me is a long one and their names are given here in alphabetical order. The following persons all kindly allowed me an interview or sent me written or other submissions: Ray Allen, Sadie Attfield, Arthur Attwood, Richard Balfe MEP, Canon Owen Beament,

Alistair Beattie, Ron Bell, Tom Bell, Tony Benn, Charles Bird, Denise Bontoft (Permissions Assistant at the Random House Archive and Library), Alan E. Bryett, Steve Bullock (Leader of Lewisham Council 1988–93), Tony Carter, Irene Caton, Ken Chapman, Jean Clark, George Coombs, Jeremy Corbyn MP, Councillor Angela Cornforth, Ron Cowell, Stan Davison, Eileen Day, Janet and Jack Dunn, Andrew Dunning, Councillor Les Eytle, Sean Geraghty, Asquith Gibbes (former Principal Officer at the Lewisham Racial Equality Council), George Goodfellow, Bert Gramston, Len Gray, Pat Greenwood (Senior Reporter, *S.E. London and Kent Mercury*), Ida Hackett, Joe Harris, Victor Henning, Colin Hibbs, Eric Hodson, Dolly Hyne (former Lewisham Labour Party Councillor), Charles Job, Derek Johnson (Business and Civic Co-ordinator, London Borough of Lewisham), Richard Kavanagh, Tom Kelly, Jean Kysow, Tony Link (former Lewisham Labour Party Councillor), Waheeda Malick (Policy and Quality Officer, London Borough of Islington), Jim Mallory (Leader of Lewisham Council 1995–98), Cyril Marshall, Roy Martin, Gordon McLennan, John McLoughlin, Sue Mead (formerly at the Lewisham Racial Equality Council), Tom Mellish (Senior Policy Officer at the TUC), Roland Moyle, David Musther, Fred Ninde, Mick O'Connor, Abe Oppel, Ron Pepper, Mike Power (Campaigns Officer at the TUC), Maura Rafferty, Russell Read, Joan Ruddock MP, Ken Savage, Alan Saward, Elizabeth Sclater (Social Inclusion and Equalities Manager within the Policy and Partnerships Unit, London Borough of Lewisham), Doreen Scott (Assistant Secretary BPTUAA), George Scott, Andrew Spencer (Head of the Community Sector, London Borough of Lewisham), Shaun Spiers (former MEP), Gary Stempel, Mary Stott, Dave Sullivan (Mayor of Lewisham and former Leader of the Council 1985–88), Jack Thain, the Baroness Glenys Thornton, Grace Triance, Heather Wakefield, Lou Waller (Community Sports Worker at Millwall Football Club), Carol Whiteside, Roma Williams (former

Lewisham Labour Party Councillor), Ken Wintle, Mel Wright.

I wish to record my thanks to staff at the British Library at St Pancras, to Chris Coates, Librarian at the TUC Archive at the University of North London, Tish Collins (Librarian) and other staff at the Marx Memorial Library, staff at the library at Heythrop College (University of London), staff at the House of Lords Records Office, Elaine Temple, former Information Technology Adviser and Roger Barrington (historical researcher) at the Public Records Office at Kew, staff at the London Metropolitan Archives, Charles Fonje and Richard Temple at the Modern Records Centre at Warwick University and the National Museum of Labour History. I must thank the staff at the National Film and Television Archive and the staff at the RAF Personnel Management Agency at Innsworth, at the Air Historical Branch at Scotland Yard and also the staff at RAFATRAD Ltd. Ron Roffey, Honorary Archivist for South East Co-op, was most generous in allowing me to carry out research in the Co-op Archive when it was temporarily housed in the empty former Co-op department store in Powis Street in Woolwich – an experience I will never forget since I found myself in the midst of that historic treasure trove which houses the movement's history, under the gaze of the portraits of many of the early Co-operators. I wish to record special thanks for the superb help given by the staff at the British Library of Political and Economic Science in their temporary abode in the magnificent Southampton Buildings in Chancery Lane, and John Coulter and his staff at Lewisham's Local History Library.

I wish to end by apologising to anyone whose name I might have inadvertently omitted and also by expressing regret that a number of those whose help I sought by letter, telephone and email, were unable to spare the time to speak to or make contact with me. Hence there may be some serious omissions from this account.

I would also like to appeal to all organisations to remember to put dates on all their correspondence, minutes and notices. It is extremely frustrating to researchers to find fascinating documents, and letters which carry no date or only give the day and the month – but not the year – of meetings, conferences and demonstrations. Similarly press cuttings are often left undated.

I give special thanks to all my family who supported and tolerated me during the entire process and preparation of this work. They did their best to turn a blind eye to the proliferation of plastic storage bins, boxes and dusty files which encroached on our living space, and learned how to keep out of the way during the difficult episodes.

[1]

18 December 1996: A Celebration of a Great Life

> 'A great socialist and humanitarian was being honoured. It was a celebration of a great life lived.'
>
> Joan Ruddock MP

> 'If I'm indispensable then I'm going, because you should never get into a position where anyone is indispensable.'
>
> Les Stannard to Richard Balfe MEP

Eighteenth of December 1996. It was a cold, clear morning. The small chapel at Honor Oak Crematorium was packed. Those who could not get into the chapel stood silently in the gardens and grounds outside, the mourners tightly wrapped in coats and scarves. Les Stannard's widow, his daughter and other members of his family were joined by friends and colleagues and by representatives of every kind of community group in Lewisham, in Greater London and beyond. There were people of all backgrounds, classes, ages and colours. There were those holding strong political beliefs and those who held none; people from strong religious backgrounds and those with no recognised faith. The Leader of the Council stood alongside councillors and officers of the Council; there were MPs and MEPs. Les's proud and grieving colleagues from Lewisham Pensioners' Forum were joined by a number of other pensioners' forums and by mourners from the National Pensioners' Convention, the British Pensioners' and Trade Union Action Association, Pensioners' Voice, the Greater London Pensioners' Association and the Greater London Forum for the Elderly. Every political party was represented. There were the leaders of the ethnic minority community groups, members of the Carers' Association and the Lewisham Association of People with Disabilities, friends from Millwall Football Club and its Anti-Racist Committee and the Millwall Over 50s Club, representatives from the press. The Mayor and her Deputy were present as were many former mayors and councillors, and senior police officers. Many of Les's ETU and EETPU trade union colleagues were present as well as members of other trade unions and of the Lewisham and Deptford Trades Council.

It was a funeral such as is rarely seen in south-east London or indeed anywhere else – a funeral described by one who attended as 'a final farewell, fit for a king'. Many remarked on the extraordinary mix of people there. That mix spoke perhaps better than any words of the man we had come to mourn – that he could reach and touch not only people who shared his commitment and principles but also those who differed from him and from one another. People whose lives, whose upbringings differed greatly from his, those for whom the very word 'Communist' was anathema yet who had come to know and admire the man unequivocally. People who came from privileged backgrounds and those whose lives had, like his in many ways, been embedded in struggle. Three years later close friends and colleagues could not find the words to convey their feelings about the funeral because all they could remember of the day were the tears they had shed. John Rampling describes Les's death as a staggering shock to all those who were close to him at the Pensioners' Forum.

Les Stannard's funeral will always be remembered by those who attended. He had requested that it should be held there where the funerals of members of his family had taken place and close to Hilly Fields where he used to play as a small boy, imagining he was in the country away from the crowded streets of Deptford where he was born and lived for almost his entire life. He would forget himself in the fresh air and bright green grass and stay away from home longer than planned, returning to a scolding from his grandmother who worried that something might have happened to him.

The service was taken by Canon Owen Beament, parish priest of the parish of All Saints, New Cross, Chaplain of Millwall and a long-standing friend and colleague. No record has been kept of his whole address yet all who heard it were moved by his words and the tributes he paid to this strong, yet gentle man who had devoted his life to fighting for justice for his fellow humans. Father Owen described 'Grandfather' Les as one of the most remarkable citizens of Lewisham and stressed: 'Let us be aware that what he did for us and for other people grew unquestionably out of the lasting love and strength of his family.'

A small group of comrades from the Communist Party of Britain proudly held a banner outside saying simply 'Farewell Comrade – Les Stannard' in large letters. Many of them later expressed bitter disappointment that the address, beautiful though it was, failed to pay tribute to Les's long life as a political activist. No one had mentioned that Les was a socialist – a truly democratic socialist. For most of those who knew him Les and political activism were synonymous; he showed us clearly that life and politics cannot be separated. His family may have begun with his wife and daughter, his brothers, nephews and grandsons – but anyone who knew Les at all well would confirm that he was motivated above all by a belief in the family of humankind.

Yet, as one friend commented later, 'the funeral was in

the family tradition – he was theirs and his public life was something else.'

As this work will show, this was strangely true of Les Stannard's entire life.

[2]

The Early Years

Leslie Francis Stannard was born on 7 August 1919 at 15 Rutt's Terrace, Dennett's Road, Deptford in south-east London. Records show that it was a fine day. Nine months had passed since the signing of the Armistice and Britain was still mourning the thousands of young men who had been killed in the Great War.

The family home was in the parish of St Paul's, Deptford, the fine church built by Thomas Archer in 1730. No mention of Les's christening has been found in any of the Deptford church records, but the family has no doubt that all three sons were christened and his war record gives his religion as Church of England.

The Times for 7 August 1919 gives us an idea of the world Les was born into, from a Western point of view:

The British Fleet was in control of the Caspian Sea.

A British Trade Expedition was on its way to Siberia, via Norway.

Allied British, French and American troops had entered the city of Budapest following its occupation by Rumanian forces.

A report from the Dardanelles spoke of a reawakening of the Turkish people's trust in the British.

On 5 August in Lucerne, Switzerland, a debate had taken place on the political system of socialism at the International

Socialist Conference. Discussion took place on the relations between the Workers International and the methods of the revolutionary Soviet government.

Five hundred municipal employees (dustmen) in Kensington and 300 in Westminster were on strike and had not returned to work following a Borough Council resolution passed the previous week. Consequently notices advertising the resulting vacancies at all levels were posted in Labour Exchanges and elsewhere so that the strike action was effectively broken by the policies of the coalition government of the time.

A bakers' strike was set to continue and the Food Controller appealed to those who could do so to bake their own bread at home. Simultaneously the government was waging war on profiteering which, *The Times* hoped, would have a steadying effect on workers' unrest which had been caused by the rising cost of living.

In Ireland, attempts were being made to remove suspicion and to bring understanding on the position of Ulster and Sinn Fein. Fifty Chinese people applied for membership of the Friends of Irish Freedom Society in Long Island, USA, in support of the cause of Irish Independence.

The Railwaymen's Union called for action by its members in support of dismissed members of the police force.

The Hospital Sunday Funds distributed £82,402 to 228 cottage hospitals.

The best champagne cost less than £1 a bottle and the best sardines cost a few pence per tin.

There were outbreaks of rabies in Farnborough and Woking and muzzling orders existed in many areas.

In the Commons the Prime Minister, Lloyd George, moved a vote of thanks to the officers and men of the armed forces and to Marshal Foch – for the part they played in winning the war. The vote was carried unanimously but Labour and Independent Liberals opposed the grants of money on the grounds that they were excessive when compared with the gratuities paid to the rank and file.

The King awarded the Order of Merit to Lloyd George in a letter dated 5 August.

Clearly, the more things change, the more they stay the same. Those who knew Les well will have a fairly good idea which of these events would have captured his interest and on which he would have had a great deal to say!

The name Stannard originated in Suffolk and is recorded in the Domesday Book. Les's parents were Charles W. Stannard and Edith Florence Victoria (née Bryett) who were married at St Catherine's Hatcham Church in New Cross Gate. He was the first of their three sons. There were no daughters. The second son is Stanley and the youngest, Ronald, died a few months before Les. The family lived for most of their young lives with their maternal grandmother, Elmira Hepzibah Bryett, née Gatfield and, until 1930, with her husband George Bryett. Les's mother, Edith, had two brothers, Frederick Arthur and George whose widow, Nell, still survives him. Frederick was killed at the Battle of Mons on 24 August 1914 – just three weeks after the start of the First World War. Nell remembers the day when the letter announcing Frederick's death was delivered to his mother Elmira at her Rutt's Terrace home.

The Stannard family has been traced back to Les's father's great, great grandfather Joseph Stannard and his wife, Mary Anne, who were both born in Suffolk in approximately 1800 or 1801. Their son Thomas was baptised in February 1838 at the Church of St Mary Magdalen in Bermondsey and his son Francis (Les's paternal grandfather) was born in Rotherhithe in 1862 or 1863. We know that Francis Stannard worked as a parquet floor layer and that Thomas was a leather dresser in one of the big Bermondsey leather factories.

On the Bryett side of the family, the oldest ancestor known to the present generation of Stannards was Robert Bryett, born in Exeter in 1790. His son, also Robert, was born in Southwark in 1813 and was married to Mahala Henry whose family came from Colchester. Their son, Robert William Bryett (Les's maternal grandfather) was born in 1837 and died in Stepney in 1864. His wife was Hannah Amelia Ingram and their son George W. Bryett, Les's grandfather, was born in Poplar in 1867. Many of the Bryett ancestors are buried in Brockley cemetery.

It was thought that the name Bryett might be of Russian origin since one (unrelated) Bryett family in London believe that their surname derives from the Russian Briot or Briat but was changed to Bryett in order to accommodate English pronunciation. Further research has established that Bryett is almost certainly a Huguenot name and this link has been established from a 'sacrament certificate' for Marc Anthony Bruyet of the Parish of St Dunstan's in Stepney dated 29 May 1709. It was signed by two witnesses and by the Minister of St Martin's in the Fields. Under a statute of 1708 for the naturalisation of foreign Protestants all Protestant refugees who took the oath of allegiance and supremacy in a court of law and who could produce a sacrament certificate were deemed to have been naturalised (Kershaw and Pearsall, p. 85). The Huguenots were French Calvinist Protestant refugees who began to flee to England from the mid-16th century onwards after the massacre of St Bartholomew's Eve in 1572. They settled in various parts of the country – including Plymouth, which is not far from where Robert Bryett lived, in Exeter, in 1790. It is interesting to know that Les, who throughout his adult life fought so passionately on behalf of immigrants and asylum seekers, may not have known that his own mother's ancestors had sought haven in England because of the political/religious conflicts between France and England in the 16th century.

It is worth noting that both the Bryett and Stannard families, four generations before Les and his brothers were born, had moved to the London area in the first thirty years of the 19th century at the height of the second phase of the Industrial Revolution.

All that has been discovered about the Gatfield family is that they owned a number of provision (small grocers') shops, two of which were in Deptford.

George and Elmira Hepzibah (the maternal grandparents) were married in 1894 in the Church of St Jude in Peckham and they started life at 14 Rutt's Terrace, which so adjoined number 15 that they looked like one large house. Les's mother Edith was born at number 14. Her father, George Bryett, worked as a tramcar conductor (believed to refer to a horse-drawn omnibus), but in those days people could just drift into jobs if they had some relevant experience and Stan thinks his grandfather also worked as an electrician. The trams which operated throughout most suburban streets were all powered by electricity.

Les's father Charles was born on 14 February 1894 at 122 Keeton's Road, Bermondsey – now part of the Southwark College campus. In 1904 he and his parents lived at 2 New Upcot Street (now demolished) in Deptford. The street ran parallel to Sharrat Street. (Rutt's and Keeton's were both named after the men who built the terraces.) Charles Stannard worked at one stage of his life at the Charlton Works in the trolleys and trams section. We do not know whether Edith worked outside the home before Les was born.

The three boys all attended Waller Road Primary School (now Edmund Waller School) at the bottom of Rutt's Terrace – known as the 'posh' side. Les was there from the age of five to 11 (1924 to 1930). The house backed on to the school playground and, at playtime, Edith would bring out three cups of cocoa and leave them by the fence where her small boys could just reach them!

Number 15 Rutt's Terrace was a small, homely and cosy 'two up, two down'. The front door opened directly on to the front room. The three boys shared a bedroom, which was not unusual; indeed it was quite the norm, in those days, for children to share their parents' bedroom. The other two bedrooms belonged to the Stannard parents and to the Bryett grandparents. It appears that Charlie and Edith lived in Peckham when they were first married but that, at some period when Charlie had no work, Elmira insisted on their coming to share her Rutt's Terrace home. The house was rented. Elmira reorganised her house so as to accommodate all seven of them. 'This is how communal living like this came about,' says Stan. Grandpa Bryett was still earning sometime in the 1930s but these were times of high unemployment. 'Our dad did have a bad spell out of work and only got the job at Charlton in the mid-thirties. He used otherwise to take on painting and decorating work with our cousin John Hoadley's father Jack.' (John Hoadley's paternal grandmother was Elmira's sister.) 'Families were a good thing,' recalls Stan who, just like his brothers, believes a great deal in keeping families together. 'The war changed all that though. Families were broken up and it was never the same again.'

Rutt's Terrace still exists but the old houses were pulled down and it is now a featureless modern 'Close' – the only remaining building from the old days is the pub, the Rising Sun, which is also closed. Charlie Stannard, and his sons, as they grew up, were almost certainly regular visitors to the Rising Sun and there is reputed to be a photograph of Les in his first pair of long trousers standing outside it. John Hoadley said that his father Jack knew Charlie Stannard as a very likeable man, devoted to his wife and children. Hoadley also remembers hearing that during World War I the Rutt's Terrace residents used to gather in the Rising Sun every evening and prepare the vegetables for their evening meal while they had a drink.

Nell Bryett, the widow of Edie's brother George, describes number 15 as a very welcoming home, to which the boys' grandmother Elmira brought a warm and loving spirit. She was a child of the Victorian age and she raised the children accordingly! She was a strong influence on all the sons because their mother Edith became seriously ill when they were all still quite young and never regained her health. The three boys were aged between 16 and 20 when their mother died.

Elmira (or Nan as she was known to everybody) was a much loved grandmother. Stan comments that perhaps the boys took her for granted! She was kind but serious about their behaviour, frequently warning them not to get into trouble. He remembers that she always prepared a glass of milk and sandwiches for them when they came home, whatever time of the day. The children adored their mother and grandmother and also loved and respected their father, but it seems that the women were the dominant force for good in the family. Stan recalls that their father was also a good and loving influence and remembers him caring for Nan in her old age and taking her out in her wheelchair. The boys also knew their Stannard grandmother who died in 1935 but not their Stannard grandfather. Grandmother Stannard had several daughters and they lived at various addresses. She eventually settled somewhere off the Old Kent Road and died there. 'Mother was too ill to go to the funeral,' remembers Stan.

Stan's memories of his maternal grandfather George Bryett are sketchy – he was only eight when George died and Les would have been about ten. Of course he was very much part of the communal family and had more time to take the children out than their own father when the latter was on shift work. 'I was just a small child myself so I remember him as an old, kind, grey sort of gentleman,' says Stan.

In 1936 or '37 the family all moved to 3 Rutt's Terrace when Elmira, who knew the landlord, heard that it was available to rent. The house was a little bigger and had a garden so it turned out a beneficial move for the family and they were happy there, despite the fact that Edie was soon to die.

We have a good description of Nan from her daughter-in-law Nell Bryett, who describes her as a very modern woman

– she was big and tall, much bigger than her husband, and had a beautiful face, and dark hair and eyes. Elmira was very clothes conscious and wore the most beautiful hats, some of which she made herself. She was always keen to learn, especially about modern office innovations, and would ask Nell to explain them to her since, presumably, she did not get out of the house much. She did, however, love Brighton and used to like to go there for the day whenever she could. Another description comes from an old friend, who describes Nan as a most lovable woman. 'You always felt you wanted to go and sit on her lap!' The relationship between mother and daughter was a close one, based on mutual affection and respect, and came to strength when Edie began to show signs of the illness which was to cause her premature death. Some months before she died they took Edie to Brighton by car. She managed to go out a bit but on the whole was not happy there and wanted to come home. Nell described Edie as a lovely person both in looks and in character – she had beautiful dark hair and dark brown eyes and a slim face. She couldn't do enough for her mother who used to remark, 'She's an angel, isn't she?' Elmira had more than her fair share of tragedy, having lost a very young son in the war and now her daughter who was only just into her forties.

'When mum began to get ill, Gran used to do all the cooking and mum just made the beds,' says Stan. It is an interesting observation that, as the children were all boys, they never made their own beds; there were no duvets in English homes in those days so that bed making was a much more time-consuming task. Stan also remembers that even when their mother was ill the boys had a nightly change of clothes. 'We never wore our working clothes in the evening and when we came home to dinner our trousers would be folded and our clothes neatly hung up. We never cleaned our shoes either – dad used to clean all our shoes for school or work to make sure that we went to school clean.' It may seem surprising to the majority of young people growing up today that Stan remembers that, unlike many other children, he and his brothers always had pyjamas and shoes. 'Not all kids had them,' he adds, 'and all the men repaired their own shoes; our dad used to repair and polish our shoes in the kitchen.'

Soon, however, Edie was unable to do much and a bed had to be brought down to the dining-room. Her family is well aware that her illness could well have been cured today. Stan remembers those last days: 'Subconsciously I suppose we knew but we still hoped nothing was going to happen to her. You couldn't walk into hospitals then as you can now so we couldn't be with her. I remember so well – the telegram coming from the hospital when I had just come home from work and I was washing.' Edie died at St Alfege's Hospital. The children were now left in the care of their capable and loving grandmother.

Edie and her mother were both ardent co-operators and always used the Co-op shop, except for the occasional trip to the corner shop. Edie was a very well-educated young woman and well informed on current events and politics. Mother and daughter also belonged to the Co-op Women's Guild and regularly attended the meetings at Monson Road. Edie spoke a great deal to her sons and made sure they listened to her. Even towards the end of her life she would teach them and talk to them – though she was often in pain – about the serious political issues of the day. At the age of 14, when he left school, Les became a member of the Co-operative movement's Comrades Circle and used to attend regular discussion groups. Stan remembers accompanying him to the tea and grocery factories in Woolwich, the home of the Royal Arsenal Co-operative Society, but while at some stage he himself dropped out, Les continued to attend the lectures. Nell has no doubt that had Les been able to stay on at school he could have continued into higher education.

Nell believes that Stanley's character resembled that of his uncle Frederick Arthur who was killed at Mons. His nature was carefree and cheerful. Ron, the youngest son, used to go to stay for periods with his Aunt Nell when his mother was ill but, naturally, would feel homesick and want to return home. Nell remembers him as a happy boy who always laughed. When he married his wife Daphne in what was considered to be a very promising match he quipped, 'D'you see, Nell? Local boy makes good!'

Les is described as having a different nature and more a Bryett in character. Brother Stan recalls that he was always the one to get the clip round the ear because Les was big enough to run away and Ron was the little one. 'Of course we used to fight and we were all quite mischievous.' Les could be cheeky at times. 'One evening we were playing outside and when our mother called us Les would not come in.' This is probably the oldest and commonest story about lively children to this day. 'The more she called out to him to come in the more he refused to. They had no mercy in those days and he was clumped round the head. Then he threw his cricket bat against the front door and split the panel which made my mum even more cross! I can't remember whether he said sorry!'

Les inherited his mother's dark colouring as well as absorbing her ideas. He was quick, and also quick to lose his temper when provoked. He was a very bright child who always persevered with things. He would take on something and devote himself to it – nothing would come in his way. He tended to keep things to himself as the oldest brother and did not discuss much with Stan and Ron. He idolised both his mother and grandmother and would always ask their advice, and his grandmother's in particular, as his mother became ill.

Stan remembers that every Sunday morning their father would take them to visit one of their much-loved Bryett great-aunts who lived in Friendly Street, but, as he got older, Les proudly followed his father's example and used to take his two brothers along. This was an example which stayed with him till the end of his life.

There were few buses in those days and the family mostly travelled on trams. As small children the three boys used to go to Blackheath and Greenwich Park on the open-topped 48 bus or they might all go together to Telegraph Hill Park and Edie would pack them a small picnic of lemonade and cake. Another favourite outing was to Greenwich Pier where the children would play at the water's edge (though they could not actually paddle!) which they used to think of as a little beach. They would then walk up one of the steep hills which led through Greenwich Park, through the main gate to the Folly Pond on Blackheath. I remember Les recounting (one day when we were visiting the Hilly Fields area for a meeting) that he used to love to go there alone as a growing boy. He used to think of it as the country, compared with the built-up area in which he lived, and he would spend a great deal of time there alone and receive a scolding from Nan when he got back for not having told her he was going to be out so long. The boys all had bicycles which they started to pay for when they left school at the rate of 2/6d per week. Stan remembers their father sometimes asking them, 'Why aren't you going out?' and when they replied they could not afford to he would give them 6d each – 1d for transport each way and 4d for the cinema. Consequently, Charlie would go without lunch the following day.

At other times the boys played football in the street and cricket too – they had stumps up by the wall at Rutt's Terrace. In the winter there was the cinema which Stan describes as 'a fleapit'. Stan also gives us the first recorded events relating to Les's lifelong attachment to Millwall Football Club. 'We used to walk along Dennett's Road, down Kender Street, through Besson Street, then to Monson Road and Coldblow Lane. We didn't always have the money to go in but they used to open the gates in preparation for letting the crowd out and we children would rush in to see the last 15 minutes for free!'

Stan remarks again that though their family was poor they

were not as poor as some people. At Christmas they used to hang up a pillowcase and 'when it was dark we would put our hands in. We always had a torch. The pillowcase would be filled with clothes – practical things – and apples and oranges and perhaps a few nuts.' It is perhaps worth recording that this was a typical Christmas present for children in those days, even those from middle-class, better-off families. 'We children would join together to buy a gift for our parents through the Christmas Club. We would put in a penny a week through the year and buy them something like a pottery milk jug.' On some Christmases they would be joined by Aunt Nell, who represented something between a mother and a big sister to the boys – she was only about ten years older than Les. Christmas lunch was eaten in the front parlour, not in the kitchen as on normal days. It was rare for them all to eat together when the boys were working, except on Sundays. As small children they always had their tea before their father came home and his meal would be kept for him. Stan remembers helping with the washing up sometimes. Les, however, would invariably be off somewhere!

As the children grew older they would go down to Brighton occasionally with their friends, one of whom was the son of the owner of the Rutt's Terrace corner shop. 'He was the rich kid on the block,' says Stan. 'The time we went to Brighton with him he had a motor bike. We took a tent and slept on the Downs, and on another occasion we slept under the pier.'

Tom Pyke (one of Les's fellow Millwall supporters) has told me that Les gained a scholarship to Brockley Central School in Walbutton Road, where he was a pupil from 1930 to 1933. The schooling was free and the value of the scholarship was about £13 a year. Ron Stannard also attended this school, leaving in about 1938. It was unusual for parents to be able to keep their children at school after the school-leaving age of 14 and it can be safely assumed that Les left school as most young lads did, in order to find work.

Brockley Central School opened in 1874. Initially named Mantle Road School, it changed its name to Brockley Central in 1914 and has now been renamed Telegraph Hill School. Frederick E. Rogers became head in 1910 and was still there during Les's last years. At that time 'central' schools came between the secondary modern and the grammar schools; they took pupils who had not passed the 11-plus or in some cases when the grammar schools were over-subscribed. Les passed the Junior County Scholarship and sat a final exam six weeks later. The school had previously been co-educational but was a boys' only school by the time Les went there. The uniform consisted of grey shorts and trousers, black shoes, green and yellow striped ties and green caps. According to another former pupil, Mrs Irene Caton, discipline was strong and teachers had no difficulty in controlling classes of 46 children. These were the days when children respected policemen and park keepers and probably anyone in uniform, and called them 'sir'. Evening dances used to be held at the Boys' Hall and former pupil Jean Pearce (Payne) recalled that in 1929 their teacher (Miss Odam) 'advised us not to attend, as dancing close to a male partner was not a ladylike pastime! Naturally many of us did go and I spent most of the evening scared stiff that a boy would ask me to dance. I soon got over that!'

The curriculum was intensive and included every academic subject except Latin as well as commercial subjects. All the pupils learned French. The standard was high and this is borne out by Sue Mead's observations about the time when she used to help Les with correspondence when Lewisham Pensioners' Forum was first established. 'His standard of English (in letters and reports) was far superior to that of young people today, and this from someone who left school at 14!' The examinations taken were the Oxford School Certificate (the same as were taken at grammar schools) and also those of the London Chamber of Commerce. Some of the pupils later went to grammar schools and continued on to university while others went straight into employment. All the children studied Shakespeare and mental arithmetic, and the blackboard featured strongly in the teaching. Like all the children at Brockley Central Les was expected to come in at least 15 minutes early every morning to copy work off the board. Homework consisted of two subjects every night and was intended to take one and a half hours. The children were not given lines to write as punishment but a section of the Bible or lines from Shakespeare to learn, and they would be word perfect by the following morning. Mrs Caton spoke to me about having the cane at this school, though it was used very rarely and across the hand. She believes that the ethos of the school contributed to the kind of man Les grew to be, that discipline was the contributory factor. Interesting memories of one of the form-masters, Charles B. Atkinson (known as Attie), have been recorded from one of Les's fellow pupils, Alan Saward. Attie (who taught Maths and French and who was later co-author, with W. G. Bate, of *Commercial School Certificate Arithmetic*) had an innovative way of dealing with children who talked in class: rather than use the cane, he would simply ask the offender to go and get him a glass of water and this would effectively remove the source of distraction. The sound of the headmaster's approach would take the heat out of any encounter such as a playground fight. On one occasion when those involved in a fight returned to the classroom with the rest of the class, Attie moved his table to one side and produced a pair of boxing gloves and told the fighters to settle their argument. The boys sparred and bobbed and weaved, taking considerable care not to hurt each other. People passing by in the corridor were astonished at this extraordinary lesson and Saward could not remember any playground fights after that!

Although Les spent such a short time at Brockley Central he retained a loyal fondness for it, not surprising for someone so attached to people, both family and friends, as he was. In 1995 he submitted a piece to the local press, entitled 'A

Non-military Reunion', which, while referring to the recent VE and VJ Day celebrations, drew attention to a 'unique event' in Lewisham – a social gathering of the Brockley Central Old Scholars Association. He invited former pupils who wished to attend to contact the Association c/o the Lewisham Pensioners' Forum office. Subsequently Irene Caton who, together with Charles Bird, keeps the Association alive, received a letter from Les expressing his regret at not being able to attend the event owing to an important pensioners' meeting which he could not miss.

As he grew older Les became involved in numerous interests and occupations outside the home. We do not know whether all his youthful social activities centred around political issues, but it will not surprise people who knew him at the end of his life that he was nearly always out. He seemed to have become political from the time he left school and it was a family joke that he should have been in Parliament.

The 1930s were years of social and political ferment in Europe and it was inevitable that Les, with his enquiring mind, high intelligence and lively spirit, would be drawn to wanting to understand the ideas underlying the political debate. He could not have been unaware of the drastic effects of rising unemployment on working-class families. His sense of injustice had been fuelled early by what was taking place in his own close-knit family. His recently widowed grandmother, who would almost certainly have wanted to return to paid work, was cast in the role of carer – taking it upon herself to look after her sick daughter and the three growing sons whose father was also unemployed from time to time. Les's daughter remembers her father's amazement at the way his grandmother managed to provide a healthy diet for the family. There were no fridges, freezers or microwaves and certainly no convenience foods but Elmira knew how to prepare wholesome meals when money was short. However, finding the money to pay the doctor's bills was an ever-present anxiety, even though the doctor did not always leave a bill; when Les came home for his mother's funeral, and for some time after, there were bills still waiting to be settled. This experience stayed with him for he was to pay tribute to his parents and grandparents when he received the London Borough of Lewisham's Community Award in 1993. Like so many of his generation who worked to elect the first Labour government in 1945, he considered that the principle of a free National Health Service for all must remain at the heart of any society which claims to be just and civilised. Another outcome of this experience was that it contributed to Les's highly advanced perspective on the position of women in society – unusual in a man of his generation.

There were other powerful forces, however, which were to have a strong impact on his thinking and to shape his political views. Les joined both the Co-operative movement's Comrades Circle and the Young Communist League and he never deviated from their related philosophies. He had been open to co-operative ideals throughout his childhood. There can be no doubt that the influence of his mother contributed greatly to Les's character and outstanding talents as a communicator, negotiator and political activist. He will undoubtedly have been aware that this was a period of rising unemployment and widespread unrest. Kath Duncan, who was to become one of the greatest influences on his thinking, was known as the Leader of the Deptford and Greenwich Unemployed. Les would have been just old enough to join the crowds and to listen to her fiery speeches and to be amongst the followers who welcomed her back to Deptford after a month spent in Holloway jail after she had been charged for being 'a disturber of the Peace of Our Lord the King'.

Les as a young man remained devoted to his family – all the boys were family orientated. The way he combined this devotion with an active political life remained a remarkable characteristic to the very end; his political life constantly took him away from home, yet his family remained a central touchstone for him. The death of their grandmother in 1962 must have revived painful memories of their mother's death when they were still so young. Les's nephew Michael Stannard remembers that when in the last ten years of his life he once asked Les about his mother because he (Michael) was thinking of compiling a family tree, Les was so overcome with emotion at the thought of his mother that he was quite unable to speak and the conversation had to be brought to an end.

While he was still at school, or possibly just after, Les had a casual job collecting glasses at the Rising Sun and it was there that a friend of the family offered him a job to train as an electrician. At that time electricity was just beginning to be installed in place of gas lighting and there were a number of different companies operating in their borough. This was an exciting new prospect and a real job. He started straight from school; and the normal practice, at the time, was that you remained a 'junior mate' until the age of 16 when, in theory, the firm you worked for was obliged to employ you for seven years.

It may surprise some young readers that at the tender age of 14 Les and his contemporaries should have been so politically aware and active. Although it is true that there were then far fewer tempting distractions for young people, the 1930s saw a growing mood of opposition and outrage against what was taking place at home and throughout Europe, particularly in Spain. Possibly the anti-Vietnam War demonstrations of the 1960s, the anti-nuclear demonstrations of the 1970s, the Poll Tax riots in the 1980s and the massive anti-capitalist demonstrations which marked the end of the second millennium come closest to resembling the kind of feeling which Communists and co-operators of all ages went through in the years preceding World War II. Although, at this stage, Les was involved in what might be described as the youth movements of both organisations, he remained actively aligned to both of them for the rest of his life. The three-part pattern of his life was already set. Love and strong attachment to his family was combined with a political fervour dedicated to bringing about justice and change; there was room in his heart and mind for only one other passionate interest and that was Millwall!

[3]

Membership of the Co-operative Movement

Les Stannard joined the Comrades Circle at the age of 14 when, in his own words, 'the movement was actively involved in local affairs'.[1] The world-wide Co-operative movement came into being in Britain as a consequence of the Industrial Revolution which brought Les's ancestors, together with thousands of others, out of a rural existence into the harsh, new industrial scene in London. The history of the British movement was written by Arnold Bonner in 1961.

The early co-operators

'*Salus populi suprema est lex*' (The good of the people is the highest law) was inscribed above the entrance to the Co-operative College in Loughborough, and from all that we know about Les Stannard it was also the principle by which he lived.

The Co-operative movement was started by the Rochdale Society of Equitable Pioneers in 1844 under the influence of Robert Owen (1771–1858). Co-operation is based on the principle of mutual assistance in trade, manufacture, the supply of credit and other services and profit-sharing. The

[1] In his submission to the RACS Political Purposes Committee 1983.

underlying principles of mutuality and the sharing of skills are the oldest principles known, older even than those of the Labour Party. Bonner reminds us (p. 1) that the notion of co-operation is older than humanity since the work of bees, ants and other animals is carried out co-operatively.

In Britain, the major type of co-operation is through the Co-operative Societies such as the Royal Arsenal Co-operative Society (RACS) whose shops used to sell at current market prices, returning the bulk of their profits to their members as 'dividends'. The retail outlets are now federated nationally in Co-operative Wholesale Societies which carry on wholesale trade and production. For a long time there were hundreds of individual co-ops controlling a large share of the retail market but, paradoxically, they did not co-operate with one another with the result that they began to lose customers to the new supermarkets.

The early movement suffered many conflicts and changes and was challenged by other reformers (such as Dr William King) who shared many but not all of Owen's beliefs – they disagreed profoundly, for example, on the role of the family, but both men believed that poverty, disease and crime were largely the consequences of the existing economic and social system. Their ideas and hopes live on in the co-operators of today. At the Annual Congress of the movement in Lincoln in 1908 the Women's Co-operative Guild outlined the difference between a co-operative 'combine' and capitalist 'combines', describing the Co-operative Wholesale Society (CWS) as

- being made up of working-class consumers not a combination of capitalists;
- governed by working-class consumers not by a few millionaires; and
- dividing its profits among all its members by a dividend on purchase (after essential deductions); profits are not divided among a few individuals as interest on capital.

Owen was in his forties when he started his career of social reform, which was based on his belief that the human character is not a given but can be formed – a theory which has continued to occupy the minds of philosophers and social scientists to this day, under the general title of the nature/nurture (or culture) debate. Current thought emphasises the strong influence of the genes on our characters, arguing that too much emphasis has been placed on the pre-eminence of environment and upbringing in the last 50 or so years. The debate will, no doubt, continue but no professional social scientist will ever be able to discount the enormous effect that the family and society have on the growing child. Robert Owen held some fairly revolutionary ideas: he believed that changing the conditions in which people lived (and he meant poor people) would lead to changing their characters and would wipe out anti-social qualities such as idleness and dishonesty. Interestingly enough he did not have anything to say about idleness and dishonesty amongst the wealthy and privileged! He denounced all organised religion as well as marriage and the family – on the grounds that families teach children to promote the interests of their own families against those outside it.

The Women's Co-operative Guild

The Women's Co-operative Guilds were established through the inspiration of Alice S. Acland in 1883. A full history of the movement is given by, amongst others, Gaffin and Thoms in their centenary history of the Co-operative Guild – *Caring and Sharing*. Acland had met co-operative leaders in northern England through her husband and was impressed by the value of co-operation; she also felt that women should have greater opportunities for self-expression outside their homes. Since the movement was founded upon a membership of consumers, women were involved in it from the start (within the home) because of their purchasing power. Acland urged them to begin to have meetings, readings and discussions. She became editor of the 'Women's Corner' of the *Co-op News* and soon started a debate about women's ideas on how they wanted their lives to develop – this at a time when women did not have the vote. Mrs Acland was a gentle mover and she spoke about women being sunbeams and encouragers, whose influence should be quiet. This can be seen as an English characteristic since, rather than embark on sudden revolution, the English have tended to change the order of their social life not by one great sweep, but by gathering up the best things of the past and adapting them to progressive necessities.

Two other important activists in the movement were Woolwich-born Mary Lawrenson and Margaret Llewelyn Davies. Lawrenson's suggestion was for the setting up of a League and this was inaugurated at the Co-op Congress in Edinburgh in 1883. It had a number of objectives, including the dissemination of a knowledge of the principles of co-operation, and the improvement of the conditions of women all over the country. The guild held democratic self-government as its chief principle. (Not all the women belonging to the guilds shared Lawrenson's views: in 1888 some of the Woolwich group rejected her emphasis on the carrying out of good works!) She did make an enormous contribution to the work of the guilds and she believed that their success would depend on the true education of women. It was soon recognised that working-class women should meet, and conduct their business, 'without the aid of a leader of more exalted station in life'. (Attfield, pp. 83–4).

Links between co-operators and trade unions began to be formed in 1891 and the guild supported bringing women into the trade unions. The 1907 Co-operative Congress affirmed the principle of a co-op minimum wage for men and boys and the guild then approached the Amalgamated Union of Co-operative Workers with proposals for a women's scale which subsequently became endorsed. Throughout the twenties and thirties the guild took up political and social issues of special concern to women – before this they had experienced difficulties in their efforts owing to a fairly strong religious opposition within the wide Co-op movement. Peace was a major issue for Guilds-women between the wars. The guild was affiliated to many peace organisations and in 1935 the RACS branches joined in the conduct of the Peace Ballot, organised by the League of Nations as a demonstration of the British strength of feeling against war. The guild was also responsible for devising the White Peace Poppy in 1934 (Attfield, p. 91).

In 1926 the guild had 58,000 members, whose principal aim was to work 'through co-operation for the welfare of the people'. Over the years the guild steadily built up, within the Co-op movement, the principle of a standard of wages below which the movement should not fall. An indication of the strength and independence of spirit of the women co-operators is shown by this quote from the Annual Report for 1898: 'We don't mix in wi' t'men's squabbles; we sits still and listen, and we votes' (Webb, p. 81).

However, the relationship between the Co-operative movement, the guilds and the Labour Party was frequently uneasy. Attfield tells us (p. 92) that in 1928–29 the guild was fiercely against the Labour Party yet, in 1936, at the height of the anti-Fascist campaigns, the guild followed the TUC in banning Communists from holding office! Such changes of policy and conflicts of loyalty continue to this day, as was shown by Co-op South-East's decision not to ballot its members but to deliver a block vote for the election for London's Mayor on 4 May 2000.

The New Cross branch of the women's guild of which Edith Stannard was an active member opened in 1918 – there were other branches throughout south-east London. This was one of a number of branches which were quick to take up the left-wing issues of the Labour movement. They sent donations to strike movements, took up international questions such as the defence of the Soviet Union and in 1933 championed the cause of the Meerut prisoners in India. The New Cross branch, amongst others, collected for the miners' lock-out relief fund. Even in south-east London there was not uniformity in the political stances of the branches; some preferred to give their attention to charitable causes (Attfield, p. 92). In 1934 the membership of the New Cross branch stood at 142 and approximately 90 women attended regularly and participated in a wide range of activities (*Comradeship and Wheatsheaf*, August 1934, p. xxv). Not surprisingly, in view of the seriousness of the Comrades Circles philosophy (see below), the women's guilds also had speakers at their meetings on co-operation, business and the economy, social services and international affairs. In 1934 they had a speaker from the *Financial Times* and another lecture was entitled 'The Co-operative Movement as Social Uplifter and its Influence on Peace' (December 1934, p. xxvii). However, they also had arts programmes and on one occasion a speaker on 'Left Wing Theatre' (*Comradeship and Wheatsheaf*, July 1934, pp. xxii).

The Suffragettes

The women of Great Britain gained the vote in two stages: women over 30 gained the right to vote immediately after World War I, but it was not until 1928 that women over 21 achieved the same right. The Women's Co-operative Guild was active in the campaign for votes for women and made clear its indignation both at the anti-suffrage utterances of certain MPs and, more importantly, at their own movement's refusal to place the issue on the agenda of the 1907 Congress in Preston (Webb, p. 97). Guild members took part in a lantern procession to the Albert Hall on 27 May 1909 organised by the London Society of Women's Suffrage.

The guild and the old-age pension

Discussion on the old-age pension was central to the guild at least from 1901 when proposals were being made for co-operative schemes to fund pensions. Following the Old Age Pensions Act of 1908 the guild continued to press, year after year, for a reduction in the pension age from 70 to 60 and for an increase in the amount of the state pension. Ninety-three years later, when the link with average earnings has still not been reinstated and when the New Labour government is working on funding future pensions through private finance, the Co-operative movement continues to argue the case for the pension scheme to be funded and administered on the sound basis of mutuality.

The Co-operative movement, the guilds and political parties

The guild followed the traditions of the movement, holding aloof from party politics and believing that people of all shades of political opinion should belong. Yet there was confusion and constant debate in both the guild and the union on what were and what were not 'party questions'. During the 1880s political socialism was spreading through the working-class organisations. The TUC took steps to bring about Labour representation in Parliament and, eventually, to create the Labour Party. At the same time the movement was being encouraged to follow the same path and at the 1890 Co-operative Congress the Secretary of the Women's Guild, Margaret Llewelyn Davies, presented a paper on 'The Relations between Co-operation and Socialistic Aspirations' – showing the similarity of the aims of both philosophies and arguing the need for parliamentary action. The 1912 Congress supported a 'closer alliance' between co-operation and the other Labour forces and thereafter a majority of the guild was in favour of an alliance. In 1920 Eleanor Barton was accepted as prospective candidate by co-operators, the trade unions and the Labour Party. She was not adopted but gained second place in the constituency of the Kings Norton Division in Birmingham. Margaret Llewelyn Davies retired in 1921. Gaffin and Thoms (p. 91) write that it was suggested at the time (though denied by her) that her retirement had been brought about by unease about her personal independence and what might be described as a tendency to be less than accountable to the wider movement. What is certain is that (judging from the letters she received at the time of her retirement) she had inspired great devotion amongst guild members and the character of the movement changed considerably after her departure.

Co-operation and education

One of the strongest features of the movement is its emphasis on the crucial importance of education – all co-operators would, by definition, need to study in order to understand the principles of business. The importance of education was not, however, restricted to the learning of the mechanisms of profit and loss or the balance of probabilities; the emphasis was on the development of people's minds through a broad education which would enable co-operators, amongst other things, to understand the system in which they lived and to determine their own destinies. The Workers' Educational Association (WEA) which was formed in 1903 was largely supported by co-operative support.

The journal *Comradeship and Wheatsheaf* reflects the philosophy of the movement in the first half of the 20th century. Originally launched in October 1897, its first editor was Charles Herbert Grinling and it was conceived on the same lines as other co-op magazines – social in character with the aim of explaining co-operative principles. It was issued by the RACS educational department and was a broad-based quality, monthly journal with an internationalist political slant. It included articles about the different arms of the movement, political articles and serious book reviews, as well as the more usual domestic kinds of articles which featured in women's magazines. Regular notices featured the women's and men's guilds' programmes and their annual reports. In those days, much as today, the term 'a new world order' was in common currency and frequently the title of a lecture or conference. Due to financial pressures *Comradeship* was reduced to but a few pages by the 1950s and featured less and less in the way of educational content (Attfield, pp. 68–9).

The Education Act of 1918 (the Fisher Act) gave local education authorities the power to subsidise classes run by recognised adult educational organisations and, while the RACS Education Committee criticised the Act in many ways, its members also took advantage of its power and negotiated with the then London County Council (LCC) with the result that the LCC funded classes on any subject which were organised by RACS. Thus, John Attfield tells us (p. 57), between 1918 and 1938 RACS gained a reputation in the general Labour movement for the progressive and ambitious nature of its educational work. Joseph Reeves, who founded the movement, undertook innovative work in young people's education and, in the aftermath of World War I, and within the changed political climate, he developed the Society's work on the basis of 'education for social change'. In this work he had the backing not only of the RACS' own education committee but also of a number of gifted young socialists determined to devote their time and energy to workers' education. These classes, which were supported by thousands of young men and women, took place in working-class areas such as Woolwich, Peckham and Deptford. Attfield tells us that 'by avoidance of trivialisation, or degeneration into "bun-fights" or leisure-orientated activities, their success was demonstrated. This all built an outstanding educational enterprise and marked the high point in the educational achievement of RACS since 1877'.

These events took place long before Les was born but the movement's educational programme continued to develop and gain strength well into the 1960s. The National Guild of Co-operators (NGC) was founded in 1926. This was a guild to which both men and women belonged and was seen as a threat by the existing (separate) men's and women's guilds. Furthermore it lacked a long-established machinery of loyalty to the Labour Party (since it was a new development) at a time when loyalty to the Labour Party tended to imply hostility to the Communist Party (Attfield, p. 92). Between 1931 and 1933 five new NGC branches were set up in New Cross, Deptford, Abbey Wood, Lambeth and Lewisham. There were Labour Party attempts to drive out the left in the men's guild so the New Cross men's guild decided to switch to being an NGC. Annual reports show this group to have been involved in militant struggles against Fascism and unemployment, collecting for the hunger marchers and participating in many demonstrations for peace (*Comradeship and Wheatsheaf*, August 1933).

The Comrades Circles

The Comrades Circles were formed in 1907 and progressed so successfully that a national body, The British Federation of Co-operative Youth, was formed in 1924. It received financial support from the Co-operative Union and a member of the education department staff acted as a joint secretary. Bonner (pp. 186–7) describes the Federation as 'a lively, vigorous, but perhaps somewhat aggressively independent body, ... which undoubtedly assisted in producing co-operative leaders'. By 1938 there were 231 circles with 8000 members.

The New Cross Comrades Circle was established in 1935 and it is possible that Les might have originally attended either the Bermondsey or the Rushey Green branch. The Woodcraft Folk also came to receive official recognition and had a membership of 5000 in 1938, but John Attfield notes that the movement generally tended to favour the Comrades Circles over the Woodcraft Folk (pp. 102–3).

It is notable that there was a belief at this time, in some sections of the movement, that the junior classes and their studies and methods were somewhat outdated and too serious for the children of the time. The New Cross Circle lectures and study programmes (notified in *Comradeship*) were organised as weekly meetings in cycles of four. They were composed, usually, of two course lectures on sociology or industrial history and a topical lecture (from an external speaker) focused on serious co-op, social and political affairs such as the study of Fascism, or citizenship or modern economic problems; a social evening would complete the cycle. Peace was studied at an early age. There was a lecture entitled 'Should Communism and Fascism be abolished?' and another on Aldous Huxley's *Brave New World*. Those who considered such courses too serious wished to establish youth clubs which would focus on handicrafts, table tennis and dancing as a different way of introducing the co-operative message. A Youth Section was thus set up in 1937. (Those who knew Les later in life would expect that, even as a young lad, he would have been more in tune with the activities of the Comrades Circle than with learning dancing and handicrafts!) The Youth Club motto was *I serve* and its code included the following statement: 'I desire to join the Co-op Youth Club in order that I should learn something of the art of citizenship . . .' It went on to say, 'I will have courage and perseverance in the struggle for right' and it went further, stating, 'I believe that the resources of the world and the accumulated knowledge of past centuries should be in the common inheritance of all mankind and I pledge myself to work for a community wherein all men shall live co-operatively in peace and happiness.' The co-operative ideal bears more than a passing resemblance to Marx's philosophy.

Another interesting educational development at this time was the 'Wayfarers' organisation set up by Leslie Paul in 1925 in Rushey Green. Here is an example of Paul's philosophy, published in the journal *The Folk Trail.*

'We wish to give every child an opportunity of entering the world of man [the use of 'man' to indicate men and women was common practice at that time] with a body that is capable of withstanding the evils of industrialism and a brain that is attuned to clear and reasoned analysis of life and not equipped with just a few dogmas . . . if children are given an opportunity to think for themselves, are kept untainted by the propaganda of imperialist and ecclesiastical organisations, are given every chance to take their own line of action or study they will act as they should act and behave a little more rationally than our fellow creatures are behaving now' (*The Folk Trail*, London, 1929, p. 19).

While we have no evidence that Les was ever a member of the Rushey Green group this book aims to demonstrate that his reasoned and undogmatic approach when lobbying and negotiating both at local government and at parliamentary level seems to point to his having been inspired by the early education he gained in the Co-operative movement as well as by his mother's influence.

[4]

Membership of the Communist Party of Great Britain

Les is believed to have joined the Young Communist League in 1936 at about the same time as he joined the Electrical Trades Union (ETU). Harry Bacon tells us that many of the Bermondsey friends whom he used to accompany to all-night parties also belonged to the League. While, like most teenagers, Les was beginning to experience the excitement of parties and a social life away from home, as a passionate and well-informed young man he was also well aware of the powerful forces shaping his world at this time – mass unemployment, the threat of Fascism throughout Europe and, in particular, the Spanish Civil War. Les would have been almost a year old when the Communist Party of Great Britain was formed on 1 August 1920 under its first General Secretary Harry Pollitt. This was a coming together of various leftist groups and, at that time, it acknowledged the authority of the Communist Party of the Soviet Union.

The Party won two seats in Parliament in the 1945 election – William Gallacher for West Fife and Phil Piratin for Mile End. Its strength and influence, even before the collapse of the USSR (in 1990–91), was not as strong as that of other European Communist parties and, of course, there were many defections following the 1956 Hungarian uprising. At the beginning of the Cold War the CP strategy was to maintain the earlier (1920) split from the Labour Party but with the intention of supporting that party at the ballot box.

The Young Communist League produced a journal, *Challenge*, the thrust of which was to challenge young people to draw attention to low pay, unpaid overtime and poor working conditions by joining trade unions and organising. It had a strong educational element, a regular page of book reviews, and an advice column which (quite remarkably for those times) included information on sex and birth control for newly married couples and young people generally which they would almost certainly not have found in any other journal. *Challenge* also played a central part in the campaign to raise funds for the victims of General Franco, and YCL members collected money and food for Spain from door to door all the year round, even on Boxing Day. A British Youth Spanish Food Shop Committee was set up to co-ordinate the campaign as winter approached. Critics of the movement remarked that the YCL was neglecting poor children in the UK; the response of one YCL branch was to hold a large Christmas party for the children of unemployed workers to which 40 Basque children were also invited.

The quality of writing in *Challenge* was high and serious issues were discussed – for example, the January 1938 issue had an article about the threat of overpopulation but went on to argue that the globe could give life and security to twice the number of people then regarded as too many.

It would seem that the Young Communists were trained according to the principles which Marx upheld when teaching his own young adherents almost a hundred years earlier. Liebknecht (quoted in Wheen, p. 194) observed: 'He [Marx] kept impressing on us "young fellows" the necessity for logical thought and clarity in expression and forced us to study . . . while the other emigrants were daily planning a world revolution and day after day, night after night, intoxicating themselves with the opium-like motto "Tomorrow it will begin" we, the "brimstone band", the "bandits", the "dregs of mankind" spent our time in the British Museum and tried to educate ourselves . . .'

As far as we know, Les and his young YCL contemporaries did not have access to the British Museum Reading Room but, following his own traditional education as a working-class boy from Deptford, one can understand how he came to be fired by a political idea. Although he was too young to volunteer for the International Brigade he was certainly involved in the massive Lewisham effort to raise funds for the Republicans. He joined the Party, and, in so doing, gained new insights and a new level of education. He became a very different person from the young lad who left school. In the Party he learned about Marxism, he learned to think about the world in historical and material terms and he gained an economic and class-based understanding of the workplace. Without a doubt his clear understanding of the meaning of the dialectic was at the base of his exceptional ability when discussing issues with those whose views were totally opposed to his own. Richard Kavanagh put it like this: 'As Young Communists we were encouraged to read – even the heavy Marxist stuff. We came to see the Soviet Union as a "workers' state" – the whole Communist Party movement was linked with the world movement of the working-class. We translated that into our daily work. Our aim was to see how to get rid of capitalism and introduce socialism. But in the USSR nationalism became the dominant force and those at the top manipulated us and let us down. Class was our ground work, our basic philosophy and our launching pad. The notion stayed with you even if you lost more battles than you won. Les retained the class instinct throughout – he was not swayed by momentary slip-ups.'

When one considers the effect that Karl Marx's philosophy has had on millions of people throughout the world and the number of world leaders who were inspired by him, irrespective of the way their own philosophies eventually diverged (for example, compare Gandhi with Mao or Mugabe), it is remarkable how many highly educated people have never read Marx's own work or even a summary of it. Whilst some would argue that his writing is too dense and difficult this cannot be said of the work of modern historians who have written about him. It is not surprising then to learn that when Francis Wheen began to research for his biography of the 'flesh and blood' Karl Marx, many friends looked at him 'with pity and incredulity' (Wheen p. 4). 'Why . . . should anyone want to write about – still less read about – this discredited, outmoded, irrelevant figure?' Yet, as Wheen goes on to say, Marx was writing about and predicting what is now termed 'globalisation' as far back as 1848! What is more, contrary to the commonly held view of Marx as a demonic and evil figure, the man himself, like Jesus Christ, would be horrified at the crimes against humanity which have been committed in his name.

If the Young Communists like Les and his contemporaries learned about Marx's philosophy and its purpose of understanding the world in order to bring about change, they also soon learned and had to live with the views of those who classified Communism as an ideology with all the distasteful, pejorative and loaded connotations of that imprecise and biased word.

During the height of its power Communism inspired countless people in Britain, of all classes and backgrounds. When one hears intellectuals and middle-class people talk about it now they often seem surprised at themselves and think of the time when they joined the CPGB as just a thrilling phase they passed through. Doris Lessing has described it as something like a psychotic affliction that many of her generation suffered, adding that at one time everyone one knew was a Communist but now not one of them remains so. It is not difficult to understand that working-class people do not hold these views, even those who did not remain in the Party. For them Communism was no mere intellectual dalliance, but represented a coherent programme to improve working-class lives. For Les's fellow workers in the contracting sections of the electrical trade, for example, Communists within their trade union fought for their rights to better working conditions, sick pay, holiday pay and job security at a time when contracted workers had none of these and could be sacked, literally, at a moment's notice. Such things were of little concern to the privileged middle classes. For them, perhaps, Communism was just an inspiring if transient good cause, an ideal appealing at the time but later discarded as unrealistic and utopian. For those such as Les's old friend, John Esterson, who continue to adhere, 75 years later, to the Communism they first learned about in the 1920s, it remains a strong belief that, for the working-classes, there is a better way to live than under capitalism.

The National Guild of Co-operators was equally active in the struggle against unemployment and Fascism, collecting for the hunger marches and taking part in peace marches. Andy Hawkins used to attend the passionate rallies for Spain at the Albert Hall where representatives of all political parties would appear on the platform – the Liberal Edmund Davies, Harry Pollitt of the CPGB and Michael Foot (to name but a few) with Alan Wilkinson, the fiery redhead from Jarrow, taking the collection and Paul Robeson entertaining everyone. 'I used to go there straight from work,' says Hawkins, 'and open up the little brown envelope which in those days held our weekly pay, taking five shillings out of it and emptying the rest into the bucket as it came round, such was the emotional fervour of that time.' J. Fyrth (p. 19) has described the Aid Spain Campaign as 'the biggest movement of international solidarity in British history', bringing together people of all views, Liberals, Labour members, the Women's Co-operative Guilds and the Communists. More than 2000 Britons joined the International Brigades.

John Rampling was witness at this time to the bloody battle of Cable Street which took place on 4 October 1936, when the CPGB led a demonstration against Mosley's British

Union of Fascists march through east London. About a quarter of a million people prevented the Blackshirts from marching through the street, which was lined with Jewish tailors' shops. 'I came back to find the resistance of the people against Mosley,' says John. 'There were many Jewish people amongst the demonstrators, though there were people of all backgrounds because, substantially, the Fascist movement was about opposition to all immigration. The Fascists hated all the immigrants, of whatever nationality, particularly because so many of them were so clever! A big barricade was built during this historic march and counter-demonstration, and Mosley and his followers were pelted. The opposition called out slogans as well as spontaneous jibes such as "Did the orange hit him?" to which the instant reply was, "No, but I wish it had!" There is a big mural now, at the other end of Cable Street, depicting the event.' A week after the march the windows of every Jewish shop in the Mile End Road were smashed. These events led to the passing of the Public Order Act.

It is not surprising then that Les was engaged by Communism. In Nina Fishman's view (p. 231) it was chiefly concern about Fascism which roused the new recruits into the CPGB at this time, rather than the experiences of hunger and unemployment; she argues that the Young Communists did not have the experience to view the domestic struggle as the crucial influence shaping their own lives. This might have been true of some, yet Les and his fellow Young Communists in Deptford were captivated by the rousing speeches of the Scots Kath Duncan, who recognised that all the issues both at home and abroad were urgent and could be tackled simultaneously. Kath not only immersed herself ceaselessly in the Deptford Spanish Aid Committee, collecting money to buy ambulances for the Spanish Republican Government and interviewing personally men for the Brigades, she also stood for the repeal of the 10% cut in benefits and the abolition of the means test. While she and other Deptford residents confronted Mosley's Fascists in Cable Street and, later, in Bermondsey, she simultaneously engaged herself in opposing the increases in gas charges which the South Metropolitan Gas Company planned to levy on the poorest people, while decreasing charges to the business community and the wealthier classes. It will be abundantly clear to anyone who knew Les in his trade union days and in his final years at the Pensioners' Forum, that Kath Duncan's inspiration and the principles she stood for remained with him for the rest of his life. Surprisingly, the issues which she fought for, especially that of means testing, remain relevant and central to this very day.[1]

Throughout the 1930s the General Secretary of the TUC Walter (later Lord) Citrine and Ernest Bevin (then the General Secretary of the TGWU) realised the implications of Fascism for the trade unions and were ahead of the Labour front bench in declaring the need for Britain to oppose Fascism. Fishman records that in most working communities and factories Communists were usually the first and only political activists propagating the case for opposing Fascism both at home and abroad, and the Communists argued for a defensive alliance between Britain, France and the USSR to combat Fascism.

At this time (as Richard Crossman noted in May 1937) even left-wing Labour people were failing to reach millions 'who still read the racing page' (Crossman, R., quoted by Ben Pimlott, in the *New Statesman*, May 1937). John Rampling observes that the Labour Party at the time of Oswald Mosley possibly saw nothing to choose between the Fascists and the Communists, seeing the Communists as fascist too, since both groups were strictly governed from above, much as Catholics also are! Paradoxically, though, it was the CPGB not the Labour Party that was the catalyst in the fight against the evils of Fascism. Any similarity between the Communists and

[1] For an account of Kath Duncan's life and work see Steele.

the Fascists was in the way they were hierarchically governed and controlled; their principles and their philosophies were diametrically opposed.

In 1935 there was a *modus vivendi* between the CP and the TUC. The CP Secretary Harry Pollitt approached Walter Citrine in March 1934 offering to place the Party's service at the unions' disposal. In return he asked for a formal united front alliance between the TUC and the CPGB. The result was that two circulars were sent from the TUC to affiliated unions and Trades Councils recommending that the CPGB and 'any fascist organisation' should be debarred by rule from holding union and Trades Council office. In the same circulars (which came to be dubbed 'The Black Circulars') information was sought about Communist 'infiltration' in official activities. The circulars were opposed by the AEU, the T+GWU, the NUR and at least nine other unions. Bevin did his best to distance himself from them, arguing that 'a trade unionist has a right to his political freedom' (Fishman, p. 86). A motion by the AEU for both circulars to be rejected was defeated but, later, both unions and the TUC failed to put the circulars into practice and no affiliated union changed its rules. Furthermore, few comments on Communist infiltration were subsequently received.

Fishman has given us a brilliant, analytic term 'revolutionary pragmatism' in her account of the Communist Party approach to managing the economic struggles in the workplace during the inter-war years. The conflict was recognised to be between trade union loyalism and rank and filism and the term is applied to the way the CP leadership succeeded in welding these two conflicting elements together. The leader Harry Pollitt and his Central Committee colleague, Johnny Campbell, always advised that loyalty to the union must come first so party activists developed a supremely pragmatic approach in their work on behalf of their work-mates, combining the guidelines with their own talents and judgements relevant to local culture and tradition. Thus they learned how to lead economic conflict yet also to survive on the shop floor. In describing the contrast between the practical commonsense approach and profound Communist belief (practicality with Utopian faith) activists operated in the belief that the proletarian revolution would ultimately take place. Theirs was a faith which was fundamental to the working-class nonconformism – indeed many Communists had come from a lay-preacher background. These CP activists who worked patiently to bring about change had stamina and this, combined with their belief, sustained them in their painstaking, boring lives as shop stewards and branch officers. Fishman argues that historians and labour leaders dismissed these activists as a small element and that they failed to recognise their achievements (Fishman, pp. 333–6).

While there was a revolutionary rhetoric and commitment in terms of the CPGB's broad ideas, in reality (or in practice) it was a pragmatic organisation. Fishman's analysis relates to a period preceding Les's own trade union activism after World War II, but it seems to hold a key to his approach. He gained not only political but also intellectual inspiration from his Communist training which helped to guide him in a way which was idealistic, yet also rational and pragmatic throughout his life. When World War II came the CP was in favour of banning strikes and prior to this Communists in the workplace were very often instrumental in settling disputes rather than taking the 'revolutionary road' of the Trotskyists – who believed in having more and more strikes until the downfall of capitalism was attained. This was never the approach of the original CPGB except possibly in the early 1920s.

Les stood for Parliament (representing Deptford) as a Communist in the 1950 General Election. He received 562 votes (1.3%) and lost his deposit. He also stood three times in local elections, in Vale Ward in 1949, in St John's Ward in 1959 and in Marlowe Ward in 1964. He was never elected. As his old friend and colleague Charles Job remarks, 'He stood as a Communist candidate at a time when the Party was under fierce attack from the press and media generally (particularly in '59 and '64) – an act of considerable courage.' Previously he was elected to his local branch committee, and at the London District Congress of the Party he was elected to the important London District Committee – a rare honour. Les was one of the first members Stan Davison would contact when he wanted a really able London member to attend national meetings and conferences. His old friend Alfred Stockwell (who died on 26 April 1999) describes how he first encountered Les during the run-up to the 1950 General Election. Walking through the street in Lewisham he heard someone talking over a megaphone, and found Les standing at a corner making an address holding on to an old pram, weighed down by a battery and loudspeaker. He seemed very agile, an attractive man with brownish hair. 'He had no car, or anything like that, and presented rather an odd sight,' remembers Mike Power (now Campaigns Officer at the TUC), whose mother's home was one of the committee rooms for the election campaign. Mike and his older brother attended Lucas Vale School in Tanners Hill at that time and Mike recalls that on one occasion his brother's teacher was telling the class about the forthcoming election, mentioning the Conservative and Labour candidates. His brother put his hand up and asked, 'What about Les Stannard?' and was met with a frosty silence – an indication of the establishment view of Communism. Alf Stockwell recalls that, at that time, slogans used to be painted on the roads with whitewash. Theirs was 'Campaigning on behalf of the CP candidate, Les Stannard'. Party supporters would estimate how far a bucket of whitewash would last and then knock on a comrade's door somewhere along the way to find a fresh bucket of whitewash prepared. One supporter who was actively involved in the whitewashing activity was Mrs Louise Pope of Pagnall Street. Alf says that although the campaigning mostly concentrated on poorer families they had considerable support from better-off families too. The whitewash practice was subsequently prohibited following a by-law brought in by a Labour councillor, Walter Green, who had argued that the writing of 'Keep Left' on the roads was liable to cause an accident! Alf says that he did not see much of Les after the campaigning and that Les seemed genuinely surprised at not having succeeded. Richard Balfe MEP, who was Les's fellow member on the RACS Political Committee, remarks that standing for the Communist Party and not for Labour was the wrong move at the wrong time and that Les might well have reached Parliament as a Labour candidate since this was a real avenue of social mobility at the time. However, Balfe remarks that Les's contribution to society was possibly even greater than an MP could achieve and that his tireless activity throughout his career and after retirement brought positive and permanent changes to the lives of many people.

[5]

A 'Spark' for Life

Les began training as an electrician after he left school in 1933, together with his lifelong friend, Harry Bacon. They did not join as apprentices but both started as junior mates, becoming electricians' mates when they reached the age of 18. Electricians' mates were semi-skilled assistants. There was no age limit for this job level – some remained at that level throughout their careers; they received 80% of the electrician's wage and some went on to be fully skilled. Harry and Les completed their full training during the war years.

Les joined the Electrical Trades Union in 1936 and remained a member of this union and the subsequent Electrical, Electronic, Telecommunications, and Plumbing Union (EETPU) for 52 years when he joined SOGAT in 1988. In 1991 SOGAT became the GPMU (Graphical Paper and Media Union) and this was the union that Les was a member of at the time of his death. He was a member of the ETU London South-East Branch Committee for 27 years, holding the post of Chairman for ten years, and Treasurer for three years. When he joined the staff of Express Newspapers in 1974 he became a member of the Press Branch.

The proud and honourable Electrical Trades Union was born in 1889 at a time when, Gordon Schaffer tells us, London's half-starved labourers fought the first battle against the oppression and exploitation of Victorian England. At this time the Amalgamated Society of Engineers existed to guard the craft standard of skilled workers from the millions of unskilled ones and was not a weapon against capitalism. On 30 November 1889 a conference was held by a small Manchester organisation known as the Amalgamated Society of Telegraph and Telephone Construction Men. Most of the delegates were from Lancashire and Yorkshire but there were also representatives from a London organisation, 'The Union of Electrical Operatives'. It was unanimously agreed at this conference to change the name to the Electrical Trades Union (comprising the London and Manchester organisations) and its rules were modelled on those of the Amalgamated Society of Engineers. The union was registered with the Union of Friendly Societies and amalgamation between them was agreed in principle in 1889 and formally accomplished at a Liverpool conference on 6 December 1890. The ETU was thus formed away from the ASE because that organisation had refused to support the labourers' bitter struggles. The ETU was never insular in its outlook – its very first balance sheet shows an advance of £10 to an Australian strike fund (Schaffer). It was also, from the start, a progressive and forward-looking union, against life membership of its officials and supporting innovative rules on the power of membership vis-à-vis the Executive.

These were the days when the advice subsequently offered by Norman Tebbit to get 'on yer bike' was first given. Junior mates were not allowed contracts so Harry and Les used to go out on their bikes looking for work. If they returned to Les's home together Nan would give them cups of cocoa and scold them for not trying hard enough to find work – which they considered unjustified! Harry remembers one particular day when they both went to a firm called Berkeley Electric. They were interviewed by an engineer called Mr Stokes who had a bad stoop and thus appeared to be focusing his gaze on their shoes rather than their faces! Since Harry's father had been in the army his shoes were invariably highly polished –

not so Les's shoes! Harry got a job but Les didn't, so Les returned a fortnight later with highly polished shoes and thus he too got a job.

Although these were times of rising unemployment and anxiety in many working-class families Les was beginning to enjoy a normal social life with friends of his age. Occasionally they would go to the Amersham Arms in New Cross and Harry remembers Les performing a very talented and popular 'turn' called 'That Old Coat of Mine' (accompanied on the piano). This would involve stripping down to a pair of French knickers, borrowed from a friend's girlfriend! They would then have a whip-round, buy more beer and take it back to finish off the evening at the home of Harry's future mother-in-law in Clifton Rise. Harry's and Les's fathers also used to meet socially at the Rose and Crown in Greenwich. Charlie Stannard sang accompanied by Harry's father at the piano.

One of Harry and Les's earliest jobs was the changing of gas lamps to electricity in all houses in Deptford. When he received the London Borough of Lewisham's first Community Award on 26 January 1993, Les in his acceptance speech mentioned by name the two Labour councillors, Chisnall and Wild, who had persuaded the Deptford Labour Party and the old Deptford Borough Council that every street in Deptford should have electricity installed.

There was a cinema strike during Easter 1938 which affected the New Cross Cinema, known as the Kinema. The strike also took place in Manchester and Hull. The issue was the principle of the 48-hour week, which had been agreed locally by the union after World War I. Tom O'Brien (later Sir Tom), General Secretary of the Cinema Exhibitors Association, had installed his employees to replace the ETU strikers. The position was a delicate one as the CEA had signed an agreement with the National Association of Theatrical Employees (NATE) in 1935 providing for hours in excess of 48. There was an ETU motion at the 1935 TUC Congress against the CEA which was attacked by Tom O'Brien on the grounds that it was 'innocent on the surface and wicked underneath'. He argued that, at that time, the employers were largely in control and would not accept a 48-hour week. The matter was returned to the TUC Congress the following year, but the position was unchanged. On this occasion Tom O'Brien described the ETU as 'manifestly Communist-ridden' (Lloyd, p. 212). A shade of things to come. Les and Harry had no work themselves at this particular time and spent their days leafleting in support of the ETU strikers. The cinema was highly popular in these pre-TV days so when Harry and Les organised a Saturday night picket at the New Cross Cinema people did not take very kindly to the two young lads who were trying to stop them from going in for an evening's entertainment. Harry remembers that when he and Les attended the next meeting of their SE Branch they were so full of themselves for having carried out the picket that they couldn't keep quiet. They were evicted from the meeting and not allowed in again until they apologised. The ETU lost the strike, none of the strikers' demands were met and the men never got their jobs back. The Hull strike lasted for a magnificent 30 weeks but was also abandoned due to blacklegging by non-members. As John Lloyd puts it (p. 213), the workers lost everything – 'no 48-hour week, no increase in wages, no recognition, no guarantee on victimisation'.

Harry Bacon and Les Stannard volunteered to join the militia at the age of 20. The general attitude of the ETU and other unions at the start of World War II was different from that in the Great War: they were now conscious of the growing menace of Fascism. Workers were willing to sacrifice themselves because their experience had taught them that there could be no peace and no progress while Fascism menaced any people in the world. Ernest Bevin, the Minister of Labour at the time, had an obsession to beat Nazism and Fascism, and the hatred of Fascism was a driving force.

[6]
The War Years

'Capitalism carries in itself war, as the thunder cloud carries the storm.'

Jean Jaures, French socialist murdered in 1914.

Les and Harry Bacon volunteered to join the RAF as electricians just before World War II was declared. Les had been working for six years, had firm political views and was well informed and clear in his mind about the dangers confronting the rest of Europe – racism, Fascism, widespread unemployment and the threat of domination by a brutal power. Forty-one years later, when he was interviewed as he arrived in Liverpool to join the March for Jobs on 9 December 1980, he had this to say: 'I have come to take part in the march because I don't want to go back to what my parents and I suffered in the 1930s.' He was speaking from bitter experience of those harsh years when his father was frequently out of work and his grandmother was taking care of the three growing boys.

Les commenced service on 7 September 1939 and was attached first to 1 RAF depot and 1 Recruits Centre at Uxbridge, then to 24 Squadron based at Hendon. Before he left the country with his first squadron he and Harry returned briefly to Deptford on leave and decided they would go along to the usual ETU SE Branch meeting at the Amersham Arms. To their surprise they were not welcomed, because they were both in uniform. Les knew his mother was dying and, following her death on 22 November 1939, he was given leave to attend her funeral and arrived at his home in Rutt's Terrace – again in uniform. We do not know how much leave he was allowed and whether he had any time to spend with his family after the funeral but from what we know of his strong bond with his mother it is not hard to imagine that it must have been a grief-stricken young man who returned to his squadron and to prepare for war. Les and his colleagues travelled by boat to Marseilles and then on to North Africa.

War records detailing Les's postings give the following particulars of the squadrons and other groups or wings to which he was attached during the period he was abroad. They were 24 and 112 and 148 Squadrons; 202 Group (RAF Middle East Forces); 256 Wing; 136 unit; MAD (Mobile Aircraft Division), which later changed its name to Advanced Aircraft Depot; and MAAF (Mediterranean Allied Air Forces). Although he was released from both 112 and 148 and attached to the other units, these two squadrons were the ones he was attached to most of the time.

24 Squadron was based in Hendon. It was employed chiefly to ferry VIPs around during 1940.

112 Squadron was originally formed in 1917 and reformed on 16 May 1939 aboard the aircraft carrier *Argus* at Southampton, for transportation to the Middle East. It arrived in Egypt on 26 May 1939. Gladiators were received the following month and when Italy entered the war in June 1940 the squadron flew fighter patrols over the Western Desert while a detached flight was operating in the Sudan. In January 1941 the squadron moved to Greece to provide air defence and fly offensive patrols over Albania. When the Germans invaded Greece from Bulgaria the squadron provided fighter cover for the Athens area and evacuated first to Crete and then back to Egypt. In July 1941, 112 Squadron

was re-equipped with Tomahawks for fighter sweeps over the desert and in May 1942 it began fighter bomber missions. The squadron flew ground attack operations in support of the 8th Army throughout the campaign in the Western Desert and, after the rout of the Axis armies at El Alamein, it deployed westwards into Tunisia (Halley, pp. 188–9).

148 Squadron was re-formed in June 1937 and disbanded again in May 1940. It re-formed in December 1940 from detachments of other squadrons at Luqa, Malta, from where its Wellingtons attacked ports and airfields in Italy, Sicily and Libya. The squadron moved to Egypt in 1941 and was disbanded again in April 1942. On 14 March 1943 it was redesignated for special duties from the Special Liberator Flight (X Flight). The Liberators and Halifaxes were engaged in dropping arms and supplies to resistance forces in Greece, Albania and Yugoslavia. It was involved in bombing missions during November 1943. In January 1944 the squadron moved to Italy and added a Lysander flight for pick-up missions. Liberators were replaced by Halifaxes at the same time and Poland and Northern Italy became the main area of operations for the squadron. Halley tells us: 'As the Russians overran Poland, missions over the Balkans again formed the main bulk of the squadron's work, the final effort over Poland being an attempt to supply the Polish resistance forces in Warsaw by long-range sorties from Southern Italy. As the war drew to a close, trips were being made to Northern Italy, Austria, Czechoslovakia and Southern Germany and, after a period of general transport duties in Italy, the Squadron moved to Egypt where it disbanded on 15 January 1946' (Halley, pp. 220–21).

256 Wing went from RAF Station Uxbridge to Southampton then to Mex, Alexandria, Port Said, Ikingi, Maryut, Aboukir, El Dhaba, Cairo, Amyria, Maaten Bagush, Shafakhana, the Western Desert, and Ismailia.

202 Group existed originally as 'Egypt' Group from 18 April 1939 and became 202 from September 1939. In

December 1941 it became AHQ Egypt and it was re-formed in July 1944 to administer RAF units taking part in Operation Anvil, later 'Dragoon'.

According to the records Les started at the rank of Aircraftsman 2 and his trade is given as 'Electrician'. He was promoted to Electrician 2 and to Leading Aircraftsman by 1941. His proficiency level is given in every instance as Class A and described as Superior. His character throughout is described as Very Good. Les gained special qualifications for his proficiency in working on Hurricanes, Halifaxes, Spitfires, Mosquitoes, Ansons and Oxford Mustangs. He received a Good Conduct badge Class 1st/A in September 1942 and was awarded the Africa Star in October 1944 and authorised to wear the clasp to the Africa Star ribbon. The Africa Star was awarded for entry into an operational area in North Africa between 10 June 1940 (the date of Italy's declaration of war) and 12 May 1943 which marked the end of operations in North Africa.

It is well known that most war veterans never so much as whisper a word about the worst horrors they witnessed on the battlefields or other arenas of war, still less do they ever disclose anything about the physical or mental suffering they endured. Les was hospitalised twice – first between October and December 1942 and again in January 1944 – but the records do not elaborate.

David Musther was a pilot in 112 Squadron, though not at the same time as Les. In 1995 they established contact and the paragraphs which follow are Les's own words to him:

'I arrived at Helwan [Egypt] in Easter 1940 to join 112 Squadron then flying Gladiators. I was an electrician and moved with them to Sidi Haneish soon after the Italians joined the war. I was loaned to 202 group after Xmas 1940 with a wireless mechanic named McIntyre – we worked on a R/T [Radio Telegraphy] system above Saloun Pass before Bardia was captured by the Army. Shortly afterwards we returned to Amyria just outside Alexandria – to rejoin the Squadron before their departure to Greece.

'In Iannina [Greece] near the lake – the R/T and electrical generators were based in a field away from the air-strip. After the retreat back from Iannina we were based just outside Athens [possibly in Piraeus] and we went by Sunderland Flying Boat to Crete just above Suda Bay. Part of the Squadron went to Heraklion the other side of the island. And they were still there when the German parachutists dropped.

'We evacuated Crete in an old ship called the Itria – we went to Abakir before going back to Helwan, in June 1941 – to what was supposed to be a Wireless and Electricians Pool. [The background to this story is that Les was on the last boat to leave Crete during the German invasion. The squadron laid landmines on the airstrip while the British troops were evacuating the island when the Germans invaded.]

'The Depot CO was a first-war pilot, Group Captain Rees VC. Our Warrant Officer Reader rucked with the authorities – he didn't want to lose the men he worked with and we all rejoined the squadron in Haifa. After that we returned to near Kasferet on the Suez Canal where the squadron was re-equipped with Tommy Hawks. Two of the sergeants among the electricians and wireless mechanics were named Drake and Howlett. One of the sergeants among the fitters was Wensley.

'I missed part of the advance in the desert due to hospitalisation but returned to the unit when it was just outside Agilea in Libya – following a retreat we were based at Gazala – El Adem and again at Sidi Haneishi. By that time the shark had been painted on the aircraft.[1] I remember the stand-down[2] from flying over Bir Akeim where the free French were

[1] 112 Squadron flew Kittyhawks at this time. These aircraft had sharks' teeth painted on their engine covers to make them look fierce when strafing Rommel's Africa Corps.

[2] Release from operation for a period.

defending. The stand-down was to allow us to put our clean dhobis on whilst the Duke of Gloucester inspected the ranks.

'I was posted to 136 u.u. which was famed and moved from outside Cairo to Benghazi after El Alamein to join a repair depot for fighter aircraft. Late in 1943 I was posted to 148 Squadron at Derna and later we went to Brindisi Italy before I returned home in September 1944.[1]

'Since that time I have lost touch with many of our colleagues, although I did meet a 112 Squadron MT driver at a pensioners rally in Norwich 3 or 4 years ago[2]. I would like any information you may receive about people on the squadron about that time, including the only disciplinarian "Smudge".'

During the preparation of this biography an advertisement was placed in the *Help – Calling Old Colleagues* section of the RAF magazine *Air Mail*. Unfortunately none of those mentioned above have come forward but we did receive memories of Les from two men who knew him, both of whom remember him as 'Joe'. Bob Parson writes: 'I knew him in Helwan in 1940 and remember one incident which occurred in the desert when water was very short. Apparently Les heard that an officer had used water to lay sand-dust in his tent; he started a campaign about officers "stealing the troops' water".' Des Cocking met Les at Amyria in December 1940: 'Being in the same Signals Section I got to know him quite well as a great character and pal. He was as "red" as anyone I have ever known; he was a great organiser and when we were at Iannina in Greece he set up "Smokey Joe's", a small café serving egg and chips and plenty of wine – the source was unknown but it was always free! He left Greece with me via Crete but left 112 Squadron shortly after returning to Helwan.'

[1] Les was one of 339 men to join the unit from various squadrons in September 1942.

[2] This was Russell Read who is now a member of the Norfolk and Norwich Pensioners' Association.

Bill Steeples, another old friend in 112 Squadron, also has vivid memories of 'Joe's Café' which was little more than a space between two houses covered over with sacking. He remembered that one of Les's assignments was to run the electricians' tent which was involved 24 hours a day in battery charging for both aircraft and batteries. He remembered another event from those memorable and bizarre days which, though sad, still brings a smile to his face. 'There was this poor Greek woman who had gone quite mad and used frequently to emerge "completely starkers". She took a shine to Les and from time to time used to descend on the electricians' tent where he was working. His colleagues would receive a frantic phone call, "Come and get me – that woman's here again!"'

Les was released under Class A (priority) on 12 April 1946 probably because of the importance of his trade in post-war Britain. He then remained in Class G reserve (which meant that he could be recalled immediately if the national interest required it) and was released from this reserve in 1959 when he had reached the age of 40.

Les's old friend, the late Alfred Stockwell, remembered that Les always underplayed the dangers he was exposed to during the war and frequently said to him, 'You were more bleedin' likely to have been killed in the London air raids, Alfie, than I was in the middle of the desert.' That is a remark which is typical of the Les we all knew.

[7]

Return to Civilian Life

After the war the young men who had learned their electrical trade while serving with the armed forces needed assistance. The government owed a duty to all those who had played a part in the war and the new Labour government had pledged a policy of full employment.

Les and Harry came home in 1945 and discussed their future with Les's father, who worked in the trolleys and trams department at the London Transport Charlton works and told them there was work there for them. In due course Harry decided to join the Charlton works and stayed there for the remainder of his working life. There is little information on Les's activities when he first returned from the war but he chose not to join Harry but to go into the contracting industry (there is a note in the ETU South–East Branch Minute Book stating, 'Brother Stannard commenced work on 2 December 1946') and he remained in that industry until he joined the staff of the *Daily Express* where he worked from 1973 till he retired in 1984.

The London South-East Branch of the ETU

As members of the SE Branch of the ETU much of the history of this period of Les's and Harry's lives is tied up with the branch committee which continued until the newly structured EETPU replaced the old ETU, under General Secretary Frank Chapple in 1961. The branch meetings always took place at the Cranbrook Arms in Brookmill Road. Harry became the first Assistant Secretary and later Secretary, and Les was elected and remained Chairman for 10 years as well as holding the post of Treasurer for 3 years. Earlier the branch Chairman, Bill Smith (then in his sixties) had become an enormous influence particularly on Les's life since he had kept up a correspondence with him throughout the war years. 'Bill Smith was like a father to us,' says Harry. 'He was a self-taught philosopher and he put us on the right road – teaching us not to be impulsive and to quieten down.' Smith is believed to have been a member of the Labour Party. He was to become Les's mentor and it is not hard to detect his influence on Les's thought on many issues and, in particular, on his commitment to the state pension: as far back as the 1958 Policy Conference Smith was arguing for a non-means tested overall rise in the pension (1958 Conference pp. 35–6).

Harry recalls that during these post-war years the branch committee had a contingency fund to help members in distress. All retired members used to be sent £2 at Christmas (equivalent to about £50 in the 1990s). Young Les made a proposal to the committee that members like himself could improve on this by actually visiting the retired members to see how they were faring. It is an indication of his concern for pensioners even at this time and is confirmed by his family, all of whom have commented on Les's unusual fondness and affection for the elderly members of his own family from a very young age.

The Minute Book of the London SE Branch meetings of the ETU (for 1946–47) is a rich historical document, covering the wide range of issues discussed and causes supported in those early post-war years following the election of the first Labour government. In October 1946, for example, we find the members agreeing to send financial support in response to a letter from Great Ormond Street Hospital for Sick Children. A collection was made in support of the catering trade workers who were then in dispute. It is notable too that at almost every branch meeting it was Les who seemed to propose admittance of a new applicant or the readmission of those who had fallen behind with their dues. In February 1946 a motion from Brothers Stannard and Gries refers to the dismissal of two workers from Deptford Borough Council for misconduct; the meeting agreed to the dispatch of a letter expressing concern over the dismissals and calling for an investigation by the appropriate committee.

In January 1947 the minutes record a request to Deptford Borough Council to grant living accommodation in the borough to a GP, Dr Chunda, who because of the housing shortage was forced to live outside the borough in which he practised. These minutes also record a motion, moved by Les, regretting the Labour government's action in employing troops in the road haulage dispute and making a number of proposals including the operation of a national wages policy. The pattern of his political activity for the years ahead and his belief in the importance and value of the resolution was, by now, well established.

Post-war homelessness in London

Les was soon heavily involved in political activity through his union branch. After the war, in 1946, there were half a million families waiting for homes in London. Local authorities were supposed to requisition empty properties in order to house homeless people but Tory councils (where the most spacious properties were) refused to use their requisitionary powers. One property identified was Duchess of Bedford House in Kensington. It had been offered by the government to the Tory council which had a list of 4000 homeless families. The council refused the offer and wanted to return the property to its owners, the Prudential, for high-rent reletting. On 6 September 1946 a Communist councillor on the LCC (London County Council, predecessor to the GLC) led a meeting aimed at identifying suitable empty dwellings and next day arranged for homeless people to arrive at 2 pm with their bedding and possessions. The occupation was carefully planned and over 100 families filled Duchess of Bedford House and neighbouring buildings. Further moves into other properties took place, for example the Ivanhoe Hotel in Bloomsbury. Food and small cooking stoves were taken in to the squatters by pulleys. On 9 September the London District of the CPGB asked the Minister of Health, Aneurin Bevan, to receive a deputation in order to discuss more occupation of empty properties but on the very same day there was a cabinet meeting and within 24 hours it was made clear that the government was determined to crush the movement. As Branson comments (p. 118), the involvement of the CP greatly embarrassed the right-wing Labour leaders. This is part of the statement from Number 10: 'His Majesty's government takes a very serious view of the forcible seizure and occupation by unauthorised persons of private premises in London . . . this action has been instigated and organised by the CP and must result in hindering rather than in helping the arrangements made for the orderly rehousing of those in need of accommodation . . . unless steps are taken to check lawless measures of this sort, the rights of the ordinary law-abiding citizens are endangered and anarchy may result' (quoted in Branson, p. 124). Harry Pollitt's response to this statement came on 12 September at a London demonstration. He said that 'all the talk about the sacred rights of private property, about the forces of anarchy which have been let loose, is done to preserve the system of rich and poor' (ibid. pp. 124–5). Writs were issued against the trespassers on 11 September. Electricity and water were cut off (but in one case, at Fountain Court, Westminster reinstalled them when supporters of the squatters arrived with candles). Eventually, following discussion at CPGB Headquarters, withdrawal from Duchess of Bedford House was recommended and a statement was issued.

On 17 September Nye Bevan announced that no legal action would be taken against squatters who left voluntarily and promised that they would not lose their places in the housing queue. The case of the five conspirators (all Communist councillors) was heard at the Old Bailey at the end of October. One councillor, defending himself, drew attention to the men and women squatters who had stood up heroically in the Blitz, as well as to the soldiers, sailors and airmen – 'the people to whom we owe our present freedom'. All five were found guilty but to everyone's surprise they were bound over to keep the peace for two years. Forty-nine years later Les was to express precisely the same sentiments at the 1995 VE Day celebrations when he called on the Mayor of Lewisham to act towards the borough's elderly population in accordance with the words he had spoken about the borough's support for the 'wartime generation' while simultaneously the Pensioners' Committee was about to be axed.

The London SE Branch of the ETU played an active part in these events. On 10 September 1946 Les Stannard, then Chairman of the branch, moved (and gained unanimous agreement for) an emergency resolution which was sent to the Prime Minister, the Deptford Labour Party, the Deptford Trades Council, the *Daily Herald* and the *South London Press*. The resolution said:

> That, we, members of the London South-East Branch, Electrical Trades Union, deplore the government's action and Mr Bevan's speech regarding the squatters.
>
> We demand the immediate supply of gas and electricity to all premises occupied by the squatters.
>
> We demand that local authorities requisition immediately, all empty premises suitable for housing the people;

and that the government override local authorities who refuse to take such measures.

There should be no evictions of persons already in occupied premises, and all writs and warrants issued to those in occupied premises and to those who have assisted their fellow workers, be withdrawn immediately.

In conclusion, we further demand that the government state in the press and to local councils the number of empty hotels, flats, houses, camps and public buildings suitable for temporary accommodation, and what they propose to do with them.

The ETU Annual Policy Conferences

From 1947 Les and Harry used to take it in turns to seek nomination to attend the ETU Annual Conferences and Rules Revision Conferences. They were close friends who constantly argued with each other – Harry remembers that Les would get annoyed with him for not having written out and sent off a resolution to the Conference, reminding him that he was paid to do it. 'He was upright in what he believed,' says Harry. 'So we would have a row about it and go for a drink the next day as though nothing had happened.' In 1947 Les was one of two members of his branch nominated to attended the 1947 Policy Conference. He did not win the nomination but he put forward no fewer than ten motions or resolutions to go forward to the Conference. At a meeting held on 26 February 1947 Les shrewdly and cleverly proposed (and it was agreed) that the relevant section of the minutes of the previous meeting should be altered so that his ten motions should go forward as a motion of ten clauses! At the age of 28 he was already showing signs of the highly effective and persuasive politician he was to grow into. He spoke at such length about his resolutions that at 9.25 p.m. it was proposed that a special meeting should be held to discuss the matter in full. At a special meeting called for 8 March 1947 members agreed this ten-clause motion with 14 votes in favour and six against and it was sent to the ETU Executive Council.

The resolution illustrates Les's shrewdness and skill in persuading his fellow branch members to support him. The text of the resolution covers support for Attlee's statement that there would be no coalition government, supports the measures necessary to overcome the fuel crisis and puts forward nine measures needed to be taken in order that Labour's programme 'Let us Face the Future' should be carried out. It is, indeed, an all-encompassing resolution covering the speeding up of the nationalisation programme, increasing wages, the co-option of a representative of the National Union of Miners (NUM) on to the government's committee, and the proposal that representatives from the NUM, the Coal Board and the TUC (in an emergency committee) should have plenary powers to carry through immediate measures to solve the crisis. Further clauses recommended an immediate reduction in the size of the armed forces, increasing taxes for the wealthy, and entering into a trade agreement with the Soviet Union and all democratic countries in Europe.

The 1947 Conference also debated the air force strikes of 1946. A historic meeting at the Memorial Hall, Farringdon Road was organised by the London area of the ETU and the London region of the AEU in their determined and dedicated support of Arthur Attwood and other strike leaders. Four men had been court martialled after the RAF demonstrations which had taken place in India earlier in the year. The demonstrations (which have also been described as strikes or mutinies) arose because of the slow pace of demobilisation and repatriation at the end of the war and the appalling conditions which were suffered in the camps in India and elsewhere. This little known event in British history and the important part played by the ETU in achieving the release of the men, have been brilliantly recorded in a brief work by David Duncan.

The ETU was from its very earliest days a forward-looking and progressive union, strongly supportive of gender equality. At the 1946 Rules Revision Conference women achieved completely equal rights with men. We also find, in January 1947, the admission to the branch of a number of women employed at a firm called Pearce Signs. The ETU was also always in the vanguard of working-class education and was the only union owning its own residential college (Esher Place, bought in 1952). The union affiliated to the National Council of Labour Colleges in 1926 and, by 1947, postal students to that college numbered 1085 and class students 321. The London School of Economics was then offering a course in Trade Union Studies. The importance of continuing education was thus in the minds of the SE Branch members and we find a reminder from the Chairman at the meeting of 18 February 1947 that free correspondence courses were available. At the 4 March 1947 meeting Brother Stannard put forward a motion as an amendment of branch standing orders with the following words: 'that one hour of one meeting each month be reserved for invited speakers from the United Nations Association and other bodies'. This is an indication of Les's vision – possibly influenced by Bill Smith but also by his early education in the Co-operative Movement and the Young Communists League.

[8]

The Fifties

> 'There has been, in the history of the Trade Union, no bonnier fighter than the Contracting Electrician. His staunchness in fighting for recognition and maintaining Trade Union principles, often at the cost of severe personal sacrifice and family privation, has been surpassed by none.' From an undated ETU publicity leaflet, entitled *Electrical Workers Employed in Contracting.*

Between 1951 and 1952 Les worked at and was Shop Steward at Camberwell Borough Council and was involved in the Direct Labour scheme through which the Council would employ staff directly instead of using contractors. Harry Bacon remembers that Les's employers before 1961 were first Electrical Installations and after that a company called A to Z. George Coombs reports that between 1953 and 1955 Les was working for a firm called Edmonsons which had a contract at Heinz and that Les, as Shop Steward, organised the ETU structure for the electricians there too. It is believed that he joined Associated Fire Alarms in 1961. This was a vast contracting organisation which at various stages took over and amalgamated other alarm companies. Les was Chairman of the AFA Minerva EMI Joint Shop Stewards Committee for 12 years.

The contracting industry is a vast one: a shop steward is elected for every site opened and a senior shop steward elected to be responsible for all the sites in an area. Throughout those years Les and his colleagues worked extremely hard to improve the appalling conditions which prevailed in their industry. Workers were paid on an hourly basis and were considered troublemakers if they tried to achieve better conditions. Bert Gramston recalls that workers who had succeeded in improving conditions on one site would suddenly be moved to another and find themselves back to square one again. They had no sick pay, no bank holiday pay and just 6d per week for a holiday stamp. Workers in this industry were aware that other workers in the same places had such benefits as sick pay; they felt enormous anger at their situation. The system was known as 'cards and coppers' – contracted workers could be sacked at a moment's notice at any time including Christmas and Easter. Les would have received his cards and coppers on many occasions (particularly because of his activities in the guerrilla strikes – see below). Gramston recalls a Miss Richardson who would call you and just say, 'Take your fucking card – there's your money and go.' Lloyd (p. 500) confirms that for many decades electricians in the contracting industry had been the backbone of the union, most of the union activists coming from this section. He adds that there were sharks in this 'rough, tough, young man's game' amongst both workers and employers. It was difficult to elect shop stewards as many sites were not properly organised and often shop stewards found it hard to find work due to an effective 'blacklisting' of militants by employers.

The guerrilla strikes of the mid-fifties

A number of Les's old friends and colleagues recounted to the author their vivid memories of the so-called 'guerrilla strikes' which took place between 1952 and 1954. At this time electrical contractors' earnings fell behind those of general labourers on building sites. Disputes took place around the London exhibition areas such as Olympia, Earls Court, White City and the Festival of Britain site on the South Bank. Employers had been making extra payments for exhibition work and wanted to stop them on the grounds that the work was taking place in congenial surroundings and was not particularly highly skilled. The ETU held out and the extra payments were retained. In April 1952 the Festival Hall site dispensed with a directly employed workforce and gave the contract to an NFEA (National Federated Electrical Association) member contractor. The ETU workers went on strike and a meeting was called of the London contracting shop stewards; the unanimous recommendation was to strike in pursuit of negotiations.

Three thousand members attended a massive and theatrical rally in Central Hall, Westminster (spilling over into Church Hall) on 6 June and the strike which had begun on 28 May 1952 extended nation-wide for the first few days of June. In 1952–54 Les was Shop Steward with a large electrical contracting company called Rashleigh Phipps, then engaged on a big site in Tottenham Court Road. Although a return to work was agreed it was also agreed that the Executive would be supported in the second half of the struggle – namely for an increase in wages, fully paid holidays and a sick-pay scheme. The 1952 wage negotiations continued and General Secretary Walter Stevens made it clear that electricians' wage levels were deteriorating rapidly. The employers made some concessions on the rate of pay and conceded the principle of two weeks' paid holiday starting in 1954. After a further four months of negotiations over wages and conditions deadlock ensued, and in August 1952 the ETU chose 16 major sites throughout the country to start to strike from 24 August. The NFEA was unresponsive and the union refused arbitration on the grounds that previously the NFEA had not followed arbitrators' recommendations. The degree of NFEA procrastinating at this time was truly remarkable and when it did eventually offer a small increase it also wanted reductions in overtime pay. The union appealed for a better offer but was ignored so indefinite strikes were planned, starting in January 1954 (Lloyd, pp. 300–303).

The newspapers were furious with the union: they claimed that support for the strike was low and kept emphasising the Communist angle. 25 January 1954 saw 7000 members gather in London following a mass march the previous Sunday with placards and slogans denouncing press abuse and distortion of the strike. By this time everything was affected including the docks, the BBC and the House of Commons, and strikes were affecting other cities. The Crufts Dog Show at Olympia had to be cancelled. 6000 members attended a dramatic rally, addressed by General Secretary Walter Stevens, at Earls Court, and on the same evening there was a torch-lit procession through London. The strikes continued.

After a return to work was voted for by aggregate voting in Port Talbot, Liverpool, Belfast and London, another rally took place at the Albert Hall to hear a report back on the most recent National Joint Industry Council (NJIC) negotiations, which only amounted to an offer to meet again. No sooner had the workers returned to work than the employers began to procrastinate again and the union now agreed to arbitration. The final result was an addition of a halfpenny to the earlier offer of twopence. Not surprisingly the final settlement was felt by many to be poor. John Lloyd writes that the positive side of this dispute was the actual organisation of the strikes themselves, earning them the title of 'guerrilla strikes'. He describes as 'swashbuckling romance' the way that, with careful planning, the workers brought about national, local and company strikes for indefinite, weekly and one-day periods (Lloyd, p. 309). Len Gray and John McLoughlin recollect these times vividly: Les would be brilliant in the organising of the strikes, always at the forefront, moving resolutions on contracting wages. They remember going to the mass meetings with him at Central Hall, the Albert Hall and Olympia. The Central Hall meeting, which was addressed by the Assistant General Secretary of the ETU, Bob McLennan, lives on in the memories of all those who were there. From this time onwards everything that the ETU did was referred to as 'Red' by the newspapers and it is detectable that preparations for the 1961 witch-hunt were being hatched. The guerrilla strikes broke the wage freeze which had been imposed by the Chancellor in the Tory government, Selwyn Lloyd.

History repeated itself in the summer of 1999 when an unofficial strike by members of the AEEU (Amalgamated Engineering and Electrical Union) including workers in the electrical contracting industry threatened to close down sites such as the Millennium Dome, the Royal Opera House and the Jubilee Line extension. The long-running dispute was, as ever, over pay and conditions and brought embarrassment to the union modernisers who were accused, among other things, of never speaking to shop floor workers or to shop stewards. On this occasion the union did not ballot for a strike and members eventually agreed to what they considered was an acceptable pay settlement and returned to work.

A Contracts of Employment Act 1953 document gives Les's date of employment with AFA as 12 August 1963, with new conditions on remuneration operating from 22 September 1964 following a collective agreement. This indicates that the new legislation might have stipulated new documentation. It is also of particular interest since the clause outlining the statutory notice of termination by employers (starting at one week and increasing to four weeks after five years' service), as well as new conditions relating to sick pay, holiday and bank holiday pay and the pension scheme, had been achieved as a result of hard-fought negotiations in which Les was one of the chief actors on the union side.

Throughout the fifties, the London SE Branch of the ETU was particularly active. Branch activities were such that one could be called upon to take part at short notice, even on a Saturday – or risk being fined half-a-crown which was a considerable sum for workers at that time. Harry Bacon recalls innumerable visits which he and Les made to the House of Commons to see MPs on particular issues. On one occasion they met John Selwyn Gummer (later a minister in the Thatcher government) who boasted to them that he was the grandson of a miner, to which their swift response was that he should be ashamed of himself for belonging to the Tory Party. On another occasion, during the Suez crisis in 1956, Harry and Les were the only two members of their branch allowed to go in to meet MPs. This was at the height of the crisis when huge demonstrations were taking place against the start of another war. Like so many young men who had not long ago returned home after serving in World War II, they were determined to fight against it. Harry described the scene outside the House of Commons: 'There they were – the police on horses and motorbikes driving us along Whitehall. I had never seen that before and have never seen it since. I saw women there, getting hold of the police and bashing them with their handbags. It was real.'

A decade later Frank Chapple and Eric Hammond were looking at ways of improving living standards for contracting electricians but their proposed deal was finally blocked on 27 July 1966 when the Wilson government imposed a total wage freeze. Did Chapple at that time give any credit for the work done over many years by people like Les who had worked so hard to negotiate with employers for decent pay and conditions? As the shop stewards' official handbook says, 'there is a vital need for shop stewards . . . in order that the interests of members of the union are protected . . . members should take pride in accepting the position and the responsibilities that go with it'. As many who knew him repeated, no shop steward could have carried out those responsibilities with more honour, integrity, fairness and dedication than Les Stannard. Doug Smith has pointed out that political activity is not considered to be charitable work. When such action is undertaken by charities on behalf of children, elderly or disabled people it is regarded by society as 'good work', but when it is carried out within trade unions it is considered anti-establishment and even disruptive!

John McLoughlin recounted to me his memories of this period, when he was working in the lift and escalator industry. It was the custom then for electricians to visit one another's ETU branches for social reasons and also to exchange information and discuss problems. John remembers visits from Harry and Les and says that he and his colleagues could not fail to notice the efficiency with which they conducted the SE Branch business and the concern they showed for the welfare of their members, something which John found stood him in good stead when he took over the duties of Secretary in his Beckenham branch. John was to get to know Les even better when (in 1959) the former joined a Victoria-based firm, Thorn and Hoddle, which had a large contract at British Oxygen in Wembley. Les was a Senior Shop Steward on another site and had responsibility for the welfare of all electricians employed by the company in Wembley, Greenwich and Edmonton. Within six months of joining Thorn and Hoddle John and his fellow workers were shocked to hear that the company was to be wound up and that all the employees would be laid off. Les immediately called a meeting of all the shop stewards and, demonstrating the negotiating skills which came to be recognised and greatly admired years later in the pensioners' movement, he achieved something unheard of at the time (when the 'cards and coppers' system was operating), securing redundancy payments for every worker, depending on his length of service. Alison Purshouse remembers Les describing those events many years later. 'He was proud of the achievement of securing redundancy pay for his brothers and he told me about the backwards and forwards nature of the negotiations and how protracted they were. He seemed almost surprised at his own success!' Les's brother, Stan, drew attention to the way that shop stewards used to be 'bought off' by employers – 'but they would never buy Les off. He would always stand up for the men and try to meet the foreman half-way.' He goes on to say that employers and some colleagues used to 'use' his brother in disputes, because he was always so good with people. At about the same time John McLoughlin found Les's experience and support invaluable when he (John) attended his first Policy Conference and had to make his maiden speech to 600 delegates and the union leadership on the platform.

The concept of the resolution

At the 1952 Policy Conference Brother Stannard seconded a resolution against rearmament moved by the General Secretary Walter Stevens and carried, with only five of the 320 delegates voting against. One of those opposing said that, although he was pro peace, he was against Communist infiltration. Press reports of the time portray a degree of anti-Communism which can be compared with the kind of vicious homophobia of the late 20th century. The *Daily Worker* and the *Daily Herald* of 29 May 1952 gave their different perspectives on this resolution, which stated that war preparations for 1952 meant that the government would spend, on arms, four times more than on health, and six times more than on education.

Les ended a brilliant speech with these words: 'Friends, Hitler said "Guns before butter". We have got to reverse that policy and make it "Social services before slaughter". I ask Conference to support the motion.' He was subsequently quoted in the *Daily Worker* of 30 May 1952 as pointing out one of the consequences of the steel shortage: that it had compelled the abandonment of work on two housing sites in Camberwell, where he was working at the time.

On behalf of the London SE Branch Les also moved a motion in support of the removal of foreign troops from British soil, arguing that America was using its wealth and raw materials to hold the British nation at its mercy. The motion ('Foreign Troops in Great Britain') was supported by the Executive Council and carried unanimously. The wording was as follows: 'This Conference views with concern the increasing number of foreign troops in Britain. It believes that the presence of these troops adds to the tension existing between the great powers, and calls upon the government to take immediate steps to ensure that these armed forces are withdrawn.'

At the 1954 Conference in Margate Les seconded a motion calling upon the government to launch a nation-wide campaign to remove all foreign troops from Britain. He quoted from Ludwell Denny's book published in 1930 which stated quite simply, 'Britain will be our colony before she is done – not in name but in fact.' Many would now hold that he has been proved right.

At the same conference Les spoke passionately in seconding an Executive Council motion (which was carried unanimously) calling on the government to meet with representatives from America and the Soviet Union in order to discuss the banning of the hydrogen bomb and the strengthening of collective peace through the United Nations Organisation. He began: 'Six months before the war in Europe ended, the most deadly weapon known to us at the time dropped on a shop in the borough where I live. That rocket immediately killed 150 people. When we look at the development that has taken place since, we can see a new stage in world affairs. The rocket, like the bow and arrow, is hopelessly out of date . . . it must be obvious that, unless the people throughout the world prevent maniacs from making such weapons, the whole future of the human race will be placed in jeopardy . . .' His speech demonstrates how thoroughly he researched his subject; he refers to the opinions of Professor Powell, a leading scientist and Nobel Prize winner, and to the fact that Britain was spending 134 times more on atomic research than on research into cancer.

At the 1956 Policy Conference in Hastings Les spoke on a motion on colonial policy, drawing attention to the fact that colonial exploitation was still being pursued in many parts of the world. The resolution was carried unanimously. This was the wording: 'This Conference is deeply perturbed that in many parts of the world colonial exploitation is still being vigorously pursued, and the colonial peoples, in pursuance of their independence and sovereignty as laid down in the Charter of the United Nations and the Declaration of Human Rights, are subject to the military might of an oppressing power. Conference reaffirms its demand for immediate withdrawal of all armed forces from colonial territories and the granting to the colonial peoples of the democratic right to elect their own governments, and pledges its support to the colonial peoples to obtain complete national independence. Conference calls further upon the Labour movement to launch a nation-wide campaign to bring to an end immediately the State of Emergency in British Guiana and the wars now taking place in Kenya, Malaya and Cyprus.'

The strong commitment which Les displayed throughout his career to the power and effectiveness of the resolution cannot be over-emphasised. He continued to use this to great effect in the pensioners' movement until he died. To quote Asquith Gibbes: 'Resolutions and petitions both have an important place in the Labour movement and Les was a great believer in the resolution as a weapon to bring about change. Often at LREC [Lewisham Racial Equality Council] it was Les [as a member of the Executive] who would be behind an effective resolution. The important thing is that he always knew when the time was right to move a resolution – timing is essential and Les knew exactly when the time was right.'

[9]

The Sixties

In 1961 John McLoughlin was working for a firm called Auto Call, a subsidiary of Associated Fire Alarms where Les was Senior Shop Steward. John notes that whichever branch of the electrical industry he was engaged in, Les always played a leading role in the fight to improve the wages and conditions of his fellow electricians. That year the ETU experienced a cataclysmic event which brought irrevocable change and continues to occupy the minds of those who lived through it, as well as those who study the history of the trade unions.

Communism is put on trial

> 'The more you find out about this case the less you know.'
> Glyn Powell, trade union historian.

> 'It was a campaign to get rid of Communists in the ETU.'
> Woodrow Wyatt MP, *Confessions of an Optimist.*

The ETU suffered a tragic blow as a result of the 1961 court case in which a civil action against the leadership was won by John Byrne and Frank Chapple. The background to this case must be included in the story of Les Stannard's life for two reasons: first, the judgement led to marked changes in the ETU, which was subsequently restructured and sought to persecute members who belonged to the then CPGB, and secondly, the case itself may have been more concerned with persecuting the Communist Party than with questions of union democracy. Some contemporary historians are beginning to express the view that its chief objective was to purge Communists from the union.

The trial, which gained national prominence, came about as a result of concerted effort by former Communists and sympathisers, such as Les Cannon. Cannon was Acting Education Officer at Esher College but was sacked from the post in April 1957. He was well versed in Communist Party ways and organisation and now passionately turned against it. The movement was powerfully backed by the media and by Labour revisionists with the support of activists from the Catholic Church (Catholic Action) who had been making virulent attacks against Communism for many years. The *Catholic Herald* actually recommended which candidates Catholics should vote for! Throughout the fifties and sixties all these forces were lined up against the Communist Party. Roy Martin described the same kind of situation prevailing in the RACS with Catholic Action as a powerful right-wing force in the bitter divisions of the time. It should also be remembered that there were personal jealousies and fights for succession to the post of General Secretary of the ETU following the mysterious death in a car crash of the former outstanding General Secretary, Walter Stevens. The circumstances surrounding Stevens' death remain questionable to this day.

Following Labour's historic election victory in 1945, the party lost the 1951 election and did not regain power until 1964, under Harold Wilson. Traditionally the Labour Party was supportive of anti-Communism at home and, as is usual when out of power (as well as sometimes when in power), keen to keep the left in general and its own left wing in particular, at further than arm's length. Within the ETU itself, attempts had been made to bar Communists from holding union office as far back as 1942. In 1943 a resolution to that effect was put forward but withdrawn for lack of support. At the 1949 Annual Conference, a long and earnest debate took place on a motion decrying the current Communist witch-hunt as an attempt to weaken the trade union movement. About 25 members spoke and a number of amendments were made to the original resolution with the final amended motion, which was passed with only seven votes against, reading as follows:

> This Conference, recognising that Trade Unionists are recruited in the workshops irrespective of any racial differences or political and religious beliefs, is satisfied that the merits of a Trade Unionist can only be judged on standards of:
>
> 1. Loyalty to the Trade Union movement
> 2. Adherence to Trade Union principles; and
> 3. Consideration for the rights and interests of fellow workers at all times.
>
> In consequence of which this Conference declares itself resolutely opposed to any suggestion, from any source, that discriminating action should be taken against any member of the Trade Union movement on account of race, religion or political faith.

One speaker in support of the motion was none other than Brother F. J. Chapple who argued that 'The constitution of our union is strong and democratic enough to protect us against the encroachment ... by the Communist Party or [someone] in the guise of St Columbania [*sic*].' He went on to dispute the insinuations of certain people who talked about 'Communists organising in secret bodies in order to decide the policy of a particular union, unions or any other bodies'.

Unions were accustomed to the intermittent attacks on Communism – the period of the black circulars (1935) was not a distant memory. At the same 1949 conference Foulkes had hinted that there was outside interference in ETU affairs, and called for a return to the Tolpuddle principles (Schaffer, p. 920). This conference was attended by Harry and Les's mentor Bill Smith, and the black American singer Paul Robeson who, during the same week, had been attacked by the *Daily Express* which simultaneously attacked the ETU President (then Frank Foulkes) for inviting Robeson to the conference. 'Was it', asked the *Express*, 'because of his reputation as a highly-paid singer or . . . an impudent attempt to foist propaganda for international communism among the delegates?' The President, in reply, said that Paul Robeson was 'not a crusader but a whole crusade in himself . . . and that if our members want a crusader on this platform in the interests of the international working class . . . then he is coming!'

The infamous 1961 court case

A writ was issued on 10 May 1960 and the case (Byrne and Chapple v. Foulkes and others) was heard at the Royal Courts of Justice by Mr Justice Winn. It took 42 days to try – from 17 April to 16 June. Over one ton of ETU papers were shuffled, 1,365,000 words were spoken and the cost was £90,000 – a very high sum 40 years ago.

The charge was that Frank Haxell and Frank Foulkes (Secretary and President of the ETU respectively) were also members of a number of special committees of the Communist Party of Great Britain whose function it was (though they denied it throughout the trial) to secure the election of Communist leaders in the union and, thus, to control its policy. The judge found for the plaintiffs, who had claimed that the elections for the union's chief officials had, for some years, been 'fraudulently conducted by means of unlawful conspiracies, to substitute, miscount, destroy or invalidate ballot papers'. Five of the original 14 defendants were found guilty. One of these (George Scott) was exonerated but Chapple and Byrne did not agree with the judge's ruling: they cross-appealed and lost their case and Scott was the only one of the original 14 to be found 'not guilty' twice in the High Court. Subsequently the new leadership (headed by Chapple and Byrne) charged Scott again on those charges thrown out by the judge and removed him from office, barring him *sine die* from holding office in the union (personal communication).

Considerable support is now given to the view that ballot rigging was not what this historic court case was about; neither was it about whether or not the CPGB had knowledge of any conspiracy. There is, on the other hand, recorded evidence that ballot rigging was a common practice, indulged in by different groups in the union. Les Cannon (a former member of the CPGB who had left the union before the Hungarian Revolution) said this in an interview, with Nicholas Wooley just before he died (*The Listener*, 28 January 1971): 'The rules were bent by both sides because there were big branches of the Union led by Communists and big branches led by anti-Communists.' The judge rejected many all-embracing allegations that were made at the trial. He restricted his judgement to one election only, saying, 'My considered judgement upon all these topics is that, when fully examined, as they have been in at least adequate detail, they do not amount to or establish any fraudulent practice by the defendants.' (Quoted in *End the Ban*, a leaflet produced by Communist Party members of the EETPU). It might be added that there were no powerful establishment figures, nor newspaper supremos, prepared to attack the anti-Communists who, by some accounts, followed ballot-rigging practices as a matter of course.

C. H. Rolph (*All Those in Favour?*, pp. 66–7) wrote that it had been 'widely known' that the ETU (membership approximately 250,000) was run by Communists and that the non-Communist majority was electorally apathetic.

Additionally, since it controlled one of the most vital industries, the union was in a position of unique power. Powell ('Turning Off the Power – Communism, anti-Communism and the Electrical Trades Union', unpublished paper, 2000) questions this supposed apathy: in 1961, even if every CPGB member had been a trade unionist (which they were not), this would have constituted less than 0.29% of the total trade union membership of around 9.5 million workers. Had apathy been a factor in the British trade union movement it would have needed every non-Communist member, even Labour activists, to be apathetic in order to explain adequately the Communists' success. Furthermore if, as Haxell had recorded, the ETU membership had increased to 240,000 by 1959 and if electoral turnouts ranged between 10% and 13%, 24,000 members could easily have outvoted the 900 Communists in the union. There were over-exaggerated assertions about the efficiency of the CPGB machinery yet not much evidence for the discontent among rank and file members for their Communist leaders; apart from the anti-Communist exceptions the membership seemed to be neither content nor discontent with its leaders (it does not follow that they were apathetic) so the question needs to be asked – how did the Communists retain their leadership if they were so universally unpopular and why did the anti-Communists not outvote the Communists?

Powell describes how Woodrow Wyatt had held discussions with the TUC General Secretary (Sir Vincent Tewson) as far back as 1956 about 'alternative methods' which could be used to deal with Communists in the ETU. Following Haxell's election to General Secretary in 1955 such 'alternative methods' included the press and media support already mentioned, insidious lobbying and, ultimately, the weight of the British judiciary. Accusations had begun to appear in the press in 1957 and the TUC had urged Foulkes and Haxell to sue their accusers but they did not do so. A *Panorama* programme shown on 9 December 1957 followed the publication of a pamphlet by Woodrow Wyatt entitled *The Peril in our Midst*. It showed union officials (with faces hidden so that their identities were concealed) revealing irregularities with the union's elections that were 'the result of Communist machinations'. One of the participants later expressed regret at having taken part and the union refused to debate the issue with Wyatt (who was described as 'the notorious Communist baiter') because they did not want to give him and the BBC the chance to film and then cut to suit their purposes. Written evidence was also produced in a letter (9 August 1958) from Mark Young (who had been expelled by the Communist Party) to the *New Statesman*. Frank Foulkes accused the BBC of McCarthyism against the union leadership, saying that they used the American 'Big Lie' technique of demanding that a person who has been lied about should prove his innocence in *Panorama*. A second TV programme, *Face to Face*, with John Freeman interviewing Foulkes, used the kind of close-up techniques now known as 'trial by TV'. Even George Brown MP – who was no Communist – complained about the loaded prejudiced atmosphere of the interview (Lloyd, p. 448).

The brutal and unjust ban on Communists

Following the 1961 judgement former geographically based ETU branches were closed down and a new vertical structure was established, based on the different industries in which workers were employed. The ban on Communists holding office came into effect on 31 December 1964. Not long after a journal called *Flashlight* was set up which aimed to restore democracy in the union. It was widely sold and Les played an active part in the distribution and sales.

In the words of Maura Rafferty, Les and many like him were 'hounded out of the union'. And in his own words on 26 January 1993 when he was awarded Lewisham Council's first Community Award, Les had this to say: 'I thank my former colleagues (who are here tonight) who often encouraged the employers to give me work (in the electrical contracting industry) when my name was mud.' The court case and the wholesale restructuring resulted in a brutal purge against anyone on the left for which many honourable left-wingers suffered disgracefully. As George Sinfield pointed out in the *Daily Worker* of 2 February 1965, 'the ban on holding office was applied only to Communists – not to members of the Tory, Labour or Liberal Parties', and Bert Ramelson told a Communist Party Executive Meeting that the ban 'prevents willing members from doing important jobs at the same time as adhering to their personal political loyalties'. The ban, he said, was spiteful and an offence to democracy. It continued to be enforced in the late seventies and early eighties and again in 1989 in the year when the EETPU was expelled from the TUC.

In the 1980s Communist Party members of the EETPU issued a leaflet entitled *End the Ban* (undated), which presented a strong and carefully argued case for equal rights in their union and an end to the discrimination against Communists. The leaflet referred back to the 1961 trial: '. . . a traumatic experience for Communists throughout the country, the majority of whom both reject and condemn the use of fraudulent means to win elections. No amount of righteous indignation from fellow trade unionists can equal the heart-searching most Communists experienced then and since.' The writers of this courageous and impressive document went on to expose as lies the sweeping and untrue statements and innuendoes which continued to be made, suggesting continuous interference by the Communist Party in EETPU affairs. They argued that the fact that five union officers, who were Communists, had been found guilty in the 1961 trial had been used against every Communist EETPU member ever since. This was a strong moral issue and, more importantly, it was wholly undemocratic and a violation of a basic human right.

Within the broad church of 'the left' these were harsh times. One of Les's old friends put it like this: 'If you were regarded as left wing (a vague term then as it is now) you were *ipso facto* regarded as a Communist even if you were not! To discover that the people you respected and supported were being accused of playing fast and loose with the ballot box was not a subject you would broach. If they were friends of yours or your family's it was uncomfortable. The ETU was the best, and the best administered union in the country then – always to the forefront of fighting for the wage structure. It supported all the causes people wanted. So when they were smeared like Scargill was at the time of the miners' strike we did not discuss it. I know that Les was very upset about it. It pulled the rug from under people's feet. One said it put the ETU back 25 years. In our heart of hearts we still don't believe it happened.' Another said, 'It felt like the officers of the ETU were just playing the same game that goes on in the City where all kinds of practices take place "legally". I do believe that corruption runs throughout our country and the cleverer and the higher up the social scale you are the better you are at it.' Yet, these same people on the 'left wing' were so confounded that they themselves omitted to take into account the ballot-rigging practices of the anti-Communists! It is even more remarkable that the CPGB itself did not take a determined stance to defend its own members nor to expose the electoral practices of the right wing in the union.

Mark Young, whose 1958 letter to the *New Statesman* had been one of the catalysts in the events leading up to the court case, re-emerged prominently in the mid-sixties and, following the 1971 Rules Revision Conference, stood for General Secretary in the 1972 election. On this occasion Chapple received four times as many votes as Young. While Young was by no stretch of the imagination a left-winger he was a popular choice for members who wanted to vote against Chapple but thought it unwise to vote for the real left-wing candidate. Tom Bell recalls that, at this time, Les

Stannard believed that his branch should vote for Young despite the hurt and anger which fellow left-wingers continued to feel towards him following the catastrophic events of 1961. 'Use your heads, not your hearts,' advised Les, the true pragmatist, but they didn't and ultimately came to see the victory of Frank Chapple and to have to live with the consequences.

The following quotation from Mr Justice Winn's judgement will no doubt continue to be well noted by historians: 'This action does not raise any general question whether it rebounds to or reflects adversely upon a man's credit as an individual or as a witness that he is a Communist. I have done my utmost throughout the trial to make that clear. Communism is not illegal in this country, nor are Communist gatherings or activities proscribed, provided always that they are not aimed against or calculated to subvert the state: in this action I have heard no evidence of gatherings or activities of that character.' He also said, 'I am not prepared to have the adjective "Communist" used pejoratively, nor am I prepared to allow attempts to be made to influence my mind to suppose that because a man is a Communist, he is not to be believed on oath, or trusted to conduct affairs honestly and straightforwardly.'

He went on to think aloud: 'Only a recluse in an ivory tower would fail to appreciate the tendency of all forms of single-minded devotion to an ideology, whether religious, political or economic, to degenerate into fanaticism, and a state of obsessive delusion that the only criterion of good and ill in conduct is utility for the achievement of chosen ends.'

Such an observation should go down in history as relevant to many contemporary conflicts. The judge's afterthought is an indication of the enormous power of the establishment which was brought to bear on the judgement since, had the evidence of rigging by anti-Communists been given equal weight, the case would surely never have been won! Indeed it begs the question – why had Foulkes and Haxell's barristers not produced evidence of ballot rigging by the other side? Moreover the judge's remarks about single-minded devotion to an ideology could be applied as much to the Communist baiters as it did to the Communists themselves!

One crucially important fact that may be overlooked in the examination of the presence of Communists in the ETU is the strong support from rank and file members for the Communist shop stewards – irrespective of their own political allegiances. Glyn Powell cites a building trade shop steward who described to him the genuine credibility that Communists gained which came through their actions in support of members' well-being; they were elected as shop stewards because of their hard work on behalf of their members, despite the fact they were Communists. Precisely the same observation about Les Stannard has been made by Sean Geraghty and many of his other colleagues who voted unanimously for Les as their shop steward in the *Daily Express* Press Branch in the years following the court case when, in theory, he was banned from holding office.

Another question which, perhaps, needs to be asked is whether people like Les, who worked so tirelessly for justice and dignity for their members, did so because they belonged to the Communist Party or whether they were members of that Party because it was within it that they found the set of principles closest to their own attitudes and beliefs. As that outstanding centenarian socialist Manny Shinwell was fond of saying, 'Socialism is an attitude.'

The years spent at Express Newspapers

In 1967 Les, still employed by Associated Fire Alarms, was engaged in the installation of a new fire alarm system at the Express building in Fleet Street. As a CP member he was banned from holding office but he was elected, on the insistence of his fellow workers, Chairperson of the Associated Fire Alarms Shop Stewards in London and nationally. Effectively the ban was being defied because Les was held in such high regard by his colleagues and they had so much confidence in him that they did not care about his personal politics but wanted him as their Chairperson. While Les was working on the Express site for Associated Fire Alarms a permanent vacancy arose; he applied for and was offered the post and thus joined the *Daily Express* staff. The *Express* later amalgamated with the *Evening Standard* and eventually both papers were bought by the *Daily Mail*. Les now joined the EETPU Press Branch and was soon elected Chairman of the Electrical Chapel. Sean Geraghty, who was Secretary of the Press Branch, recollects that at this time, when Communist electricians were finding difficulty in finding employment, they followed a policy (set up by Sean's predecessor Ben Bleach) whereby Communists (who were not permitted to hold union office) could be considered when job opportunities arose.

It need hardly be emphasised that electricians are highly important in the printing industry since if they stop work everything stops. The print industry operates a 24-hour day all the year round. Their world does not stop whatever holidays the rest of the world are observing or enjoying. Thus negotiations over pay and conditions were crucially important. Ron Cowell recalls the way that Les stood by his principles when negotiating a comprehensive salary for the Chapel members rather than a rate of pay plus overtime. He and his colleagues adhered strictly to the value of this principle. Les was excellent in negotiations and as part and parcel of that achievement all Chapel members at the *Daily Express* gained a good working system and a good salary. Union rules forbidding Communists from holding office meant that Les could never be a Father of the Chapel (this was the term for the shop steward in this part of the industry). His FOC was Ron Cowell who praises Les both for his negotiating skills and for his adherence to principle. George Coombs, who became Les's foreman chargehand, remembers how Les always worked hard, consistently always turning up for work early. 'He always tried to back up what he tried to teach and, though we had our differences, Les was always charming as well as being a great negotiator who would slowly try to talk people round to his way.' Asked about relationships between workers and employers, Sean Geraghty remarked wryly that the workers only ever met the employers over arguments or negotiations and cared little about what the employers thought about them as people; yet Ray Allen (former Electrical Engineers Manager at the *Express*) had this to say about Les's membership of the union's negotiating committee as deputy to FOC Ron Cowell. 'The committee had to meet us to negotiate prospective redundancies – what I recall about Les (in backing up his FOC) is that he was very astute, and an extremely able and fair negotiator.'

[10]

The Seventies and Eighties

In 1976–78 the word 'Grunwick' became familiar to everyone in Britain, especially during the mass pickets of the late summer and autumn of 1977. Grunwick Processing Laboratories Ltd was formed in March 1965 by Anthony Grundy, George Ward and John Hickey. It started with processing black and white films, later moving into mail-order colour processing. The staff in this latter section were almost all immigrants, East African Asians, mainly women, and the predominant language was Gujarati. The strike was started by six individuals who had never been in a union, nor on strike before. It centred on the fundamental right of workers to join a trade union and to be represented by it. This right was denied by the employers and the dispute became long, bitter and at times violent. Other issues, crucial to the rights of working people, were also raised, such as the vulnerability of immigrant workers, the oppression of female workers, the rights of workers to picket in support of their colleagues, the political role of the media and the outcome of the intervention of the law in industrial disputes. There were over 550 arrests – more than in any dispute since the 1926 General Strike.

Readers are referred to the work on Grunwick by Jack Dromey and Graham Taylor (amongst other accounts) for a full account of the strike and the unprecedented war of ideas which centred on it. There was a huge and continuing demonstration of solidarity by fellow workers, supported by numerous MPs and other important figures, thousands of trade unionists rallied in support and even card-carrying Tories joined the British left on the picket line. A picket of 140 lawyers, barristers and solicitors, law teachers and students took place on 28 October 1977 to focus attention on the inadequacies of the law and the violation of its letter and spirit by the Grunwick management. In Northern France dockers threatened strike action to cause the stoppage of lorries carrying strike-breaking processing materials.

On the other side was ranged the full might of the opposition, and the National Association for Freedom was set up – an avowedly anti-Communist movement which saw Grunwick as part of an international conspiracy.

In August the Scarman Report called for union recognition and reinstatement of the workers but, ultimately, the mass movement was broken. One view held that this was due to the intervention of the right wing of the Labour Party. It was argued that while the government and the TUC wanted to see a union victory, a preoccupation with order at any cost and fear for the future overrode everything else with bitter consequences for the Grunwick strikers. The then Home Secretary Mervyn Rees and Prime Minister James Callaghan justified their action by claiming that the electorate would be frightened by the left wing's policies.

The first police attack took place on 13 June 1977, and 7 November of the same year went down in the history of the trade union movement as one of the worst ever attacks by police on pickets. The Lewisham and Deptford Trades Council minutes for 21 June 1977 record that the Trades Council banner delegation had taken part in the mass picket on four days to demonstrate its support for the past ten months. 'The strikers were heartened and pleased with our constant support. Members of the delegation were impressed by the solidarity and courage of the Asian women on the official picket.' They had also been shocked by the strike-breaking role in which the police had been placed by their superiors and, in particular, when they had witnessed police officers taking their tea breaks inside the Grunwick factory. They had overheard police inspectors ordering officers to arrest the official pickets, irrespective of their behaviour. They had made complaints on both of these questions and this information had been taken by local MPs to Mervyn Rees. The Trades Council delegation continued to support the picket as much as possible, leaving Lewisham at 6 am three times a week. Telegrams and letters of support were sent, meetings were held with the borough's three MPs and letters outlining the reasons for the Trades Council's support were sent to the press. John Esterson remembers the occasion when the police were there on horses: 'We had our banner against a huge wire fence; the police were charging the crowd and we would have gone down with that fence. I can never forget that incident that we shared together, me and Les.' Doug Smith remarks that Les would go along to the Grunwick picket as himself but really with the Trades Council, always, with John Esterson, holding aloft that hugely symbolic Deptford banner.

Former Lewisham councillors Andy Hawkins and Jon Lansman both remember Les from this period. Hawkins knew Les from as early as the fifties. 'You couldn't be on the left of politics for long in Lewisham without bumping into Les and being aware of what he was concerned with and the influence that he was beginning to exert. I never changed in my opinions of him and the impressions I first had.' Lansman, who came to know Les much later, also records his activity in the Labour movement in the 1980s – through the Co-op, the miners' strikes and in support work in general. Les is likely to have been present too at the April 1979 Anti-Nazi League demonstration against the National Front in Southall. This was the occasion when a young New Zealand teacher, Blair Peach, who played a prominent part in the confrontation, died from a cracked skull delivered by the police who were tackling the riot. Kevin Halpin records that Les was a strong supporter of the Liaison Committee for the Defence of the Trade Unions, which is a broadly based organisation and has the support of the CP amongst others. It was in this capacity that he would have been involved in all the struggles and disputes. Sean Geraghty emphasises Les's political astuteness and his exceptional concern for workers whenever industrial action was taking place. 'He was one of those you could always count on. During the miners' strikes, the nurses' dispute, ASLEF, the Furniture and Allied Trades – he would have made sure to meet the ASLEF drivers and to visit the mining villages.' Jack Dunn had this to say about events following Edward Heath's resignation: 'The Tory Party set up about ten committees which related to every aspect of British life – the Energy Committee, of course, was about coal and other fuels. It was decided that a leader should be elected who would kill off the miners and the mining industry. The arguments put forward about pollution were spurious since there is a technique whereby sulphur can be extracted and sold for other purposes.' Dunn reminded the writer that the miners were so powerful because to a very great degree the British working class had a dependency on their power and their willingness to use it against repressive measures. He went on: 'Les did a great deal of organising in London during the 1984 strikes – he approached people and working men's clubs who could provide accommodation, he helped to find organisations which could provide refreshment; we had refectories, places for people to sleep, miners on the floor, their wives came too. Yes, Les did all of that – he supported workers in the struggle but, even more important, he recognised that it was the collective effort of the trade unions and others that could change things.' Harry Bacon also remembers the trade union activity in support of the miners though he does not think the unions gave sufficient backing to the miners. 'Les and I and others who had formed the Retired Trade Unionists Association, raised funds from the local

Labour Parties and we managed to hire a minibus and to visit one of the Kent mines. There we faced the police on the picket line. There was real solidarity then, a wonderful feeling, just like in the old days.'

Doug Smith remembers Les's involvement in the demonstration and march following the New Cross fire on 18 January 1981; he was involved also in the local and national Tenants' Associations and in the SE London Council for Workers' Control which was part of a national organisation aimed at involving workers in the management of their own companies. The issue was not only about workers having seats on their companies' boards but also about generally building up union membership. The extension of worker participation and employee involvement – the worker/director – had been a constant issue of political debate and public policy on industrial relations in the UK for ten or more years before the 1979 election.

Charles Job sums it up: 'During the post-war years there was not a march or public demonstration in which Les was not to the forefront, if it was a cause he held dear – be it against the Vietnam War, anti-apartheid or CND and, most recently, the ridiculous Poll Tax, you could be sure that he would be there, giving his support.'

During the Thatcher years (and before his retirement) Les's experience, knowledge and ability as Chairman of his Chapel proved invaluable in the difficult period which faced the trade unions. The miners' strike was followed by the closure of mines in 1984 during which time the Fleet Street electricians gave outstanding support both morally and financially to the miners in their fight for the survival of their jobs and their industry. Les had previously supported the miners during the 1972 strike which brought down the Heath Conservative government. He foresaw, at that time, that a defeat for the miners would mean that another section of workers would be likely to be 'picked off' in the future and suffer the same fate. He was proved right when the printing industry (Wapping) was the next to be taken on by the Thatcher government in 1985. Despite having one of the best organised trade union structures in the country the industry was decimated and thousands of jobs were lost, resulting in some of the most highly skilled electricians in the country never working again. Ray Allen remembers that he had just purchased brand-new machinery from Sweden at that time but with the huge changes to the printing industry brought about by the technological revolution it was too late. It was also too late for those who had recently retired – Les Stannard among them – to salvage something from the wreckage of this catastrophe. Terms of severance were negotiated to reach a reasonable deal for those who were made redundant.

Les joins SOGAT

In 1982–3 there was an attempt to enable EETPU members to join SOGAT. John Lloyd, writing of the Gatwick meeting (p. 619) which offered the Press Branch leadership the exciting vision of moving into SOGAT, notes that this would have enabled them to control their own negotiations and to become liberated from the EETPU bosses. Lloyd writes that at the request of the EETPU the TUC stopped the move by electricians into SOGAT, and those who had moved were returned to the EETPU on 2 November 1983. However, one of the Fleet Street FOCs who attended the famous Gatwick meeting (in fact every FOC was present) states that, in fact, no member of the EETPU ever joined SOGAT at this time and the ultimate decision of the Express Chapel was that it was only prepared to move into SOGAT through the TUC. Sean Geraghty was suspended from holding office, initially for 20 years (later reduced to one year), for attempting to break up the union.

Les did join SOGAT after his retirement in 1988. This was the year the EETPU walked out of the TUC over the issue of single union agreements. Consequently, because they had left the TUC and were no longer bound by the Bridlington agreement, members were now free to join SOGAT. Negotiations took place with Brenda Dean, General Secretary of SOGAT, and part of the agreement was that retired members of the Press Branch of the EETPU could also join SOGAT as honorary retired members. Les very much wanted this because he was a Press Branch delegate to the Lewisham Trades Council representing the electricians in SOGAT. Ron Cowell kindly provided a copy of the resolution relating to the transfer. At a special meeting held on 14 December 1988 at St Bride's Institute in the City, the following resolution was passed:

> The unanimous recommendation of the Branch/FOC's Committee is, that the membership of the London Press Branch transfer into SOGAT, in accordance with the agreement providing a National Branch for electricians and all members covered by the Branch.

In 1991 SOGAT changed to the Graphical Paper and Media Union (GPMU) and this was the union that Les belonged to at the time of his death. His union membership therefore spans a total of 60 years and, if one counts the three years in the electrical industry from the age of 14, the total number of years was 63!

The All Lewisham Campaign Against Racism and Fascism (ALCARAF)

Lewisham and Deptford Trades Council was the body which heralded the establishment of ALCARAF in the 1970s. The National Front in Deptford had gained 1731 votes in the 1974 by-election and the British National Party had considerable prominence in the borough. The police had made quite an issue of mugging by young black people and this had led to expressions about sending black people 'back home'. The TUC wrote to all Trades Councils advising that campaigns should be organised to show opposition to the National Front's message. A letter was sent by Harry Bacon, then Secretary of the Trades Council, to all parties, trade unions, ethnic minority organisations, and to numerous church and community groups, explaining the economic problems of the time and drawing a parallel with the 1930s and the rise of Mosley and the Fascists. The letter made clear that the closure of the south-east London factories, the loss of jobs and the housing shortage could not be blamed on black workers. MP John Silkin called a meeting to consider possible action in the light of rising racism in the borough and a further meeting called by the Trades Council at what is now the Irish Club in Davenport Road, Catford, agreed a draft constitution for ALCARAF; the organisation was finally launched on 22 January 1977 at Lewisham Town Hall and was attended by about 160 people.

Joan Anim-Addo has written an account of the Bloody Saturday March which took place on 13 August 1977 and the events which led up to it, in particular the Lewisham 24 (later 19) affair. Whilst the National Front planned their march round New Cross, Deptford and Lewisham – described as 'making a territorial bid' – the police controlled and rerouted the concurrent ALCARAF March for Peace which was led by the Bishop of Southwark and Mayor Roger Godsiff in an impressive demonstration of civic concern. The deliberate rerouting of the ALCARAF march was described by the *South London Press* (5 August 1977) as a pointless magic roundabout from Ladywell Fields and back, via Lewisham High Street. As Anim-Addo remarked, the police appeared more interested in easing the way for the National Front and turned down the Mayor's request to allow the ALCARAF march to proceed through the areas where the black community was prominent. The National Front achieved their aims while the peaceful counter-demonstration was broken up twice – at Lewisham Way and at the clock tower. It should also be noted that this was the first time that police were equipped with riot shields.

Doug Smith, the President of the Lewisham Trades Council and Chairman of ALCARAF who had earlier led a deputation to the House of Commons to urge the local MPs to ban the forthcoming National Front march, pays tribute to Les for the way he put forward strong arguments in support of establishing the broadly based organisation which ALCARAF became. The Communist Party of Great Britain, at the time, aimed for a bringing together of all groups opposed to racism no matter how disparate, and Les played a leading part in persuading the militant groupings which refused to join church representatives in this common aim. One local politician describes such militant movements as 'right wing' in that they believe in the use of violence to bring about change. This was in direct contrast to the humanitarian Communism which Doug and Les and others like them adhered to.

Asquith Gibbes sums up Les's anti-racism like this: 'For me as a black person, the distinguishing feature of Les was his deep humanity for all people – he was quintessentially a working-class person and if you asked me to choose a white person who has all the elements of a real person, who did not see colour, race, creed, or anything, that was Les. I don't think it was his Communism which made him like this – it was most unusual. There are unique people in this world and he was one of them. His concern for issues of justice and equality transcended everything.'

It was, therefore, in the nature of the man that he would want to become involved in ALCARAF. Les saw this grave issue had to be addressed – both as a Communist and because of the kind of person he was. He knew the meaning of 'partnership' long before it became the fashionable thing that it is today. With his vision he looked at a wider perspective for tackling racism through ALCARAF – he argued strongly for the Churches, the trade unions, the local authority and all minority groups to be involved in the setting up of ALCARAF so that it became a rainbow of organisations ranging from Church of England vicars to the Socialist Workers' Party and the International Marxist Group.

The Labour Party political broadcast

On 9 December 1980 a Labour Party political broadcast was dedicated to the March for Jobs which was held in Liverpool on 29 November and attended by thousands of people from all over the country. Those attending were addressed by the Leader of the Labour Party, Michael Foot, by Denis Healey, Eric Heffer and other speakers, who predicted that unemployment would reach more than 3 million by 1981; not surprisingly, those old enough to remember the 1930s were determined to remind younger people of the hardship experienced by workers at that time.

The broadcast made its central message the rapidly rising unemployment which was a direct consequence of Prime Minister Thatcher's policies: industries were being closed down and large numbers of people were receiving redundancy notices, with disastrous effects on the economy and on workers and their families. Factories were shutting down or working shorter weeks, shops were closing because people had little money to spend; it was feared that the engineering backbone of the country was disintegrating. Denis Healey, estimating that there were more than 150,000 people present, said that this was the same number as the Thatcher government was throwing on to the dole queues every month.

The opening shots of the party political broadcast were of a train pulling in at Liverpool station and large numbers of demonstrators alighting. The first words to be uttered were those of Les Stannard, replying in that unmistakable voice to a reporter's question: 'I have come to attend this march because I don't want to go back to what my parents and I suffered in the 1930s.' A little later came a close-up of Les, aged 61, in his cloth cap and with a friendly but determined expression on his face. He went on to say, 'I am hoping that this march today will convince the people of Britain that the sooner we get rid of the Thatcher government the sooner we've got a chance of rebuilding Britain's economy and putting Britain's people back to work.' This was not the end of the story however.

On 11 December, under the headline 'Party Fury over Red Star', the *Daily Mail* reported that Labour moderates were asking questions about how a Communist had come to appear on their broadcast, and it was implied that Les had been deliberately asked to speak. There was great fear at the time about 'entryism' into the party but in reality Les's appearance on the broadcast was purely coincidental – he just happened to be one of the many people being interviewed as they came off the train. As one of the organisers said, '... we do not ask to see people's party cards on these occasions. It is the sort of thing that could happen when you film a march of this nature.' The Communist Party of Great Britain's industrial organiser commented that the alternative economic strategy adopted by the TUC and the Labour Party had a great deal in common with Communist Party policies, adding, 'There is a good working relationship between ourselves and Labour Party members in many key industries.' The matter was subsequently raised at a Lewisham Council meeting and it was some time before the matter died down – much to the amusement of Les who had spoken in all innocence!

[11]

Millwall

On Wednesday 18 December 1996 at 7.45 p.m., the evening following Les Stannard's funeral, Millwall were playing Luton Town in the Nationwide Football League Division 2. A tribute and a photograph of Les appeared in the programme and, before the game began, a minute's silence was held in his memory; all the players wore black armbands. This was a rare honour usually reserved for former players.

> 'Everyone in the MFC Community Scheme valued Les enormously and when he passed away there was a dark cloud over us.' Lou Waller (Millwall Football Club Community Sports Worker and Lioness)

> 'Les has not been replaced and now it's a lonely furrow without him.' Fred Ninde (Chair, Millwall Club Community Scheme)

> 'What we've pioneered is a change of attitude . . . in the most difficult surroundings and circumstances. I believed football was uniquely able to do this. In the same way as the manager is trying to build a team the supporters can be proud of, we are trying to build a club the community can be proud of. The two together may change people's lives in a way that has never happened before.' Gary

Stempel (former Community Development Officer, Millwall Football Club)

'You have no right to say anything about violence unless you have tried to do something about it and, having begun to do the things we are doing . . . I think our actions speak for themselves . . . Our wish, our task, our commitment, was to bring Millwall to the people. We wanted to bring football home.' Reg Burr (Life President and Director of Millwall Football Club)

Les Stannard and Millwall were inseparable. He was a supporter from the age of six when his father took him to his first match and he was allowed to go along with his friends when he was about 12. He became passionate about the team, the game and Millwall's place in the community he loved and he rarely, if ever, missed a home game. A number of his fellow primary school pupils were the sons of Millwall players. This was such a close-knit community that when the players went to the Queen's Head in Dennett's Road on a Saturday night they frequently used to finish off the evening by going to Les's Nan's house for a party. Les took his daughter Lesley and nephew Michael to watch the game and, not long before his death, he had started to take his two grandsons too. Some of Michael's earliest memories are of going to Millwall when he was about nine or ten. Les, the family man, would make it a memorable occasion for the young lad, taking him home for tea afterwards and then waiting with him at the bus stop when it was time to go home. They used to stand at the Coldblow Lane end and both Lesley and Michael remember a stream of people coming up to greet Les on the terrace. Barry Fenton was the manager at this time – round about the mid-sixties – a man who did a marvellous job, and kept the team in the second division, but always on a shoestring. The directors gave him little in the way of resources but he had a good knowledge of the game and great ability in signing players. Michael remembers that Fenton would walk out of the dug-out near the goal mouth where he and Les used to stand, and Les would call out, 'Get your money out, Fenton.' Les also had a couple of favourite players – one of them, Keith Weller, was excellent. He was bought from Tottenham and went on to play for England. If any of the spectators booed or jeered at him Les could always be counted on to turn round and say, 'Not Weller's fault!'

If Les and Millwall were inseparable the same was true of Les and politics, so Millwall and politics came to be linked through him. He became utterly committed over the years to Millwall as a centre of community activity, and he worked in every conceivable way to benefit the underprivileged residents of Deptford and Lewisham – through the Millwall Community Sports Association. He may not have known the term but Les was the most gifted and natural 'networker', always getting to know new people, linking people and issues together and building alliances. As John McLoughlin says, 'The fact that he was at football did not mean he was not still involved in his trade union and political activities.' After the match, the networking would continue on the bus from New Cross back to Lewisham. While most people who get on a bus hide behind a newspaper or football programme, this was an opportunity for Les to get involved in a discussion with a man sitting about six seats away, raising the issue of the bus pass, or the GLC, or the Health Service – there was always some topic for him to get people talking about. 'Someone else would then butt in,' says John, so that by the time they got to Lewisham half a dozen people would be talking together. 'We would get off the bus and they would still be going at it hammer and tongs as the bus drove on. That was Les. He got people involved in thinking about things and in thinking for themselves.' Jim Mallory remembers meeting Les in Lewisham town centre when he bought a copy of the *Morning Star* from him. 'Les told me about the main news in the papers and I was interested and bought a copy. I was impressed as this was not the usual technique for selling papers. The next day I saw him again at the Coldblow Lane end of Millwall Football Club and it took me a while to make the connection, as selling the *Morning Star* and Millwall didn't seem a likely combination of interests!' In time Mallory came to realise that this was just one example of Les's talent in merging all his interests and concerns together. He could not have had a better centre of activity than Millwall.

In June 1986 the club was not only confronted by a terminal condition common to many League clubs but had gained a national reputation for hideous hooliganism – it came to epitomise everything that made football detestable. At the last minute the club was saved by a group of dedicated businessmen who recognised the deep emotional bond which exists between a team and the families who live in the area in which the team plays. The rescuers worked on their belief that the spirit of the team and that of the local people should be brought together, to identify with one another again. In the words of Reg Burr (Life President and Director), 'so that the man on the pitch and the man on the terraces saw each other as mates once again'. The Millwall Community Scheme under the direction of Gary Stempel was born at this time, sponsored at first by the GLC and, following the axing of that organisation, by a consortium of Lewisham and Southwark Councils and the Sports Council. In 1987 Lewisham Council became the sponsors and leader Dave Sullivan became a non-voting director of Millwall. The history of Millwall in the community has since been published by the club.

When one examines the huge financial and other difficulties faced by the club it is clear that this was a situation made for the kind of person Les was, involving the club he was attached to, his overwhelming passion for justice and equality and his detestation of racism. A heady mix. He worked closely with Gary Stempel whose job it was to forge close links between Millwall and the community through the development of different social, educational and sports initiatives. Stempel stresses that the project was never an anti-hooligan scheme; it was not the answer to football hooliganism, which has nothing to do with football and is embedded in much more complicated social issues. The Community Scheme, however, aimed to forge close links with specific target groups – the truancy project, young offenders, tennis and basketball schools and others, with the aim of changing attitudes. 'It should not be seen as an answer to this troubling phenomenon,' insists Stempel, 'but just as the manager is trying to build a club the supporters can be proud of, we are trying to build a club to bring pride to the community. The two together may change people's lives in a way that has never happened before.'

'Many of these projects bore Les's trademarks,' says Stempel 'and, in the midst of difficult times, he could be relied on to bring a smile to people's faces.' Les also became Chairman of the Millwall Over 50s Club which itself was part of the Community Scheme, as well as being a weekly social gathering. This was the one leisure activity he allowed himself during the last ten years of his life. There was one memorable occasion when the club organised an outing to the Kent countryside. 'You should have seen the look on the landlord's face when he saw that our van had Millwall written all over it,' says Stempel. 'He even tried to refuse us entry until Les went up to him and convinced him that this group was not going to wreck the pub! By the time we finished lunch we were all friends and were being asked to return!'

Les had strong and positive views about both the hooliganism and the racism at Millwall. In *Millwall in the Community* he himself writes (p. 35) about the occasion when Lesley accompanied him to the Luton match following which terrible crowd scenes were shown on television. 'At the ground hardly any turnstiles were open. Then they opened just one of the gates, very suddenly, and people got pushed through the turnstiles.' Les and Lesley were pushed through into the ground and never paid to get in. There was considerable fear that had anyone fallen over there might have been a stampede. Les later wrote to the Football Association and to his MP John Silkin about what had occurred and sent their admission money to the FA. I didn't want Millwall spectators accused of breaking into the ground. Eventually, the FA sent my money back and told me to post it on to Luton, which I did.' This is typical of the way Les always went to the trouble of putting things right, no matter how busy he was.[1] Another example of the way Les never let anything go comes from Carole Newman, Director of the Greater London Forum. In the early nineties the GLF produced a booklet called 'Lead the Way' which listed amongst other things the football grounds which had the best adapted toilets for elderly and disabled people. Gold stars were awarded to those which fulfilled all the criteria, but Millwall did not get a star because although theirs were reasonably well adapted they were not as good as some of the others. Not surprisingly Les would not let this pass; he went to the authorities to get the matter put right – and it was!

Again on p. 35 Les writes about the emergence of racism in Deptford in the 1970s and how he was part of a delegation to the Millwall directors to request that they do something to assist community relations in the area. He never wanted to see again the displays of Fascism which had marked him so permanently in his youth. Stempel pays tribute to Les for never being afraid to raise the issue at meetings and Asquith Gibbes remembers him being so incensed by racism that 'he kept knocking at my door to tell me that black people were not coming to football because of this. He reminded me that black people loved football as well as cricket and he would

[1] Readers who read this account in *Millwall in the Community* should note that despite what the caption says the man on the left of the photograph is not Les Stannard!

Les's mother, Edith Stannard (née Bryett) with her youngest son Ronald at Rutt's Terrace c.1930

Banner, Women's Co-operative Guild, Coll Misc 268 British Library of Political and Economic Science

(Left) Les's maternal grandmother Elmira Hepzibah Bryett (née Gatfield) at 15 Rutt's Terrace – early 1930s

From *Ethel and Ernest* by Raymond Briggs

Helwan, Egypt in 1942

In France, with a French family, at the end of the war

After the war. Late 1940s

'Defence not Defiance' the Electrical Trades Union logo

'Light and Liberty'. An Electrical Trades Union badge

From *Ethel and Ernest* by Raymond Briggs

The 1950 General Election. The Deptford candidates hand their nomination papers to the Mayor. Left to right: E. Miller (Liberal); Les Stannard (Communist); Geoffrey Sarjeant (Conservative); J. Cooper (Labour)

Gladys and Les on their Wedding Day at Newton Abbot. 29 March 1956

With young Lesley on a summer holiday in Torquay 1960

The family on a visit to the Cutty Sark in Greenwich. Winter 1962

The Millwall logo

With Rose Kerrigan (Chair) and Stan Tulloch (Vice-Chair) of Lewisham Pensioners' Forum at a Pensioners meeting in the 1990s

Lewisham pensioners presenting the 'Keep the Travel Permit Free' Petition to the Mayor of Lewisham, Councillor Nicholas Taylor 1989

ALCARAF (All Lewisham Campaign Against Racism and Facism) publicity leaflet

Windows smashed and slogans daubed in Catford by the National Front –

THIS IS THEIR POLITICAL PLATFORM.
DON'T GIVE THEM THE CHANCE.

ALCARAF c/o 120 Rushey Green, SE6

At Luxembourg airport 'en route' to the Seniors' Parliament 1993

Les, the Lambeth, Southwark and Lewisham constituency delegate to the same parliament, with Richard Balfe, MEP

Salud 'Mr Lewisham' – memorial cover photograph in 'The Greater London Pensioner' February 1997

Les's oldest friend, Harry Bacon (Chair of Lewisham Pensioners' Forum) and Mayor John O'Shea. Lewisham Clock Tower 2nd June 1998 at the unveiling of the stone erected in memory of Les Stannard

not give up and kept pressing for black people to become part of the entertainment.' So the seven-member Anti-Racist Committee was set up in September 1994 under Reg Burr. 'Les was a prominent member of this committee and it was set up because of his influence on me,' adds Gibbes. Millwall has now been transformed and racists have been banned from the terraces.

Wherever Les went in the community he left his unforgettable mark on those who knew him. Lou Waller remembers him most of all for never being judgemental and for always giving a chance to people, talking to them, never dictating or talking down. 'He was immensely wise and he always stood by what he believed.' Fred Ninde, Chair of the Millwall Club Community Scheme, remembers yet another side to his character – his appreciation and encouragement for those, like him, who did voluntary work in the community. He also noted Les's passionate interest in giving opportunities to youngsters from poor backgrounds who had had few opportunities. 'His view was opposed to Thatcher's "stand on your own two feet" – because he believed strongly that those who found it difficult to help themselves needed support.'

The same view is expressed by Father Owen Beament who remembers how hard Les fought to point out the many injustices which Deptford youngsters suffered. Gary Stempel sums up the Les he knew: 'I have not met anyone with so much energy and enthusiasm – let alone a pensioner aged 65-plus, and I learned so much from him. He was a man of great vision; he gave so much and never asked for anything in return.' The same sentiment is expressed by Ron Bell, Community Development Officer at Millwall between 1986 and 1996. Bell used often to give Les a lift home to Elmira Street and he remembers how, before leaving him, he might ask Les a question which would then start up a conversation and end up with Les philosophising on the world! 'He taught me so much about the 1930s and the 1950s. I do miss him; he always had time for me. What I also loved – not liked –

about him was that he always moved with the times. You could see this in the way he worked during committees – he could talk to anyone and understand what they were saying, no matter how young and different they were. He never lost the plot!'

The Millwall Anti-Racist Committee is now well established. Early in the year 2000 the Chairman, Theo Paphitis, proudly reported that a group of fans from Kosovo was to attend Anti-Racism Day at Millwall on 11 March, an event which would have brought enormous joy to Les. It was, in fact, the police who had had the imaginative idea that the Kosovo refugees should be invited. Sadly the local and national media played a disgraceful and regrettable part in the subsequent cancellation of the visit. In the light of constant press stories about the troubles which asylum seekers bring with them, it was wrongly reported that the club had been receiving racist telephone calls. The *Daily Telegraph* could not resist the temptation to combine the paranoia about asylum seekers with the stereotypical picture of racist fans. In reality no such phone calls had been received but the paper succeeded in ruining what could have been a terrific afternoon for the young Kosovans. Ken Chapman, Millwall's security adviser, describes the episode thus: 'It articulates the "problems" of being damned for what you do and damned for what you don't.'

[12]

Deptford Trades Council and Lewisham and Deptford Trades Council

Trades Councils are the TUC in microcosm – they exist to bring together all trade unions to act as a sounding board in each borough with a special emphasis on the employment situation and the lives of working people. Every Trades Council is affiliated to the TUC and there are rules of affiliation.

Records of Trades Councils show very wide-ranging concerns reflecting the national political issues of the day, such as entry into the Common Market (now the European Union), racial discrimination (at a time when some pubs were trying to operate a colour bar) and the operation of boycotts of the exports of various countries. Trades Councils are also closely tied to the Labour Party and in 1960 resolutions were sent to the Labour Party Conference asking that the social implications and nationalisation principles of the (now defunct) Clause 4 should not be changed. More immediate and practical matters which affect people's lives have always been equally high on the agenda, for example, the dangers of inflammable clothing and of second-hand oil heaters and the dangers to children of ice-cream van chimes (when crossing roads). This is an indication of the way that Trades Councils are embedded in their local communities.

It is believed that Les was a member of the Deptford Trades Council as far back as 1947. The Council itself was founded in 1898, 38 years after the London Trades Council (to which

Deptford was later federated) came into existence during the time that Karl Marx was living in London and long before the Labour Party was born. The London SE Branch of the ETU was affiliated to the Deptford Trades Council from at least 1927. The merger between the Deptford and Lewisham Trades Councils took place in October 1973.

Regrettably it has not been possible to locate the whereabouts of Deptford Trades Council's own archives but we know that it was originally called the Deptford and Greenwich Trades Council and it appears to have been a radical one which caused considerable disquiet to the TUC and, at times, to the local Labour Party, over the years. On more than one occasion there was division amongst its ranks and it was disbanded and re-formed at least twice – in 1935 and again in 1958. In 1953 a letter from the TUC notes that the previous Trades Council had refused to carry out decisions of Congress and of the Annual Conference of Trades Councils. Yet, in 1956 while all this conflict was taking place, the Council continued to give priority to matters of local concern: for example, its members raised what was then the considerable sum of £550 for the Manor House hospital with a 'Stop Watch' competition.

One of the main bones of contention was Clause 14a of the rules of affiliation which read: 'The Council shall refuse to accept the credentials of a delegate from an affiliated branch if the delegate in question is a member of the Communist or Fascist parties or any subsidiary organisation of these parties, or a member of an organisation proscribed by the TUC.' In April 1958 Deptford Trades Council asked the TCJCC (Trades Councils Joint Consultative Committee) to withdraw this rule but was refused. At their AGM in March 1960 the members resolved to allow affiliated organisations to elect delegates of their own choice without discrimination.[1]

Similarly, the London Trades Council had its own battles

[1] University of Warwick Modern Records Centre. 79/D/2 and 2/8

to fight with the TUC and for the same reasons. In 1947 a Joint Meeting of the London Trades Council, the London Labour Party, the London Co-operative Society and RACS – to plan for May Day 1948 – was terminated because the Secretary of the London Labour Party refused to share a platform with a member of the Communist Party. The London Trades Council itself was disbanded on 8 October 1953 by a vote of 41 votes to two because the TUC ruled to disaffiliate it on account of its Communist associations and activities.[1]

Les Stannard was a proud Deptford man to his fingertips. When the borough was absorbed into Lewisham in 1964 under the GLC, staunch Deptford and Millwall citizens hated the idea of their special borough losing its identity. Les had no choice but to recognise and accept the fact that Deptford no longer had the base for the kind of labour movement which he knew and loved – the big engineering companies and the docks had almost all gone. The Labour government of the time had imposed a restriction on the size of industrial buildings (the decision on size having being reached not very thoroughly by the Secretary of State for Employment who carried out his review by helicopter!). This added impetus to the work of Trades Council members and no one gave greater commitment than Les who put his heart and soul into projects to generate new areas of employment for both men and women. As Richard Balfe MEP notes: 'Les had a long Trades Council history and was a staunch trade unionist, always on the right side of arguments – the correct side.' (This is an interesting observation, coming from someone who frequently voted differently from Les when they both sat on the RACS Political Purposes Committee!)

During the seventies Les also became a member of the Deptford and Greenwich Local Employment Committee (including the Youth Employment and Disablement Advisory

[1] London Metropolitan Archives. ACC3287/02/4 1952–53

Committee); he was an Executive member of the SE London Campaign Committee against Unemployment and Factory Closures and one of the founders of the 'Lewisham Here Today' bus project for unemployed people and the Lewisham Co-operative Development Agency. He was co-opted also to the Lewisham Borough Council Employment and Industry Committee and participated in the setting up of the South-East London Institute for Workers Control.

Attempts to bring about a merger between the Lewisham and Deptford Trades Councils began in 1965. A letter from the TUC to the then Secretary of the Lewisham Trades Council, Mr T. Tilley, questioned his request that the name of that Trades Council should be changed to the London Borough of Lewisham Trades Council which, by implication, would also have covered the old borough of Deptford (records of Lewisham Trades Council 1960–70). The TUC's very wise response argued that while it could see the advantages of a merger it was clear that Deptford would object to it since the Borough Council would then be in a position to say that it would deal with the LBL Trades Council and thus override the Deptford organisation altogether. In due course, when the merger was formally proposed, it was strongly resisted by the members in Deptford. Les, not surprisingly, had a strong commitment to ensure that the borough continued to be recognised. He insisted (according to Mike Power he fought tooth and nail) that the new organisation which came into existence on 23 October 1973 should be known as the Deptford and Lewisham Trades Council and while the names have now been reversed both are included in the title to this day.

The ban on Communists holding office in the EETPU continued until 1989 and Les, who had previously been Vice President of the Trades Council, could no longer hold that office and was offered the least popular post of Treasurer of the Lewisham and Deptford Trades Council when it was merged. Meetings continued to be held at the Deptford

Engineers Club. Deptford's industrial power base was in crisis and there was much work to be done on behalf of workers whose employment was being threatened.

Harry Bacon was Secretary at the time that Les accepted the post of Treasurer and the Secretary who followed was Maura Rafferty. John Esterson, who was the auditor, spoke to me of Les's professionalism. 'He did a proper job of everything he undertook. I used to go to his house and would find everything perfectly organised – all entries neatly and painstakingly recorded, everything in perfect order.'

Maura Rafferty was a community worker at the University of London's Goldsmiths College. There were strong links between the two organisations and as the Goldsmiths community workers did not have borough boundaries, Maura became involved also with the development of Docklands through the Docklands Action Group. The Conservative Leader of the GLC at the time was Horace Cutler and, not surprisingly, the five plans which had been put forward did not give priority to ensuring that the residents of Docklands and the Isle of Dogs would benefit. Maura and Heather Wakefield (who was engaged to organise a women's employment project which still exists) helped to prepare a new plan for the Docklands Development Body – one that generated four or more female or male supporting jobs for every docker's job. The important thing to note is that as industries began to close and community workers became more involved with employment issues, contact with the Trades Councils became ever more crucial. The Goldsmiths College community workers thus fed back much of the information gathered to the Trades Council through Les, and the Lewisham and Deptford Trades Council had much stronger community links than any other. Both Maura and Heather wished to record his impressive record of commitment to women but also stress that he was so good at facilitating and encouraging other people.

Tom Mellish (who joined the Trades Council in 1978)

expresses exactly the same sentiment: 'He was loyal and would stick up for you, was always pleased to encourage younger people and showed his pleasure when they took up new positions. He gave me tremendous support when I took over the Chair telling me what needed to be done, but never in a dictatorial way.' Les was always a compromiser and a pluralist. At meetings he would bring out opposing arguments and use his sound knowledge to get to the point and to make an analysis. Rafferty argues that in this respect he was in the Euro-Communist mould.

There is no doubt that Les was a pivotal figure in this demonstration of 1970s networking and it is echoed by Sean Geraghty's observations that Les's membership of his Trades Council also raised the profile of the Trades Council in the Press Branch. Whereas it was customary for different ETU branches to be affiliated to different Trades Councils they rarely had any contact with them but, through Les, the Press Branch had a good working relationship with the Lewisham and Deptford Trades Council. Asquith Gibbes makes a similar observation: 'The LREC had an employment group in which Les was a prominent member. Because of his long-term work in the Trades Councils he saw things in a wider perspective and that he could be a vehicle between us and the Trades Councils and thereby ensure that issues of unemployment and racism were tackled by the Trades Councils. The link was also strong when ALCARAF was set up.'

Another function of the Trades Council was to be represented at the local authority, and in Lewisham and Deptford the Trades Council became a strong voice at the time of rate-capping and the Poll Tax. Tom Mellish notes that in the days of Thatcher's reign the Borough Council would regularly seek the Trades Council's views on such issues – this is less so now under New Labour. In the late seventies the Trades Council was 50 or 60 strong and used to meet at Deptford Town Hall; Mellish's memories of Les are of an effective and efficient organiser. In time we came to use the prominence of the Trades Council to promote the need for the setting up of Lewisham Pensioners' Forum with the local authority. If an issue was brought to the Trades Council Les would want to see it discussed and carried through. Nothing would be allowed to disappear and if he could not achieve what he wished at the Trades Council he would take the matter elsewhere. Perhaps it was Les's CP training in organisation and structure which made him a stickler for procedures, and this could lead to his becoming belligerent at times though never confrontational. He would sometimes need calming down! However Mellish insists that his CP allegiances never interfered with discussions. Thinking back to the Les Stannard he knew, Mellish believes that Les would turn up at things not because of his membership of the CP but just for himself. He did not seem to be part of a group. This idea is reinforced by Mike Power who recalls Les turning up at demonstrations with one of the original Deptford Trades Council banners: a small triangular affair with a little pole across it, it would hang loose in front with a stick behind it – all this to make sure that the Deptford Trades Council, as represented by only Les, would still be recognised.

Les's Trades Council work in the Lewisham and Deptford area was carried forward in his membership of the London Trades Council, of which an account was given by the late Margaret Whitham, President of the Greater London Pensioners' Association – another former colleague who paid tribute to Les's loyalty and reliability. She had known him initially in the CP from 1946 but came to know him better through the London Trades Council which she describes as strong, influential and powerful, bringing people together from all sections. 'It was more like an advanced TUC with shop stewards as well as TC delegates. Some have argued that the TUC would have gone so far as to want to see it disbanded. When it was re-formed in 1973 as the Greater London Association Trades Councils we [CP members] would be encouraged to attend and to present papers but we were expected to sit quietly in a corner! From the Communists' point of view this organisation lacked logic and clarity and Les was heard to remark to a colleague as they left one of the meetings, "Can't you tell? They lack all that we learned in our Communist training!"'

[13]

The Royal Arsenal Co-operative Society

The Royal Arsenal Co-operative Society (RACS) was set up in 1868 by workers at what was the Royal Arsenal – where the football team started its life. The society moved into Woolwich and became the dominant force in south-east London trading and politics. In 1921 the balance was tipped in favour of the Co-operative movement taking political action. There were, again, conflicts within, because, as Rhodes has shown (p. 1), although the co-operators held dearly to the Rochdale Pioneers' principles of religious and political neutrality, their ideas were also based on the French Revolution's call for 'liberty, equality and fraternity' which had political overtones. On the other hand, whilst the co-operators held closely to Owen's principles they felt they wished to disassociate themselves from his anti-religious views since to exclude people who had religious views undermined another Co-operative principle, that of open and voluntary membership! Different Co-op societies made different decisions about political allegiances at this time – RACS formed its Political Purposes Committee (PPC) in 1921. Unlike many others in the movement RACS affiliated directly to the Labour Party; affiliation to the Co-operative Party followed much later. The committee looked after the political functions of RACS. Unusually in the movement, the RACS PPC was an 'open' committee – one did not have to be a party member to stand, only a member of the 'Co-op'. Elections were by single transferable vote (a form of PR) so minorities were always represented and it was never dominated by one faction or another. While it would be true to say that the right wing of the Labour Party held the majority for most of the time, Balfe says that the Labour left wing was also represented, as well as the Communist Party, an occasional Trotskyist, even the odd Conservative, and people with no politics at all. The CP tended to have two seats out of the directly elected ones and Sid French (the leader of the CP) was a member for many years. Les was elected to the committee on the Communist vote. The broadly based composition of the PPC (reminiscent of today's New Times Network) and its system of election was extremely unusual but it worked well for almost 70 years. RACS thus differed from other Co-op societies – its 'political machinery' was not set up under the aegis of the Co-op Party and it sponsored parliamentary candidates who did not have to be members of the Co-op Party. Its principle that anyone could join the PPC was at variance with its affiliating to constituency Labour Parties in the area yet, once again, the arrangement worked.

The PPC was charged with the administration of the society's political fund. Since it was affiliated to both the Labour and the Co-operative Parties the fund was used largely to provide backing for local and national parties. Indirectly the PPC held a seat on the National Executive of the Labour Party and it also sponsored candidates for both local and national elections. Several MPs and some MEPs and some peers are indebted to the Co-op for its support.

In the early fifties there was expanding trade and geographical expansion; small societies joined RACS, bringing with them different political traditions and stronger allegiances to the Co-op Party, hence the PPC began to reposition itself and to fall into line with the rest of the Co-op movement and the Union Congress decisions.

The strong right/left divisions and the ferment within the

Labour Party in the mid-fifties which were often aligned to the unilateral versus multilateral disarmament camps (as well as to Clause 4 and to trade with South Africa) had their effects on RACS. As Rhodes tells us (pp. 192–3) the society became as much concerned with the policy as with the functions of the Labour Party. The Labour group on the PPC became less cohesive. A rift even appeared between the PPC and the RACS General Committee which was in part due to the fact that the General Committee and the Education Committee could make appointments to the PPC. The Labour group on the PPC thus objected to the fact that Communist appointees on the PPC could create pressure (reflecting their CP positions on disarmament) at the society's quarterly meetings. There were splits also within the RACS Education Committee and struggles, generally, about member democracy. The Education Committee split centred round one group wanting a non-controversial approach to education work while another wanted to continue to stress its co-operative and political content. Attfield tells us that various attempts were made to cut costs at the expense of the society's democratic structure. Much controversy arose over plans to introduce a stamp, similar to the famous Green Shield Stamp, and when the vote was carried in favour of the stamp it was regarded as representing the wishes of officials and senior staff against those of the members (Attfield, p. 73).

There were evident strains between government, employers and the trade unions in the seventies when economic growth faltered and unemployment increased, and there were strong contrasts between the dull 'going nowhere' Parliamentary Labour Party and the left-wing surge in local authorities, with Liverpool, Islington and Lambeth as prime examples.

1981 saw the emergence of the SDP in response to the gradual left-wing drift of the Labour Party. Michael Foot was elected Leader of the Labour Party and both he and Tony Benn were in favour of unilateral nuclear disarmament and against the EEC. There were more conflicts within RACS and a strong statement was issued by the committee, supporting Clause 4 and the strengthening of the Labour Party at a time when some Co-op MPs, including committee vice-chairman John Cartwright, had defected to the SDP. Yet, while the Co-operative Party supported Michael Foot's enquiry into the 'Militant Tendency', this was opposed by the PPC on the grounds that, whilst party discipline should be maintained, the rather hysterical scapegoating of groups should be avoided. In the light of this Balfe and Stannard proposed an amendment to a resolution, asking the National Executive of the Labour Party (NEC) not to set up a register of groups (such as Militant). Divisions also occurred between RACS and the London Co-operative Society London Region Political Committee, over the Section 11 seat on the National Executive.[1] Les moved a resolution proposing that RACS and the London Region Political Committee should jointly put forward a candidate. Balfe moved to support Hilda Smith, the committee chair, and the RACS followed him. In the event, both Smith and the LCS nominee, Les Huckfield, were defeated.

The PPC then became the Co-operative Wholesale Society (CWS) Ltd Royal Arsenal Branch Political Committee. Little changed at first – it retained its affiliations to the national Labour Party and the Co-operative Party. In time, however, it was over-shadowed by wider developments. RACS had been based on co-operative trade and political debate but when the pattern of trade changed so did the RACS political organisation. The CWS did not want its resources to support the Labour Party.

RACS merged with the CWS in 1985. It chose not to compete in the vast, emerging supermarket industry but remains an immense organisation, the biggest co-operative

[1] Section 11 is Division II of Socialist and Co-operative Societies section of the NEC.

retailer in Europe and the biggest commercial farmer in Britain. It has also become involved in the insurance, travel agency and car sales business. The ethical Co-operative Bank is also a major player standing out on its own in the banking industry. The Co-operative Retail Society (CRS) and CWS remained rivals until very recently but by early 1999 a full merger seemed likely to take place and any resulting deal is likely to be in convenience stores rather than in competition with the major supermarkets (see *The Times*, 8 October 1999).

The CRS and the CWS were the trading arm of the movement and there was also the funeral service, the arsenal, the 'divi' (or dividend) – all of this remains a strong movement in south London and people were part of the movement from the cradle to the grave. This was certainly true of Les. In the mid to late eighties he was very much involved in the partnership between Lewisham Council and the Co-op in the setting up of the Funeral Service with Lewisham's logo used in all the publicity. Les would not give up on it (recalls Councillor Angela Cornforth) because it offered a funeral with dignity at a reasonable price, but the project came to be threatened by the cabal of other funeral directors.

The PPC was abolished in 1992 in favour of smaller party councils which are now established or being established all over south London. Balfe has no doubt that the co-operative ideal remains relevant and important in society today and believes that the Co-operative Party should work hard to promote the political theory of co-operation in all parties.

In 2000 Tony Blair set up a Commission to report on the future of the Co-operative movement. It is believed 'that he had been persuaded that when so much of what socialism stood for had gone for good, this was one part of the heritage that could be rejuvenated to provide a real example of a different way of doing things'. The Commission's report was expected at the beginning of February 2001 (Christopher Hird, Director of Fulcrum TV, from *Red Pepper*, February 2001).

Les Stannard's work within the Co-operative movement

Les became active in the Labour movement from the time he joined the Communist Party in 1937. We know from his brother Stanley and from his aunt, Nell Bryett, however, that he was beginning to show signs of political interest when he was 12 or 13 and perhaps the biggest contribution to this awakening of his consciousness was the illness of his mother, Edith. In these pre-welfare state days doctors charged fees, although they did not always take them. After Edith's death her doctor was still owed a considerable sum and, says Stan, this made a great impression on young Les. His daughter Lesley also remembers hearing this account from her father when she was growing up. The same experience laid the foundations for his impassioned views on the way that women are penalised in respect of the state pension, for he had witnessed the role of 'carer' which his grandmother assumed in looking after him and his brothers as Maura Rafferty and Heather Wakefield point out: 'One of the most impressive things about him was his commitment to women. He used not to make grand statements about "women's rights" but he never said a sexist thing in his life. He never spoke to colleagues about these personal experiences but when he spoke about mothers going hungry and not going to the doctor because the half-crown would be needed for food for the family, we knew it was his mother and grandmother he was talking about.'

Les became a member of RACS in 1950, and became Secretary of the Lewisham North (Deptford) area Members Council. This council held meetings with other RACS committees to mandate policy. He served on the PPC for six years (from 1980 till 1986), sat on the Members Council for 17 years and on the Special Committee between 1971 and 1973. He was elected as members' delegate to the Co-operative Congress in 1970. This body is often described as the parliament of the movement (Les always termed the Lewisham Pensioners' Forum the 'pensioners' parliament'). Delegates to the Congress came from over 1000 separate Co-operative societies, including the Co-op Party, the CWS and the worldwide Co-operative movement. RACS had a membership of more than 350,000 and 9000 employees, and covered a wide area – based in Woolwich, it embraced Faversham in Kent, Woking in Surrey and Slough in Buckinghamshire. Les was a regular attender at the Lewisham and Woolwich gatherings and soon built up a reputation as a keen co-operator.

The PPC throughout its entire existence maintained a high profile in its work within the Labour movement generally and gave its support to a wider range of campaigns, causes and issues, both nationally and internationally. It held a tight rein on its own administrative costs and always endeavoured to use its grant to the best effect. These are some of the issues it was concerned with during the time that Les served on the committee: the inclusion of co-operative studies in the school curriculum and in higher education; the campaign against the privatisation of both the NHS and transport; the campaign about the state pension and the dissemination of the Pensioners' Declaration of Intent; the People's March for Jobs; and the Campaign against the Police and Criminal Evidence Bill. The committee supported or affiliated to numerous organisations: Amnesty International, the National Museum of Labour History, the Fawcett Society and various organisations concerned with disarmament. It sent messages of support and thermal clothing to the women at Greenham Common. Women's rights featured high on their agenda, with issues such as domestic violence. International issues they discussed and monitored included the turbulent situations in Iran and El Salvador and the sale of South African goods. They were represented at the 'Liberation' Conference on the Middle East and in many conferences on world disarmament. This was reflected in the donation they sent in memory of Philip Noel Baker of the World Disarmament Campaign.

Roy Martin, former Secretary of the RACS Education Members Relations Committee, recalls the unique position which Les Stannard held during the unpleasant days of left-right divisions during the fifties and sixties. This was the same period as the bitter court case which brought down Haxell in the ETU. At this time, in RACS, Martin remarks, one had to 'line up on the side of the angels'– the divisions were bitter and there was considerable animosity and nastiness on either side. Catholic Action was a strong force and influence against the left within the movement. 'Les was one of the few who was not affected – he was accepted by everybody even by his political opponents who recognised that he was straight as a die. Even when the truth was not to his political advantage he was renowned for facing up to it. Furthermore, such was his character that despite his own radical views he always stood above the cheap personality campaigns being waged at the time and, unlike others in both camps, he never attacked anyone for being a Catholic.'

In recording the contribution that Les Stannard made to the movement in the later years Richard Balfe says that Les changed the British Co-op movement by bringing the concerns of senior citizens to the agenda. He always won not by winning votes but by winning arguments.

After his death South East Co-op (the name of the new organisation set up after the merger with the CWS) set up two bursaries in Les's name as well as contributing to the Lewisham Pensioners' Forum Les Stannard Memorial Fund.

[14]

The Retirement Years

'Self – self – self . . . there are so few people who seem to realise that there's no meaning to oneself unless one is busy with something much bigger than just what one is. A cause, or a duty – something which doesn't begin and end inside one precious self-contained little personality.'

D. Jacobson, *The Evidence of Love*

'Many of us accepted an early retirement and settled for an easy life, feeling that we had done our share in the trade union movement. Not so with Les, who did even more work after retirement than in the whole of his trade union career with his involvement in the pensioners' movement. He was a born leader, and Lewisham should be proud to have produced someone who never gave up the fight to improve the lot of his fellow human beings.'

John McLoughlin, former ETU colleague

'No one will ever know how much he did. The contribution Les made to pensioners and to Lewisham will never be sufficiently recognised. He was brilliant. He never thrust his political views on you. He is still with us.'

Tony Link, former Labour Councillor, London Borough of Lewisham

'Don't forget Rose Kerrigan – he could not have done it without her.'

Dolly Hyne, former Chairperson of the Pensioners' Committee

Four flights of very steep steps, covered in old-fashioned linoleum, the colour of bulls' blood, led to the second floor offices of Lewisham Pensioners' Forum which they shared from their inception until January 2000 with the Lewisham Racial Equality Council. Pensioners are not a single mass of people as they are often portrayed by the authorities and the media; they vary from the relatively young, strong and active to the very old, sick and frail. Yet they are lumped together in the public mind and almost ghettoised as 'the elderly' rather than seen as elderly people – ourselves, grown older. A moment's reflection would make one realise that this kind of language illustrates the way older people are marginalised in our society.

Many many pensioners have climbed those steep stairs at 48 Lewisham High Street in various degrees of health and ability and ranging in age from 60 to 90-plus – an indication of their determination and commitment. During those so-called retirement years Les Stannard climbed the stairs several times a day, managing the day-to-day work programme as well as attending perhaps four meetings daily both in Lewisham and in central London.

The complete history of the pensioners' movement in Lewisham must in due course be written as a tribute to an outstanding group of committed and determined citizens who devoted their retirement years to a campaign for justice for pensioners both in their local borough and nationally. This account of Les Stannard's life summarises some of the campaigns and activities which they carried out between 1986 and 1996.

Mr Lewisham and the Pensioners' Forum

After Les's death the front cover of the GLPA journal for February 1997 carried his photograph under the heading SALUD MR LEWISHAM. In examining these last ten years of Les Stannard's remarkable life it becomes abundantly clear that his work for pensioners and the policy of his borough towards its elderly citizens were intertwined. The active political pensioners' movement in the borough began in 1979 when a group of pensioners got to know each other at the Age Concern 'Pop In' Centre in Catford. They began to define their aims and an ad hoc committee was formed. The aims of this Lewisham Pensioners' Action Group (LPAG) were to consider the needs and problems of retired people living in Lewisham and to find ways of advising and giving help. Their chief concerns were pensions, transport and health issues.

Some of those involved were Nora Sheedy, Mary Dennis and Ron Pemberton. Rose Kerrigan joined the Action Group in the early days when another group she belonged to in Sydenham closed. Les, who had not yet retired, attended the group as a speaker from the Deptford and Lewisham Trades Council in December 1981. He joined the Action Group in May 1982 and was later elected to the committee, remaining until his death. Betty Cayzer recalls that she soon became aware that Les was the mainstay of the organisation. He was always able and willing to explain things and give advice if asked, though he never forced himself or his views on anyone. In fact, at meetings he was always to be seen somewhere at the back of the room. He must have made a lot of personal sacrifices in devoting so much time to improving the lot of pensioners. At meetings he always seemed to say the right thing at the right time and in the language ordinary people understood. He had the full backing of LPAG when he set up the Forum but even when the Forum was established he continued to give his total support to the LPAG. 'There will only ever be one Les; he was an inspiration to all pensioners,' said Betty Cayzer. The LPAG is now almost 21 years old and has a membership of about 100.

In pre-New Labour days Lewisham Borough Council was both innovative and radical in its approach to the many social problems which confronted it. It was also the first and only borough in the country to establish a statutory Pensioners' Committee as part of its formal committee structure. In March 1983 it issued its first policy statement on elderly people, intended to provide the basis for a new approach to the development of services:

> The Council acknowledges and places high value on the considerable life experience of elderly people in Lewisham and is committed to safeguarding their fundamental rights of independence, freedom and choice. It views retirement as the beginning of a stage of life which offers people opportunities for positive change and life enrichment and pledges itself to develop services in ways that best enhance these opportunities. The Council will aim to provide a flexible range of services which responds to the individual needs and wishes of older people themselves, involves them in decision-making processes and respects their right to choose their own lifestyle. It not only encourages but expects them to comment on and criticise services which fail to meet their personal needs and wishes them to participate in and contribute to the running of present services and the development of new ones.

A structure of consultation was set up in September 1985 under the then Leader of the Council Dave Sullivan. He was conscious of the fact that while there were a number of organisations in the borough working with and providing services for pensioners, more needed to be done to support a movement whose objective was to represent and give a voice to Lewisham's pensioners. In the autumn of 1986 Sullivan attended a meeting of the Lewisham Labour and Trade Union Retired Members Association at the East Lewisham Labour Party. The Chairman at the time was Harry Bacon and John Rampling was the Secretary – both subsequently long-standing members of the Management Committee. Les was there; though he was not yet retired he was fully determined and energetic. Sullivan recognised this and knew also that he had met a group of highly organised and dedicated people. Groups now came together in what John Rampling describes as 'the emergence of a vitalised and turbulent force which lit the fuse that exploded into the Lewisham Pensioners' Forum'.

Lewisham Pensioners' Forum was established and a constitution agreed in 1986. The Management Committee adopted the Pensioners' Declaration of Intent and the criteria set by the National Pensioners' Convention in 1979. The founder members were Rose Kerrigan, representing the Lewisham Pensioners' Action Group, Harry Bacon, representing the Lewisham Retired Trade Unionists, and Les Stannard, representing the Deptford and Lewisham Trades Council. The first grant of £1000 was allocated and Les's old friend and comrade Asquith Gibbes, Principal Officer at the Lewisham Racial Equality Ccouncil, proposed that the then Lewisham Council for Community Relations should take care of the grant until formal proceedings were ready to begin; before long, a room at the LCCR offices was made over to the Forum.

These are the Forum's aims and objectives:

> To promote the welfare of people over retirement age and people who have retired early because of sickness, or unemployment (retired people) within the London Borough of Lewisham, so as to improve their conditions of life, relieve their poverty and provide facilities and opportunities for retired people in the Borough to meet, discuss matters of common interest and undertake action to advance their well-being.

The members of the Forum's first Management Committee were Rose Kerrigan (Chair), Harry Bacon and Stan Tulloch (Vice-Chairs), Les Stannard (Secretary), Lilian Beale (Treasurer) and the following members: Eileen Ashman, Wally Barnes, Pat Burke, John Esterson, Cynthia Howells, Rosalia Mooney, Stan Nicholls, George Parker, John Rampling and Irene Swift. The London Borough of Lewisham representatives were Councillors Peggy Fitzsimmons and Tony Link. The co-opted members were Elizabeth Gallagher, Director of Age Concern, Lewisham and her staff members Ralph Borkett, Jacqueline Jolley and Mary Lynch. Linda Fergusson represented the Lewisham Council for Community Relations and Pensioners' Link was represented by Denise Fowler.

Les served the Lewisham Pensioners' Forum for ten years and during that time and to this very day the Forum's workload was very demanding of its unpaid officers, Management Committee members and the paid staff. Les was both inspired and determined. He battled with the local authority and the government on a wide range of issues related to pensioners' rights. He wanted to ensure that retired people should have the opportunity to contribute to society and to the political debate; to ensure that pensioners are guaranteed sufficient income to enable them to live comfortably and in security for the rest of their lives. Les wanted to make certain that every aspect of pensioners' lives was addressed – from the most important national issues, such as the state pension, the National Health Service and Social Security, standing charges and free travel, right down to the smallest detail which makes life not just bearable but fulfilling and enjoyable. So while on the one hand he was actively involved in the national movement for the restoration of the link between pensions and earnings he devoted perhaps almost as much time to the maintenance of the Travel Permit for Londoners. He bore in mind also the great importance of social activity, education and leisure to the health and well-being of elderly people, and would ensure that Lewisham pensioners could reach adult education classes, leisure centres, cricket at the Oval, and the annual Christmas Police Concert at Hendon.

Les felt a great personal concern that older people should experience security, comfort and enjoyment in their final years. He was particularly keen to promote working relations between people of all ages, especially between elderly people and children, believing that older people have a great deal to contribute to children in the way of passing on a lifetime rich with experience.

The Forum's work programme was, from the beginning, a very ambitious one, covering all aspects of pensioners' daily lives, whether they were newly retired and having to learn to live on a reduced income, or so sick and frail that they needed total care and someone to represent them if they had no family. Les brought three vital attributes to the Forum – his many years' experience in the trade union movement and in the Lewisham and Deptford Trades Council; the fact that, except for the disruption of the war years, he had lived his whole life in Deptford or Lewisham; and most importantly, his unique ability to network. Les, with his colleagues, was able to bring the Forum to the attention of Lewisham residents and to members of the local authority. Within a very short time 'Les Stannard' became a well-known name in the borough and because of his apparent ability to be present in several different places at once, his face soon became familiar both to councillors and to members of the public. He also had a large circle of friends and acquaintances from his involvement with Millwall.

The Forum's Management Committee met every four weeks and the agenda would be prepared by Les and his colleagues in the Officers' Committee at their fortnightly meetings. The agenda would be drawn up not only from issues under discussion in council committees but also from a network of other pensioners' organisations and interests – the Greater London Pensioners Association, the National Pensioners Convention, the Travel Permit Working Group, Age Concern and Pensioners' Link. Issues will also have been drawn to their attention through (amongst others) the Millwall Over 50s Club, the lunch clubs and day centres and individual members.

Membership of the Forum was open to every retired resident. One of the first tasks was to establish a mailing list and to send a bi-monthly newsletter to members keeping them fully informed about both local and national news, forthcoming legislation and how it would affect local authority services. No one anticipated in the 1980s how catastrophic the legislative changes were to become for Britain's pensioners, so that their incomes would be drastically reduced and their health and welfare damaged. Many would argue that the extent to which Les drove himself throughout those ten years could well have brought about his own untimely death. Even on his death-bed he was expressing concern about forthcoming events in the pensioners' calendar and wanting to make sure that the Forum would be represented.

During the first two years of the Forum's existence the Management Committee undertook to organise all their activities themselves but they received full administrative support from the staff of the Lewisham Council for Community Relations, to which the Pensioners' Forum owes an enormous debt. Early in 1988 the local authority agreed to increase the Forum's grant so a co-ordinator and an administrative assistant could be employed, and the programme was expanded and formalised. Les's vision was, first, to strengthen the Forum's base within the borough, in order that elderly people could participate fully in the decision-making process, and, therefore, to involve all Forum members in that process whether or not they were able to attend meetings. In this respect he and his colleagues also ensured that all minority groups should be fully represented within the Management Committee and in the Forum's activities. Secondly he aimed to gain a high profile for the Forum within the local authority and he attended any Council committee meeting whose agenda contained items of relevance to pensioners: this meant that he was likely to attend committee meetings at the Town

Hall as often as four times a week, often returning home well after 10.30 p.m. when others of his age would have been comfortably sitting in front of the television or warm in their beds. Thirdly he recognised that the Forum should be in working contact with pensioners' organisations in nearby boroughs, with hospitals, the local and national carers' associations, Community Health Councils, Health Centres, bereavement groups, the Youth Service, the Adult Education Service and local and London-wide voluntary organisations.

Lastly and most importantly, Les never lost sight of the fact that, to be effective, local pensioners' groups and forums need to reflect the developments taking place within the national and international pensioners' movement. Three years before his death Les was elected Vice-President of five major pensioners' organisations: the National Pensioners' Convention, the Greater London Pensioners' Association, the Greater London Forum, the British Pensioners and Trade Union Action Association and the Joint Council for Senior Citizens. He had been involved in the setting up of the Greater London Forum in 1987 following the demise of the GLC in 1986. There had been a Forum for Elderly People within the GLC but this also met its end at the same time. Finally, Les was elected Senior Vice-Chair of the GLF in 1994. It is envisaged that a new Forum for Elderly People will be established by the new Greater London Authority which came into being in 2000.

In 1993 Les announced that he wished to resign from the position of LPF Secretary in view of his election to the five London and national pensioners' organisations and he called for a new Secretary to whom he vowed his full support. He said that his election to the national and London organisations, which he accepted as a great privilege, would not have been possible 'if Dave Sullivan, the Council Leader at the time, had not given his support to the establishment of the Forum. Neither would my recognition be possible if it were not for your [Forum members'] support at Forum Meetings and the day to day activity that many Lewisham people contribute to the national pensioners' campaigns' (1994 Report, p.12). However, he relented and continued as Secretary for the 1993–4 term though he was adamant that he would not carry on after that. He added, 'I will not be deserting the pensioners' movement, but will continue my association with the Forum through the London-wide and national organisations, as well as associating myself with the public campaigns that LPF and LPAG conduct on behalf of the pensioners' movement.'

Within months of the establishment of Lewisham Pensioners' Forum Les attended meetings in all parts of the country in support of pensioners who wanted to establish their own organisations – somehow he would find the time to fit everything in and never turned down a request for help.

His diary for the week of 10 September 1995 gives an indication of how busy he was. The day after he attended a public meeting in Leeds to assist in the progress of the Pensioners Liaison Forum there, he was at the TUC Pensioners' conference in Brighton. On Monday he had a full day in the office commencing with an officers' meeting. Tuesday was devoted to preparing for the forthcoming Pensioners' Day in Lewisham but also included a meeting of the Millwall Anti-Racist Committee, followed by the executive meeting of the Greater London Forum for the Elderly, then the South-East London Retired Members meeting at the Oval. Wednesday 13 September was Pensioners' Day in Lewisham but Les also fitted in an executive meeting of the Greater London Pensioners' Association and an appointment with the Mayor of Lewisham before Pensioners' Day itself started at 1.30 p.m. He did not forget, however, to return to one of his GLPA colleagues an umbrella which he had rescued after it had been left behind at the previous meeting. That evening he did manage to enjoy a little relaxation because Millwall were at home to Luton at 7.45 p.m. Thursday was taken up with more Millwall meetings and a short morning visit to Millwall

Over 50s Club. Friday found him, as always, at Lewisham Market collecting signatures for petitions.

Les's one morning of leisure was Thursday, when he never failed to attend his beloved Millwall Over 50s Club at the Den and later at Zampa Road, but even then his friends recall that he rarely stayed for very long, hardly stopping for a cup of tea. Still less did he find the time to join them for lunch since he invariably had to be on his way, back to the office or another meeting. On such occasions lunch would consist of a bag of fruit which he regarded as sufficient to last him until his evening meal. On other occasions, if he found himself unexpectedly having to attend yet another meeting, a bag of crisps would suffice. Such was his passion for what he was striving to achieve that all personal comforts, food, drink and rest, would be forgotten. In the fortnight before a Forum meeting Les would often come into the office with a beautifully written draft letter to go to Forum members which he would have stayed up late to write at home the night before. 'Please would you put this in order,' he would say, or words to that effect. If he was not on his way to another meeting he would stay in the office and help with the collating of the letter; he nearly always stayed to help fill the envelopes or alternatively would take a pile back home with him to complete later in the day. Les taught me a valuable lesson in how to arrange the envelopes in such a way that they could be stuck down in double quick time. Attaching stamps was also done with great speed though they sometimes landed a long way away from the normal right-hand corner!

The most lasting recollection I have is of Les as my teacher and my mentor. Sitting next to me at the desk he would answer my many questions about the history of the pension, the position of women and the ways that they have been discriminated against. He could be counted on for a broad-ranging, thoroughly informed, fair and balanced assessment of almost any social or political issue both past and present. As John McLoughlin also recalls, 'He had an astonishing knowledge of world affairs – he was not just a local Lewisham and Deptford politician. Ask him about a current issue – say, what was going on in the Middle East – and he would give you not just his opinion but a thorough analysis of the situation and the events which had led up to it.' Les's talents as a teacher and mentor are noted also by Doris Smith when recording her first attendances, with Les, at the Elderly Services Planning Group: 'He has been an excellent teacher on how to voice the problems that members of the Forum have raised with us about Care in the Community.'

In 1990 the Forum's own agenda began to place greater responsibilities and powers on the Management Committee. Two major events were the setting up of the Pensioners' Committee and the local authority's invitation to the Forum to nominate representatives with speaking rights to sit on 17 Council committees. Nominations for all these committees were made at the Forum's autumn AGM. The first nominees to the Pensioners' Committee were Rose Kerrigan, Les Stannard, Harry Bacon, Pat Burke and Stan Tulloch. The other committees on which the Forum was represented were: Central Services, Social Services, Safer Cities, Education, Housing, Environmental Services, Race Relations, Women's, Leisure Services, Transport, Disabled Persons and the Police Consultative Committee.

Meetings of the Pensioners' Forum take place every other month; in the first few years of the Forum they were held at the Riverdale Hall in the Lewisham precinct and they are now held at the Town Hall Civic Suite in Catford. Every meeting would have an invited speaker or speakers and a debate related to a current issue. The question of the state pension dominated those years and continues to this day. Before the 1997 General Election the Labour Party implied its intention to restore the link between earnings and pensions and it is clear that the late John Smith saw this as an important manifesto issue. Yet, to the bitter anger of the entire pensioners' movement, the New Labour government appears to have turned its back on restoring the link. Les was determined to ensure that politicians were accountable to their pensioner constitutents and he initiated the tradition of devoting the Forum meeting before local or national elections to a debate with prospective candidates.

The London Borough of Lewisham Pensioners' Committee

An idea whose time had come 1987. Abolished 1996

> 'The involvement of pensioners in the consultation process does not necessarily guarantee improvement in services to elderly people – particularly at a time when the government is restricting local government spending and also "capping" those authorities they think are spending too much.'
> Les Stannard, Annual Report 1991, p. 5

The London Borough of Lewisham Pensioners' Committee was the first and the only one of its kind in the country. It met for the first time on 6 February 1987 and meetings took place four times a year until it ceased to exist in March 1996. It is important to record this outstanding event since, by the establishment of this committee, pensioners were for the first time in a position to affect local authority policy and thus, in turn, bring about the changes they sought to improve the lives of elderly people.

At the first meeting of the Pensioners' Committee the Leader and first Chair, Dave Sullivan, made the following statement: 'When the Labour Group was elected in May 1986 we made it clear in our manifesto that the needs of Lewisham pensioners would have a high priority during our administration. The manifesto gave full support for pensioners' needs for adequate income, decent homes, access to health care, heating allowances, education and leisure . . . and for a wide range of social services, concessionary travel scheme etc.'

The procedures in Council committee work (between members, officers and representatives of the voluntary sector) are usually formal. Officers are paid to carry out the policies of the Council and councillors are elected to determine those policies. They earn their living elsewhere. In this process officers are in a powerful position because they have access to information and knowledge by virtue of being there full time. When councillors decide that they want something done they have to get officers to write reports which have then to go through formal committees. In a Council like Lewisham, which for some time has had a Labour majority, one gets a quite stable situation and officers know that an issue will almost certainly be supported if a leading member or committee Chair says they want to support it – for example to find resources for a project. On the other hand, councillors may ignore professional advice and take irrational decisions. A healthy mix is one where councillors can have the courage to make it clear that a matter has not been given due consideration and that the professional advice has not been appropriate.

Waheeda Malick, who was appointed by the Leader to work with the Pensioners' Forum and to act as the link officer in relations between the Forum and the Pensioners' Committee, recalls how swiftly her reaction to working with pensioners changed once she met Les for the first couple of times. 'I had never worked with pensioners before and soon realised that this man, Les Stannard, was going to mean hard work. The image I had held in my mind until then, of a pensioner sitting round the gas fire, tottering around the high street with a stick or featured in a mugging poster, soon disappeared. True, this man had white hair but he had more energy than I did; "This is what we want," he would say, and immediately I clicked and knew we were going to enjoy working together and would achieve things.'

Waheeda explains that officers would meet separately with voluntary sector representatives and with the Leader. Where the Pensioners' Committee was concerned, many barriers were broken down and one outstanding change of procedure took place when the Pensioners' Forum began to produce its own reports for Committee – something hitherto unheard of. Les and the co-ordinator would prepare the report and the officers and committee clerk, Colin Hibbs, would (without in any way altering its content) put it into official format and language. There would first be a pre-meeting to prepare the agenda and to decide tactics, depending on which department or individual officer was going to be involved. 'We certainly had battles over procedures with some departments, which was not surprising in view of the fact that procedures themselves were being revolutionised and turned on their heads. Never before had individual officers attended meetings to give account or to reply to reports. Many were put off their guard by the kind of down-to-earth practical questions which the pensioners' representatives asked.'

It was not just a question of words and dialogue – things did change. Trees around day centres got priority for being cut in winter because of the dangers of slippery leaves and because they obstructed light. When 'wheelie bins' were introduced, the engineers were invited to come along to the meeting to show how easy the new bins were to wheel – in a short time Les had them laughing when he pointed out that many pensioners were half the engineers' height and weight. 'Fill up the bin,' he said, 'then come to me and tell me it's easy for them!' He managed to make his point in a jovial way without provoking or upsetting people and, after that, pensioners were allowed to leave their bins wherever it suited them and they would be collected!

Lively exchanges took place between Les and the then Chair Dolly Hyne, 'a great enthusiast and champion of the pensioners, but nonetheless a councillor with an agenda'. Often Dolly's role was to try to engage the pensioners on issues. Les and his colleagues, in their turn, were determined to stick to the pensioners' priorities and not be led astray.

Combine all this with an unruly group of pensioners and young staff with a touch of rebelliousness about them, and it was no wonder that Colin Hibbs said that 'it was the most exciting committee around – and it worked!' Channel 4 made a film about the committee, showing how ordinary people were being recognised as pioneers by establishing a decision-making structure on every issue affecting them – practical things designed to make a difference to pensioners' quality of life. Many groups from outside Lewisham came to learn. By 1994–5 the Forum representatives on the committee were increasingly active and were responsible for raising more than half the agenda items.

Les had always read his papers thoroughly, as well as being fully versed on earlier statutes; he was thus ahead of many other voluntary sector representatives who would turn up at meetings and demonstrate in a very short time that they had not read their papers and thus could not do justice to their cause. Elizabeth Sclater (at that time Principal Officer, Pensioners, in the Equalities Unit) draws attention to another of Les's outstanding qualities: 'He was always clear and firm about what the consultation process was about and what impressed me most was that he never said anything or agreed to anything without adding that he must go back to his members and colleagues to talk about the matter. He would certainly have had his own views but every issue went back to the Management Committee and then to the Forum; then he would be able to say that he had the backing of his members. He always had to know that he had the authority to negotiate and he never forgot who his constituents were.' Similarly, Jeremy Corbyn MP notes that whenever Les visited the House of Commons to meet MPs he always began by making it clear on whose behalf he was there, since he represented different organisations on different occasions. Corbyn adds that many voluntary organisation representatives fail to remember this important point. Where Les was concerned it was a mark of his professionalism and the high regard in which he was held that his own Lewisham MPs very quickly stopped whatever else they were doing and immediately came down to meet him in the lobby whenever he sent them his card!

Elizabeth Sclater had been involved with the Pensioners' Forum in a previous post as manager of the social work team at Hither Green Hospital that dealt with the Geriatric Unit, but found herself in a very different position when she became Principal Officer. 'It was a totally different perspective when in my Council role I had to face any criticism of the Council from Les, fair and constructive though he always was: yet, from my point of view as an officer, my responsibilities were made relatively easy (compared with my opposite numbers in other boroughs) because Lewisham's pensioners were so well organised. I was able to build on the sound organisation of the Forum and learned much from Les's consummate skills in reading the political climate. Because of their membership of the wider pensioners' movement (both in London and nationally) Les and his colleagues were often better informed than I was; it was not unusual for me to want to consult them!'

She also remembers the remarkable achievements of the Forum at Pensioners' Committees when, without pulling any punches and without acrimony, the pensioners were able to show clearly the adverse effects of certain policy decisions which, had the Forum been consulted, would never have been taken. Similarly Dolly Hyne remembers that through the Pensioners' Committee many vulnerable pensioners had security locks put on their doors – something that was really needed. While being conscious of the big national issues Les would also operate on the vitally important local issues. 'He was a union man,' says Dolly, 'and you could read that every time he made a speech, which invariably would start with words like "We are going to" or "This is what is wanted".' Consider for example the availability of educational courses. People like Dolly, Les, Harry and Rose were well aware that education (however loosely described and whether offered in schools, day centres or luncheon clubs) could make an enormous difference to the lives of elderly people, especially those who lived alone. 'Just the fact that they can come out of their homes and do something for themselves will keep them alive and also save money for the Council. If they stay at home and talk to no one and eat poorly, then before you know it you have the expense of hospital and community care,' says Dolly. No wonder that Les saw the importance of fighting both for the retention of the Travel Permit and for educational and leisure opportunities.

Jim Mallory remembers well that Les was brilliant at exploiting the councillor/member/voluntary sector relationship. He always made it a point to speak to councillors first and was an expert at obtaining a paper or drawing attention to a rumour. 'He would know just the right member to speak to so that he would succeed in getting a decision modified or changed and was more effective than anybody I remember in the pensioners' movement or even across the whole of the voluntary sector.'

The Pensioners' Forum and the Pensioners' Committee – a force for change?

The Pensioners' Committee then was a unique, possibly never to be repeated, exercise in true people's democracy. It must be recognised that Les and his colleagues were themselves a unique and unusual team, brought together by strong (albeit not identical) political beliefs and a concern for justice and fairness. That in itself would not have been enough. Les's exceptional intelligence, his command of the political scene both locally and nationally, his knowledge of all the relevant legislation and of the chief actors who needed to be lobbied, and his gentle powers of persuasion made him a formidable force.

When asked about how the Forum's interventions effected change, Dave Sullivan remembers that Les would frequently talk to him in the foyer of the Civic Suite, lobbying him and persuading him, quietly, on current issues. Sullivan would then become involved and action would begin to follow. This happened on many occasions. Sullivan does not think that the Council merely paid lip service to the Forum because pensioners had become a significant force in Lewisham – a voting force apart from anything else and still seen now as a major part of the community of the borough entitled to have a voice. 'Throughout the time that the Pensioners' Committee was in existence I never saw it marginalised – in fact I saw it as quite influential: never as influential as it would have liked to be, perhaps, for every group wants its cause to be the most important. However, looking around the country many people were quite surprised that we had a Pensioners' Committee – I was asked many questions about it and I think it was quite effective.' Lewisham Pensioners' Forum was still receiving enquiries in 1998 when a pensioners' group in Manchester was considering the possibility that a Pensioners' Committee might be established there.

During 1989, plans were afoot to reduce Pensioners' Committee meetings to two a year, instead of four. Les, with his exceptional skill, managed to rouse a considerable response to counter this proposal and, in his words, 'Lewisham councillors accepted our view that matters could not be adequately considered at six-monthly intervals' (1989 Annual Report, p. 1). The Pensioners' Forum won the day and the committee continued to meet four times a year. The Forum was unable, however, to affect the consequences of new legislation – the Housing and Local Government Act which removed the rights of representatives of non-statutory organisations to vote at Pensioners' Committee meetings. This did not, however, prevent them from making important and effective contributions.

For several years there were moves to abolish the committee and to cut the Forum's grant. Sullivan remembers in particular Les's personal skill in keeping the committee going and maintaining the grant. However, the committee remained in danger of abolition; a merger proposal was agreed to establish an Equalities Committee – an umbrella group which would bring together five previously separate committees: Pensioners, Women, Race, Disabled People and the Lesbian and Gay Committee. The then Leader of the Council, Jim Mallory, argued that the separation of the different groups meant some issues were not being addressed – the experience of older black women, for example – and that they would be better served by one corporate committee. He was aware that while the Pensioners' Committee was the best organised of the groups and conducted the best lobbying, it was less supported within the Council than all the other groups because there was no older person working full time within the Council. Some might regard this as a rather weak excuse! Mallory put forward Les's own arguments that pensioners were not being listened to because of the Council's own inadequacies! Les, however, did not see that the abolition of the Pensioners' Committee was the solution to the problem. Councillor Angela Cornforth confirms the reasoning behind the decision, that many councillors considered too much duplication was taking place and that the proposed Equalities Committee would be a unit of social justice which they all wanted to see in place. Others argued that the weakness of the now-established Equalities Committee lies in the fact that it does not give any clout to individual groups. However, the Mayor of Lewisham insisted that he wants to re-establish a formal pensioners' representative committee as part of the council's new committee structure (Dave Sullivan, 22 September 1999).[1]

The proposed merger led to a series of opposing actions by the Forum which expressed great disappointment that, after setting up such a pioneering example of consultation

[1] This has not happened yet, but the Council's cabinet and scrutiny arrangements are being reviewed and new ways of engaging the community are being examined.

with its elderly population, the borough was now abandoning its own good practice. In October 1995 a Forum resolution was sent to Councillor Mallory supporting the continuation of the Pensioners' Committee in its own right, which led to a lengthy correspondence and a series of meetings between Mallory and the Forum officers. Les, the supreme networker, received the support of prominent trade union leaders and senior colleagues in the Greater London and national pensioners' bodies. There was also an exchange of correspondence between Les and the then Chair of the Lewisham Association of People with Disabilities who was even stronger in his criticism of the arbitrary way the decision was taken and the lack of consultation.

Following Management Committee consultation Les sent a letter to all Forum members on 12 December 1995 urging them to support the retention of the Pensioners' Committee, arguing that whilst realising that all London Councils were under severe financial pressure as a result of further government cuts in public spending, political purposes should not be overthrown in order that £45,000 could be saved in the Equalities Unit. He quoted from the words of the Mayor, Councillor Alan Till, at the VE Day Commemorations: 'On behalf of the Borough of Lewisham, we pledge ourselves anew to work in support of the wartime generation. We promise to do everything possible where there is need and to ensure that the people of our wartime generation may enjoy the years ahead in comfort, dignity and contentment. This, we say, is a lasting token of our appreciation and gratitude.' Les commented that the Forum trusted him to see that this commitment was applied to the financial decisions then being made in all Council departments.

The Forum lobbied the next Pensioners' Committee meeting on 6 February 1996 and a vote by the Labour Group to reinstate the Pensioners' Committee was lost by one vote with 22 councillors absent. The last Pensioners' Committee took place on 28 March 1996. At the March 1996 Forum meeting the following resolution was carried unanimously: 'That this Forum recognises that in the past ten years Lewisham Council has assisted the empowerment of pensioners by setting up the structure to speak to pensioners' representatives in the Borough. The Forum is totally opposed to the demise of the Pensioners' Committee. We instruct the Management Committee to continue to press the Council to meet pensioners regularly to discuss policies until such time as the Committee can be reinstated.'

From May 1996 (just seven months before Les's death) discussions took place on the structure of the pensioners' group which was to meet with the Leader, between Equalities Committee meetings. Clearly it could not be constituted as a formal policy-making committee (which is precisely why it was so radically opposed); the Forum was assured that it would have a strong advisory function on all aspects of pensioners' lives in the borough and that pensioners' items would appear high on the Equalities Committee agenda. The Forum's response was an emphatic 'no' but, as Mallory remarks, they were pragmatic people and one could begin to see that Les, in particular, was prepared to listen, 'in that curious way he had of combining the symbolic with the practical'. Les never underestimated the power of language (though he recognised bitterly that this new group would be a relatively toothless structure) and his proposal that it should be formally entitled 'the Pensioners' Liaison Committee' was accepted. By the following July nominations were being sought for two vacancies on this newly formed committee which continues to this day.

The most important question to be asked about the effectiveness and powers of the Equalities Committee – and any forthcoming statutory group to be established to address the concerns of Lewisham's pensioners – is to what extent it contributes to and affects the Council's ultimate policy decisions or whether, like the European Parliament, it becomes just a talking shop.

Not surprisingly the Forum also had other bitter disappointments and knocks. Throughout the period of the Thatcher government the Forum Management Committee witnessed repeated cuts to services in Lewisham. Another series of cuts suffered by local residents were those which had to be made to the numerous voluntary organisations in the borough – including the Forum itself. Les was hopeful even then of the Forum's future, remembering that the Council had given birth to the organisation in the early eighties and that the Forum was now seen as an essential part of the local democratic process which, he believed, would continue into the next century.

In 1993 Les, Doris Smith (now Secretary of the Forum) and co-ordinator Alison Purshouse took the Forum into new and important arenas – they made a presentation on the work of the Forum at the Social Services Conference and led a workshop for Social Services Directors. Later in the year they made similar presentations for retired employees at Pensioners' Open Days, organised by the Council's Superannuation Team. All these events were very well attended and the Forum team was able to raise consciousness about pensioners' lives and concerns in different parts of the country.

This chapter has sought to present a broad picture of Les Stannard's work for pensioners throughout the years of his retirement. Before his final days he was still in a position to reflect on what the movement had achieved and was acutely aware that the end of the second millennium might not bring justice for Britain's pensioners despite the growth in both the economy and the national pensioners' movement.

One close friend expressed his belief that when Les realised that he would never regain his health and strength and consequently would not be able to continue his campaign, he seemed to lose the will to live. Others disagree, arguing that Les was totally exhausted both physically and mentally. 'He was besieged on all sides,' says John Rampling. 'He gave beyond the call of duty and could give no more.'

[15]

The Forum's Activities and Achievements

> 'We need to convince the younger generations that our ideas for a welfare state and universal benefits are basic essentials for a just and fair society.'
>
> Les Stannard

Fighting for the link between average earnings and the state pension

The history of the British pensioners' movement might have taken a very different turn had Prime Minister Margaret Thatcher not taken the decision in 1980 to abolish the link with average earnings which had been built into the state pension by Secretary of State Barbara Castle in 1975. From the very earliest days of Les Stannard's involvement in the Lewisham movement, when he joined the LPAG and before the Forum was established, this was the one issue which overarched all others and on which he and his colleagues fought tirelessly at local, London and national level. During the last 20 years poverty in old age has brought a miserable existence to many British pensioners who fought in World War II and then paid, throughout their working lives, into the National Insurance scheme.

Because of the abolition of the earnings link the state pension now rises only in line with prices. Its value has fallen consistently since that time so that at the beginning of the 21st century a single British pensioner's income has fallen by approximately £104 per month and a married couple's by about £160. The increase in the year 2000 was 75p per week. This caused such outrage amongst pensioners throughout the country that the government proceeded to take a number of measures to placate them.

For ten years Les and his colleagues participated at local, London-wide and national level in numerous lobbies of parliament and in other deputations organised by the National Pensioners Convention (NPC), British Pensioners and Trade Union Action Association (BPTUAA), and the London pensioners' organisations. He ensured that the issue of the state pension was constantly to the forefront of the Lewisham Council Pensioners' Committee agenda, and at the bi-monthly meetings of the Forum. For at least 12 years (from 1984 if not before) he fought with all his might to see the overturning of this gross injustice towards a relatively acquiescent and powerless section of Britain's citizens. In June 1986 the RACS Political Purposes Committee of which he was a member agreed that a resolution on the issue should go to all constituency Labour Parties. With the 1997 General Election in sight, pensioners had reason to believe (judging from the statements of Labour politicians in opposition) that if a Labour government were to come to power the pensioners' long and honourable case would be vindicated. After all, the former Leader of the Party, John Smith, had pledged that he wanted to see the link restored.[1]

Forum records show that a report on the March 1987 pensioners' rally, at which the issues of the state pension had been discussed, was submitted to the Pensioners' Committee on 2 July 1987. The following March large numbers of Lewisham's elderly people joined colleagues in the House of

[1] *British Pensioner*, Spring 1999.

Commons to hear the second reading of Jeremy Corbyn's Private Member's Bill 'The Elimination of Poverty in Retirement', this having followed Corbyn's earlier bill on the elimination of standing charges. The Bill never reached the statute book. In 1989 Rose Kerrigan and Caroline Williams accompanied Les at an Action for Benefits press conference and lobby at the House of Commons, having been invited to speak on the effects on pensioners of the withdrawal of transitional benefits.

In the ensuing years, Lewisham residents lined up on street corners and in the market place, at rallies and at every opportunity, to sign the NPC petition for the restoration of the link. Later the petition named the figure of £75 per week as a starting point. In that year 19,000 signatures were raised in Lewisham alone as a contribution to a national petition comprising half a million signatures. This was presented at the House of Commons by Les and Fred Baker of the BPTUAA, following a huge rally of 2500 pensioners at Westminster City Hall. Ten years later at the beginning of the year 2000 the NPC was still arguing for a modest starting point of £75 per week and still the government refused.

The activity surrounding the 'link with earnings' continued unabated until the 1997 election, when, much to the anger and bitterness of elderly people and the bodies which represent them, the fine words spoken by Labour in opposition were never again repeated. The Blair government, three years later, solidly refuses to restore the link. More fine words have replaced the old ones as the government impresses the general population with the idea that pensioners are being cared for by the government when, in truth, a means test (under another name) has been introduced for the poorest of poor pensioners while the great majority who have the tiniest of small additional pensions continue to live in poverty.

Linked to the fight for the restoration of the link with earnings, Les consistently drew attention to the need for a change in social security legislation with respect to gender equality in the taxation and the welfare benefits system. Many of his former colleagues remember him, in particular, for his emphasis on the position of women and their pensions. As one of the Vice-Presidents of the NPC, Joan Hall, remarks, 'I remember that he was a great fighter for women; he was on his own in this fight as far as men were concerned. Women naturally fought for women but he was the only man who did.' Carole Newman, the Director of the Greater London Forum for the Elderly, notes that he was a strong supporter of equal opportunities. On one occasion when she was appointed as a Labour Conference delegate, she asked Les for guidance on how she might tackle the pensions issue; he replied, to her surprise, that she should speak about women who lose out on pensions because so many who were unable to pay full contributions fail to receive a full pension. These views were outlined in a Pensioners' Committee Report on 23 March 1989 and again in September 1993.

In making these proposals Les, with his legendary networking skills, drew the attention of Pensioners' Committee colleagues to the important 1985 submission from the Lewisham and Deptford Trades Council (of which he was a member) to the Council's own Working Party on the Fowler Social Security Review.

In 1995 the Forum made it clear that it rejected the recommendations of the Borrie Report to extend the principle of means testing by paying a guaranteed minimum pension to the poorest pensioners only. Les wrote vigorously on this issue in the Annual Report, making it clear that those pensioners who also received the State Earnings Related Pension (SERPS) or another occupational pension were being punished. He pointed out that the media at this time (the 50th anniversary of the end of World War II) were hailing pensioners as war heroes one moment and the next moment accusing them of being bed blockers and scroungers who had not saved for their old age. As to the argument that the country could not afford to restore the link (0.2% of GNP)

Les reminded us that Britain was still the seventh richest nation in the world. Since politicians of the two main parties had now begun to compete with one another on bringing down income tax rates, Les reminded us that his generation had paid 33% income tax in post-war Britain, to help pay for the nationalised industries which were taken under state control, and that those who worked overtime on Saturday afternoons to help rebuild Britain paid 40% tax – the same rate now paid by millionaires and chairmen of former state industries! The link with earnings is also symbolic – it maintains a connection with the working world and, for active trade unionists, it gives the dignity of still being linked to working colleagues. They argue that since occupational pensions are regarded as deferred earnings the state pension should be regarded in the same way.

In 1996 MPs voted a 26% rise (based on average earnings) in their own salaries on 10 July! A resolution was carried at the July 1996 Forum meeting: 'This LPF acknowledges the decision taken in Parliament on July 10 to link the wages of the Prime Minister and MPs with average male earnings in equivalent jobs in industry. The same principle should apply to the basic state pension. All parties should agree to re-establish the link as the first step towards improving the pension.'

During 1996 Les (as Vice-President of the NPC) accompanied President Jack Jones and General Secretary Jack Thain to meetings with Tony Blair, Paddy Ashdown and Parliamentary Under Secretary Oliver Heald (Tory Pensions Minister) to press for the restoration once again. They expressed their deep concern to Blair about the means-testing recommendations of the Borrie report. As Les remarked in his final speech at the tenth anniversary rally of LPF, Harriet Harman, then Shadow Minister for Social Security, had pinched the Lilley and Portillo policy of the 'No Turning Back Group'. He reminded those present at Lewisham Theatre that when the basic pension was first established it was intended to be paid to everyone over 70 and that in the post-war election of 1945 people had voted for Beveridge's 'universal benefits from the cradle to the grave'.

Three publications from the NPC in 1998 and 1999 (*Pensions, Not Poor Relief*, 1998; *Pensions Who Pays?*, 1999 and *The Unwanted Generation*, 1999) give a comprehensive and reasoned analysis of the state pension scheme from its inception under the 1908 Old Age Pensions Act, arguing that since 1980 Income Support (the modern equivalent of the 19th century Poor Relief) has actually been higher than the state pension, thus encouraging the view that the pension is merely a contribution to Income Support for the poorest people and a bit of a perk for the better off. The NPC makes an unequivocal case demonstrating that the United Kingdom government can afford to restore the link with earnings, and pensioners today and the pensioners of the future must ask themselves why the New Labour government has taken the decision not to restore it. On the one hand the government considers it must obey the demands of the International Monetary Fund (IMF) and the World Bank on decreasing government expenditure, while on the other hand, Labour Party principles point to the fact that social insurance is about a civilised society itself taking the responsibility for old, sick, unemployed and other poor people.

It should be noted that the government's decision not to restore the link with earnings is one of the building blocks of its policies on taxation and welfare reform – the decision had to be taken whether to put a relatively small amount on to the whole state pension or to target only the very poorest. For people who have, as yet, no need to understand what has been happening to the state pension since 1980 the emphasis on 'the poorest' has an emotive ring to it – who would argue against the poorest people getting help from the government? However, that very phrase conceals the fact that the Minimum Income Guarantee is means testing by another name, and that people who have small additional pensions are being penalised and might even be poorer than those receiving the Minimum Income Guarantee since the latter are entitled also to additional benefits, such as Housing Benefit and Council Tax Rebate!

If the matter were not so serious it would be laughable that any government should quite openly decide to defraud elderly people of the pensions they have contributed to throughout their lives.

It has been emphasised repeatedly in this work that Les had a conciliatory and co-operative nature, that he always aimed to find consensus and to win arguments by quiet persuasion. There were occasions, however, when people who openly displayed a lack of understanding or who defended unreasonable or unfair policies would bring forth his anger. One such occasion was in 1988 when Les was a member of a deputation to the Minister at the Department of Health and Social Security to speak on the issue of pensions. The Minister commented that 'Beveridge never intended the state pension to be the sole support for retired people and that they should use their savings to eke out the pension.' Les displayed considerable fury at this remark, we are told by one of his colleagues. He replied, 'When did we get a chance to save? We spent the best years of our lives fighting a war and afterwards building the country up again, experiencing wage restraint as well. There was never enough money for savings.' A deadly silence followed; the Minister seemed to realise that Les had won the argument and quickly changed the subject. Paradoxically, 12 years later the people who did eke out their pensions by making some savings are penalised by the government which makes sure that their pensions actually reduce in value, year after year! The government nevertheless continues to advise workers to save for their pensions – naturally, in that way, their entitlement to the national state pension will be eroded even further.

By May 2000, when the 75p per week increase had been announced, the pensioners' campaign began to gain momentum and media interest grew. The 75p increase was seen as one of the government's worst 'own goals'. At the Blackpool parliament Jeff Rooker, the Pensions Minister, took part in a fiery debate with Rodney Bickerstaffe, General Secretary of UNISON, tipped to succeed Jack Jones as the NPC's next President. With the General Election approaching, the government showed signs of panic and more sweeteners were offered to pensioners – an increase in the heating allowance to £150, a raising of the threshold for eligibility for Income Support and the introduction of a 'Pensioners' Credit' to help those owning moderate savings or small occupational pensions. Anything rather than the reinstatement of the link with earnings. Pensioners were enraged and Tory pensioners in particular began to attack Tony Blair for the injustice they felt – choosing not to remember that it was Mrs Thatcher who had broken the link with earnings and that, despite its failure to restore the link, the New Labour government had made a greater contribution to the welfare of pensioners than the last Tory government ever had!

As the year 2000 party conference season and the General Election approached, the future of the state pension became a major concern for all the political parties. It gripped the media as never before and pensioners had, at last, become a powerful lobby. At the Labour Party Conference a composite resolution from the unions and a number of a constituency parties was put forward. It drew on the recommendations of the Social Security Select Committee for an immediate increase in the state pension and for a restoration of the link with earnings or inflation, depending on which was the higher. The resolution was carefully worded so as to give the government room for manoeuvre. An almost unprecedented 24-hour period of cajoling and arm-twisting followed, as the Chancellor and the Prime Minister held a series of private meetings with the proposers, with the intention that the resolution be remitted. Despite such pressure the motion was debated at the conference and carried by a ratio of three votes to two. It was the first time that Tony Blair had been defeated at conference since he became Leader of the Labour Party in 1994.

The pensioners' movement strengthened its resolve and continued its campaign with a powerful rally in Central Hall and a lobby of Parliament on 7 November 2000. The debate continues.

The historic battle for the Freedom Pass

> 'I remember travelling with him when the idea struck him, as he noticed empty trains rattling back to Central London, how the bus pass might be used on the trains too. It took some master-minding to get to where it is today, but Les could slice through objections and present a simplified unstoppable case.' John Rampling

> 'I once met Les and three of his Lewisham Pensioners' Forum colleagues, loaded down with banners, books and pamphlets and waiting for a 21 bus to take them back to Lewisham at the end of a campaigning event in New Eltham. The temperature was in the nineties and I asked them why did they not take a cab. Les reminded me of the struggle they had fought to gain the pensioners' concessionary travel permit and, as the bus drew up, he said, "If we don't use it they'll have more excuses to take it away!"' Andrew Spencer

The Bus Pass, the Travel Permit, the Freedom Pass – it has undergone a number of name changes but the struggle to attain and to retain free travel for London pensioners has been long and hard. As we progress through the new century it will continue to be administered by the Transport Committee for London (TCfL). The majority of London's pensioners who carry a Freedom Pass in their pockets or handbags have little idea of the political battles which are fought year upon year to ensure the retention of the pass, still less do they realise what an amazing achievement it was to bring about the extension of the free travel facility to the railways.

The very earliest concession scheme in London was introduced by the London Borough of Camden under Section 40 of the Transport (London) Act 1969 – this gave half-fare concessions in restricted hours to people over 75. The Bus Pass for Londoners came into effect in 1984 during Ken Livingstone's leadership of the GLC. It was administered under the London Regional Transport Act. The pass enabled pensioners to travel on London buses and the underground and also to travel half-fare on British Rail. Conditions for the use of the pass are set every two years at the time of renewal, usually in March. The permit is paid for by the Social Services' budgets of the London boroughs and, before privatisation, the figure was negotiated annually with London Transport and British Rail. At every stage of renewal the unanimous agreement of the 33 London boroughs is required (by the previous 31 December) and a statutory reserve scheme can be (but never has been) put into place if agreement is not reached. The improvements to the reserve scheme are now enacted in the GLA Act which allows the boroughs to make a decision on the scheme by a two-thirds majority rather than unanimity. No one would have been happier with this enactment than Les Stannard, who knew only too well that on several occasions just one or two London boroughs almost succeeded in holding London's pensioners to ransom.

Simultaneously negotiations also took place on the 'door to door' schemes (the Taxicard, Dial-a-Ride and Community Transport) for people unable to use public transport, all of which constantly fall under threat as local authorities review their budgets every year. In effect the Taxicard scheme became London-wide in 1984. Les Stannard had a phenomenal knowledge of how local government and other committees work and was aware that negotiations needed to take place in several different arenas, with constant reporting back to members for endorsement. He also knew the importance of consciousness raising, drawing people's attention to what was taking place in the political arena and the ways in which they needed to take action in order to achieve or retain their rights.

Thus it was that the LPF battle for free travel for pensioners started on the streets of Lewisham in one small area of Lewisham Market where every Friday morning, however dreadful the weather, a group of brave pensioners from both the Forum and the Action Group stood with clipboards drawing the attention of people of all ages, shopping for their vegetables, to the fact that their own Travel Permit (or that of their parents or grandparents) was at risk. Thousands of signatures were collected over the years – not only for the retention of the Travel Permit but also in support of many other services which were under threat or facing structural change. In Les's mind the petition with thousands of signatures was the chief weapon in any battle for justice.

Outside Lewisham Les was a founder member of the Travel Permit Joint Working Party on which he represented the GLPA, the other organisations being Age Concern and the GLFE. All of these were, in turn, represented on the Advisory Panel to the London Committee on Accessible Transport (APLCAT). The LCAT was the organisation through which the London boroughs took decisions. It was composed of one councillor from every local authority. APLCAT has now been replaced (while retaining the same membership) by the London Mobility Advisory Panel (LMAP). The JWP held regular meetings with the LCAT and took part in deputations to the Secretary of State for Transport and the Minister for Transport in London. Gaining strength in the process, Forum reports presented at the Pensioners' Committee ensured that recommendations were made to the Policy and Resources Committee which, in turn, was also represented at APLCAT. All these different processes, the networking which was Les's trademark, led towards the ultimate achievement. As has often been remarked, Les was a man of all-encompassing vision. He looked at the entire issue of transport for pensioners (be they newly retired or very elderly and infirm) and worked towards ensuring that all existing services, whether regular public transport or the specialist services for those who were unable to use public transport, were maintained and, if possible, enhanced. Les was always active and positive, demonstrating that if people organise and confront authorities they can make things happen.

The issue remained high on the Pensioners' Committee agenda throughout its entire existence and the Committee Chair in 1989, Dolly Hyne, was a member of the deputation to the Ministry of Transport to negotiate the necessary resources. In the same month, the Forum was addressed by Councillor Jon Lansman, Chair of the London Committee on Accessible Transport, and a petition bearing the signatures of 14,000 Lewisham residents was presented to the Mayor, Nicholas Taylor, at a full Council meeting. The Forum also submitted a petition to the Joint Working Party at Kensington Town Hall.

During 1990 the Ministry of Transport subsidy to local authorities was threatened by the effects of the Poll Tax; boroughs therefore faced huge fare increases and the future of the Travel Permit looked doubtful. The Pensioners' Committee resolved that the borough should take part in a deputation of Council Leaders to the Ministry of Transport and the Forum was represented on a Greater London Pensioners' Association deputation to the Ministry which was headed at the time by Cecil Parkinson with Michael Portillo as the Minister.

1991 saw the arrival of proposed deregulation of London's buses. During the same year the ALA made a stated commitment to the Travel Permit and the Pensioners' Committee resolved to lobby MPs, MEPs and the Secretary of State for a Senior Citizens' Europass. In the light of a report from the borough's Deputy Chief Executive on budget implications for pensioners there was discussion on the possible introduction of an administrative charge and on the question of whether the Travel Permit should be funded centrally or from Social Services.

In May 1992 Les and Alistair Beattie (the Age Concern London representative on the Working Party) submitted a paper on the implications of deregulation; this was followed by a big conference which took place at Conway Hall in Red Lion Square.

In September 1992 the Pensioners' Committee received an LPF report suggesting that Social Services should no longer administer the Travel Permit in view of harsh cuts being made to elderly people's services. The implication of this report is that older people who used their Travel Permits felt that their peers who were unable to use them because of frailty or ill health were subsidising their free travel. A late 20th century example of the effectiveness of a 'divide and rule' policy.

Much of the pensioners' movement's activity in 1993 was concerned with the forthcoming deregulation of buses and the impending privatisation of the railways. It was feared that the London boroughs would no longer be able to maintain the Travel Permit and members of the JWP proposed to the new Minister, Steven Norris, that Travel Permit resources should be ring-fenced. At its September 1993 meeting the Pensioners' Committee resolved to refer a Forum report on the effects of deregulation on the Travel Permit to the Social Services, Environmental Services and Transport Committees and once again recommended that Council representatives on LCAT should continue to support the maintenance of the Travel Permit.

The JWP described the retention of the Travel Permit as a battle by pensioners and disabled people. It was resolved that the issue should continue to be pressed on MPs and Council Leaders. MPs in particular were slow in responding to constituents' concerns. The LCAT prepared a resolution of opposition to deregulation if this was included in the forthcoming Queen's Speech, but the proposal was dropped from the Speech at the last minute. In July 1993 the government was defeated by the House of Lords on the issue of rail franchising and this paved the way for British Rail to bid for the franchise. A further Lords debate during the same month effectively delayed privatisation.

Council elections were to take place in spring 1994 and Les worked through the JWP to ensure that pensioners would lobby their election candidates on where they stood on the issue of the Travel Permit. In June 1994 Les, as JWP representative, made a presentation to an LCAT sub-committee on the extension of the Travel Permit to British Rail. At the same time the Pensioners' Committee made an urgent recommendation to the Policy and Resources Committee to fund this extension at a cost of £45,000. The Pensioners' Committee was, at the same time, asked to investigate reports that there was to be a reduction of Dial-a-Ride services.

The deadline for agreement on the extension of the Travel Permit to British Rail was 16 February 1994 – it was the last opportunity for this to take place before further privatisation. Problems were raised by both Wandsworth and Westminster Councils. Pensioners were urged to write to their councillors and to the media. It was suggested that the extension of the Travel Permit gave Councils an opportunity to do something practical for pensioners in the light of the praise which had been heaped on their heads at the time of the D-Day celebrations. The Working Party planned a publicity launch in the event of the extension being achieved.

The Travel Permit was extended to British Rail in April 1995 – an outstanding achievement for the movement of elderly and disabled people and an example of the effectiveness of people power which ought to inspire all who work in the non-statutory sector.

The privatisation of the rail services came into effect in 1995. London Transport kept an overseeing role in setting standards and contracts for bus operators bidding for bus routes which meant that there was no wholesale deregulation in London although the routes are privatised and operators bid for the franchise to run services on them.

Les was elected Chair of the TP JWP on 7 June 1995.

VAT on fuel

In September 1994 a petition with over a million signatures was presented to the Queen, requesting not only the restoration of the link between pensions and earnings, but also more resources for community care and the removal of the threat of a second levy of tax on fuel. The pensioners' movement was victorious in one respect – the second instalment of VAT on fuel was withdrawn. One imaginative member of the Forum's Management Committee whose name was Ken Clark had the brilliant idea of writing to every Kenneth Clark (or Clarke) in the London telephone directory to ask their views on the introduction of VAT on fuel. He was able to show that the majority of the Chancellor's namesakes strongly opposed the tax. With the support of the Council, signatures to the petition were collected in every public place, there was a demonstration outside the Town Hall and the story received considerable press coverage.

The campaign for the prevention of death from hypothermia

> '40,000 people, mostly solitary pensioners, died from hypothermia in Britain in 1986.' Lewisham Pensioners' Forum Report to the Pensioners' Committee, October 1987

One of the most direct ways in which the Forum effected change in the lives of Lewisham's pensioners was in its lasting campaign to draw attention to the dangers of hypothermia. This was a period in which the Forum was beginning to present its own reports to the Pensioners' Committee and thus to influence Council policy. The October 1987 LPF Report also drew attention to contributory factors to hypothermia, namely poor diet and poor housing, stating that much colder countries like Sweden had lower death rates from hypothermia than Britain. Between 1976 and 1979 the death rate in the UK from this condition rose by 24% compared with a rate of only 6% in Sweden. The report gave ten points of recommendation and proposed that members of the committee should act as 'Freeze Line' contacts.

In 1988 the first Working Party for the 'Keep Warm in Winter' Campaign included officers from the Central Policy Unit, Management Committee members and the co-ordinator and representatives from Age Concern and Pensioners' Link. A number of events were organised to ensure that elderly people at lunch clubs and other centres would learn about the campaign. The 'Freeze Line' was re-established and winter packs were distributed giving practical advice together with simple wall thermometers. Postcards were issued as part of the support scheme for isolated and disabled pensioners and were also distributed to GPs and health centres, and emergency store items were prepared.

In winter 1988/9 the 'Keep Warm, Keep Well' exhibition toured the Neighbourhood Offices and Les proposed that for the following winter the exhibition should move to a central location such as the Riverdale Centre. By this time working relations between the Forum (and Les in particular) and Council officers had strengthened and since no real input of resources had been allocated it was agreed that a budget of £5000 should be made available for the following year.

What nobody realised at the time was that Les would accompany me, as co-ordinator, to each of the Neighbourhood Offices whenever the exhibition had to be moved and that he, personally, would put the stands up with a little help from me. This is an example of how Les would never say he could not manage something, however inconvenient it might have been for him, and he never let me down.

The 1989–90 exhibition at the Riverdale Centre was a tremendous success. With advice sessions on home insulation, welfare rights advice, safety checks of plugs and electric blankets, sessions on how to take exercise to keep warm and healthy, there was altogether a lively atmosphere of learning and co-operation between the hundreds of visitors (pensioners and their families) and the many Forum members, staff and Council staff who took turns in running the exhibition. Because it was in a central location, people of all ages took an interest and younger people talked to us about the financial and other hardships being experienced by their parents and grandparents and went away with information and ideas to pass on to them. In the words of one Council officer, 'We tried to introduce all kinds of things to raise awareness amongst people of all ages – and it worked!'

History was also made that winter of 1990 when Les (with his passion for keeping closeness between the generations) arranged for children in three primary schools (St Mary's, Ladywell, Adamsrill, Sydenham and Christchurch, Forest Hill) to work on a 'Hypothermia Project'. An exhibition of their work was held and, accompanied by a group of pensioners, they were taken on a guided tour of the House of Commons by Joan Ruddock MP, following which they were entertained to a tour of the Town Hall and lunch with the Mayor, Nicholas Taylor. Two charming accounts of these events are given in the 1990 Annual Report. In the words of Lily Beale: 'The pensioners enjoyed the day so much and learned as much as the children.'

The second phase of the campaign involved the exhibition touring every health centre in the borough with the involvement of the Transport Department and ended with a Mayor's press conference. A Hypothermia Factsheet (translated into the five main community languages) was produced and the campaign was relaunched in January 1993 (during the European Year of Older People) in the presence of Bridget Prentice MP. From that time the two exhibitions were extended to cover all aspects of health for older people. Further co-operation was received from Health First and by 1995 the touring exhibition was an established fact and continues to raise interest. Plans were made to join forces with other projects, such as the Deptford Health Challenge and pensioners were given guidance about obtaining grants for insulation from the Home Energy Efficiency Scheme.

National Health and Social Services legislation 1989: A decade of reforms and cuts

> 'It was felt that the White Paper (Working for Patients) concentrated too much on the economics of providing services – rather than on the needs of patients.' London Borough of Lewisham Pensioners' Committee Agenda Papers, 6 June 1989

The late 1980s and subsequent years saw draconian reforms of legislation in two important fields relating to the care of the most vulnerable people in society. The National Health Service (hospitals, GP practices, community health services) was the subject of the 'Working for Patients' Bill, while the residential and home care of young and old, mentally and physically disabled and mentally ill people of all ages, was covered by the 'Caring for People' Bill. Both bills received the Royal Assent and were placed on the statute book in 1990. The government then took a decision to postpone the community care legislation until 1993 at the earliest.

The appealing and emotive titles of both these bills disguised the underlying intention of the government of the time which was to reduce public expenditure drastically and to shift responsibility for health services and for care from the state sector by an insidious process of privatisation.

In brief, the White Paper 'Working for Patients' proposed the opting out of some hospitals from health authority control by transforming them into self-governing trusts; this also was to apply to community health services. The legislation relating to community care placed responsibility on local authority social services departments for the assessment of individual care needs, for community care services and also for the financial support of people in private and voluntary homes. Local authorities were also expected, indeed actively encouraged, to make maximum use of the independent and voluntary sector in delivering these services (even Girl Guides and Brownies came to be recognised as a useful asset in the eyes of some imaginative reformers!).

At the same time as the Community Charge or Poll Tax legislation was also being debated in Parliament, local authorities and the entire non-statutory sector all over the country came together in an unprecedented action to oppose these vast proposed reforms. For the Management Committee of the Forum and for Les in particular, who never did anything by halves, this came to mean daily and nightly activity in the form of meetings with other local and national organisations, reports to the Pensioners' Committee, the preparation of petitions and resolutions and attendance at numerous national demonstrations.

At the March 1989 Pensioners' Committee the Forum representatives raised their concerns about the effects of the 1989/90 budget cuts on elderly people's services, following a Social Services Report which outlined the many areas which would suffer. In 1990 the Mayor, Nicholas Taylor, called a Towns Meeting and the Council issued a document expressing its fears about the problems which would be created for local patients if hospitals proceeded to adopt the government's proposals. A Lewisham Pensioners' Forum petition opposing self-governing trusts was presented to Professor

Elaine Murphy, Professor of Gerontology and Manager of Guy's and Lewisham Hospitals.

The proposed reductions in service to community care clients heralded the introduction of such terms as 'targeting' and 'eligibility criteria' which are now commonplace in government language and founded in the Victorian philosophy which distinguished between the deserving and the undeserving poor. The language employed appears eminently sensible to the average person but terms such as 'better use and management of resources' and 'the ranking of needs' actually mask the intention to exclude all but the utterly destitute from receiving care services. Such drastic cuts might indeed make a great deal of sense for a very poor country with marginal resources but in this case the seventh richest nation in the world was masquerading as a poor one in order to justify its decision to reduce public expenditure.

The Pensioners' Committee minutes for 1 October 1991 record that the Council had submitted its own strongly worded response to the hospitals' opting for trust status and outlined the reasons for its opposition. The Forum's own unequivocal response was presented on the same day, clearly written by Les himself and endorsed by the Management Committee, but despite the co-ordinated and democratically voiced opposition of all staff at Guy's and Lewisham Hospitals, of the Community Health Councils and of the majority of Lewisham's pensioners, the consultants and senior staff at both hospitals proceeded with the setting up of trust status and achieved this in April 1991.

The Forum Management Committee was gravely concerned that if trust status was also to be gained by the Lewisham community health services, their monitoring and regulation would effectively be removed from local authority control. Thus a resolution passed on 12 June 1991 by the Pensioners' Committee established that, in the event of trust status being granted, the effects on elderly people would be reported regularly to the Pensioners' Committee.

The Forum was actively involved in the borough's social services and voluntary sector debate on the future of community care as well as in the London-wide movement and in parliamentary lobbies. The voluntary sector set up its own Community Care Forum, a shadow group which would reflect the views of community organisations to the local authority.

The 1994 LPF Annual Report gives an account of the Tomlinson Report, which sought closures of certain London hospitals, including Guy's and Bart's. Les did not mince his words: 'Tomlinson . . . was seeking the closure of too many London hospitals and his assessment was based on finance, not on the principle of the number of hospital beds that London needs.' He added that the Forum's stance on the issue was backed by Professor Jarman's research and that the charity the King's Fund had admitted that its findings two years previously now needed reassessment.

The Forum continued to keep the crucial issue of health care in the capital city as one of its major concerns, fearing that the introduction of the market system into the NHS would result in bringing hospitals into competition with one another, that waiting lists were growing and that some health services were being rationed (1994 Annual Report, p. 20). The Forum also supported proposals for a single health authority for the whole of London.

In the second year of the operation of the community care legislation Les drew attention to his concern about the growing divide between rich and poor and asked that the issue should form part of the Pensioners' Committee's work programme. One councillor asked whether it was national or local government policies which were responsible for people becoming victims of poverty.

There were campaigns throughout the summer of 1995 on the question of financing continuing care and community care. A petition signed by over 70,000 pensioners was presented to the Labour Party Conference and to the Leader of the Opposition. A delegation of 50 LPF members held a meeting with their MPs, to discuss the perilous situation within the Home Care Service, such that it was reported that resources would have to be transferred from elderly people who received only *one hour* of home care a week in order to support others who were even more vulnerable! Concern was also expressed about the indistinct boundaries between health and social services, which enabled both to have a financial interest in referring cases back and forth to each other. It should be recorded that all the political parties were now supporting a shift away from the state provision of health care in an attempt to avoid tax increases, yet in Germany taxes had been raised to cover costs! By 1996 the local authority grant had been cut by £10 million. A sombre address by the Director of Social Services to the March 1996 Forum outlined the most pertinent issues and the effects which would be felt by local residents.

The Forum's response to the Social Services Strategy did not accept the often repeated statement that older people had had more than their fair share of the cake. Eligibility criteria were becoming so tight that more and more people were being excluded from receiving services. People were to be allocated services according to their ability to pay rather than on the basis of their needs and, while there had always been clear divisions between the duties of district nurses and home care workers, these became blurred and unqualified 'personal care' workers took over some of the tasks which had previously been the responsibility of district nurses.

This was the devastating situation which elderly people faced in 1996 after seven years of active campaigning by local and national pensioners' organisations. The last speech given by a gravely ill Les, on Pensioners' Day – 25 September 1996 – less than three months before his death, was bravely entitled 'Celebrating Ten Years of Empowerment'. He placed positive emphasis on the achievements of the pensioners' movement in the borough and the Council's recognition of the Forum's immense contribution to the workings of local government, but his general tone was one of great disappointment, sadness and uncharacteristic anger at the consequences of the government's policies relating to elderly people – each one of which had actually contributed to a deterioration in the quality of life of every pensioner in Britain.

The Pensioners' Forum support for carers

Les had a devotion to the cause of carers (most of whom are women) which was deeply rooted in his psyche for two reasons – firstly his desire to see justice for people who found themselves, unwittingly, categorised as 'carers' and secondly, his personal experience of the plight of carers from a very young age. Les's commitment to carers in general and to women in particular dominated much of his campaigning work both during his working life and after his retirement. It is not surprising, therefore, that the Forum had an active working relationship with Carers (Lewisham) from its earliest days and both organisations were represented on the borough's Elderly Services Planning Group.

With the delay of the community care legislation till 1993 and the consequent lack of resources, Forum representatives campaigned for support for Carers (Lewisham). Much of what had appeared in the White Paper 'Caring for People' – that there was to be radical improvement to the situation faced by Britain's six million carers – vanished and never appeared in the subsequent bill. There was documented evidence to show that because few carers ever received a break from their tasks, 365 days a year, many of them became ill and even died before the person they were caring for! The Borough of Lewisham certainly made great strides in establishing respite care in order to release carers for short periods. Because of the delay of the community care legislation a number of insurance companies began to offer schemes for families of ageing parents in order that they could be released from the burden. Carers' organisations dubbed this development as 'cashing in on the plight of families'. The situation was exacerbated by the closure of some nursing homes in 1990 and there was a shortfall of funds available for recruitment of qualified staff to help with the care of housebound people.

Postscript: 18 months after Les's death the New Labour government came to admit that services to carers were 'patchy'. An enquiry was launched in June 1998 and in February 1999 the government announced a £140 million budget to provide respite care. The Minister called for changed attitudes to carers and the government made a long-term commitment to make amends for their loss of pensions contributions and to grant them council tax reductions. The move was welcomed by the Carers' National Association which was, nevertheless, concerned about whether the resources allocated were sufficient. One Community Care Action Group commented that in the light of the financial problems which Councils were facing (the community care budget was being cut by £4 million) the new carers' strategy was a nonsense. One Liberal Democrat MP pointed out that the sum total of the Minister's statement was worth no more than 15 pence per carer (*Independent*, 9 February 1999).

The establishment of a Residential Homes Visitors' Panel

> '. . . to bring the Forum into the residential homes, to let the residents know they can use our services, that we are there to represent all pensioners and that residents' rights are as important as everyone else's.' Alison Purshouse, Annual Report 1995

During 1988 and 1989 media reports about the alarmingly poor standards of care in residential homes, as well as serious lacks in monitoring and supervision, were causing widespread public distress, particularly amongst pensioners. I can well remember the morning following the TV report on one particular residential home in Kent and the horrified and shocked expression on Les's face when he walked into the office. Following discussion with his colleagues on the Officers Committee the issue went straight to the top of the next Management Committee agenda.

The Wagner Report on community care and its recommendations on the need for high-quality training and a career structure for residential care staff had been widely welcomed by the Forum. At the same time the Griffiths Report was causing considerable disquiet across the country and many feared that its recommendations were preparing the way for the privatisation of social services and the shifting of responsibility for the care of the most vulnerable members of our society to unpaid volunteer workers and the private sector, with a big question mark about accountability.

Following endorsement by the Forum, a process of consultation was set up with a proposal that a small group of Forum representatives might visit the residents of one or two of the local authority homes. It was agreed that the project would start on a very small scale with the five co-optees to the PC concentrating on just two homes.

The managers of the homes, the residents, the visitors and the Manager of Elderly Services all had to be quite clear about the terms of reference of the panel. The visitors were not to act as regular befrienders and they most certainly were not inspectors. The purpose of the visits was that they should be informal, friendly and neutral and it was anticipated that a relationship of trust would develop, such that residents could perhaps make suggestions about ways in which their lives might be improved. In time good rapport was established and some ideas and proposals were adopted. Whenever appropriate, issues raised were referred to the relevant officer or department.

By 1991 the panel was well established and so successful that it was agreed to extend its scope to include all the borough's residential homes and to bring in many more visitors to the panel. A Policy and Equalities Committee Report to the Pensioners' Committee of 14 June 1994 entitled *Developing User Standards in Residential Care* included data on the Forum's Visitors' Panel. In 1995 Forum representatives, through their representation on the Social Services Committee, joined the Council's own advisory panel to the Residential Homes Inspection Unit. The panel's remit was now broadened so that members began to visit private homes too. During this year the visitors took on the additional task of informing residents of the Forum's work and explaining that, if a resident wished it, professionally trained Forum representatives might also be able to act as advocates for those who had no family to represent them.

The Forum now also became involved in the debate on the future management of homes and was urging that this should remain within the current system of Social Services management – rather than that management, and financial control, should devolve to individual homes. They raised their disquiet about propositions to 'stretch' managers' responsibility to more than one home and were extremely concerned that individual homes might very well lose touch with emerging thinking on the care of elderly people in residential accommodation. More members joined the panel and their fresh insights as newcomers were greatly welcomed.

The Forum representatives on the Social Services Committee raised many of the panel members' concerns, in particular those about the lack of activity, as well as about staff shortages and other important issues. During 1995 Forum representatives began to work with Elizabeth Sclater (Principal Equalities Officer – Pensioners) on a questionnaire for residents enabling them to register their satisfaction or otherwise with their own homes and to make suggestions, in Les's words, on 'what changes could be made to make life easier and, in particular, more interesting' (Annual Report 1995, pp. 8–9). Les knew that the Pensioners' Committee had recognised the value of the panel and its contribution to Social Services work with the homes. Since it was planned to extend the scope of the panel to private homes and to nursing homes he appealed for more members to join the panel and also for more resources to employ a part-time organiser to manage this growing service.

By January 1996 further reductions in spending were being envisaged and the Pensioners' Forum diary for that month tells of how the closure of one residential home had brought a budget reduction of £3 million. Two months later the number of beds in residential homes was reduced from 300 to 180 and the proposals then, which have continued to the present time, were to develop sheltered housing and very sheltered housing as an alternative to traditional residential care. These schemes have been made possible by the establishment of the Linkline service which enables solitary elderly and frail people to call immediate medical care by the touch of a button – a technological achievement which, it is true to say, has brought peace of mind to many individuals and their families, with the important proviso that sufficient resources are there to ensure that emergency calls are responded to immediately. Consequently a Sheltered Housing Visitors' Panel has now been set up by the Forum.

Education

Les always held strongly to the socialist principle on the crucial importance of education for working-class people. We see an instance of this back in his days with the ETU SE Branch, when he proposed that a speaker on an educational topic should be invited to attend meetings on a regular basis. In addition to the importance of education and continuing education for adults he also constantly displayed enormous interest in the education of children and, in particular, emphasised the benefits which children could derive from being with elderly people.

Forum representatives attended a number of local and

London-wide meetings on education following the abolition of ILEA by the Thatcher government. The Forum was also represented on the borough's full Education Committee as well as on the Consultative Committee for Community Education. Les constantly appealed to Forum members to volunteer to join the Forum's own Education Working Party in order to help it extend its activities and research.

A well-researched document of responses to the borough's draft development plan for education resulted in the inclusion of an additional sub-clause in the revised plan, supporting education for and participation by older people.

The July 1989 Forum was devoted to education and this was followed by a formal meeting by the Forum's own education sub-committee and the new Youth and Adult Education Review Working Party. The Forum presented a paper to this group, outlining the educational needs of adults in general and older people in particular. At the Forum's request the then Ravensbourne Adult Education Institute set up computer literacy classes for older people. In this year, the Forum also pressed for pensioner representation on the borough Education Committee and on the board of governors of the new Institute.

On a related issue the Elderly People's Resource Team had developed reminiscence work amongst elderly people and Les gave his strong support to this as a means of enabling young people to understand the world we live in through what he called 'living history'. He also hoped that reminiscence courses could become part of the continuing education syllabus.

In 1990 John Rampling represented the Forum at a conference designed to develop a strategy for education provision for people with special needs and disabilities. He drew attention to those elderly people who are housebound, in hospital or residential care, arguing that they are desperately deprived of educational stimulus. This was reinforced by the Residential Homes Visitors' Panel. In the same year Marjorie

Packham and Caroline Williams attended a conference about the future of community education in the borough, which not only looked at funding but was also an information-gathering exercise on good practice.

In June 1990 the Forum joined the former Ravensbourne and South Lewisham Institutes in an Education Day called 'It's Never Too Late to Learn' and Les together with other Forum members took part in a number of workshops which buzzed with ideas on such images as 'Challenging the Images of Age', 'Education for Life' and 'Growing Old in Another Land'. The Director, Maggie O'Neill, who made the closing address, was inspired by the active interest displayed and the ideas put forward.

During 1991 Forum representatives brought their concerns about cuts in non-statutory education to the Pensioners' Committee as an emergency item. The committee agreed a number of resolutions requesting a report on community education, Lewisham's plans for adult education generally and for elderly people in particular, including those who had special needs. Other requests were for a reintroduction of music and movement classes in residential homes. The committee also requested a report on fee increases for elderly people and on a comparison of enrolment figures with earlier years.

1995 was designated the United Nations Year of Older People. The Leader of the Council was quoted as saying that the budget for community education in Lewisham was being 'sustained' from budgets outside education. In his report as Honorary President, Les praised a recent entertainment by schoolchildren at a pensioners' gathering and commented on how the head was attempting to set the children's sights for the future with this philosophy: 'If you make up your mind you can achieve anything' – a maxim which Les himself followed throughout his life, though government policies made sure that he would not achieve in his lifetime some of the aims he set for himself and for the pensioners' movement.

Les spoke also about inter-generational understanding and the ways that pensioners could pass on their experiences to children. Drawing attention to the fact that many elderly people were giving their time to listening to children read and also to passing on their experiences of wartime Britain and the setting up of the welfare state, he commented wryly on whether the Department of Education would want to fit this innovative work into a crowded national curriculum or whether, in Les's own words, 'they would view these subjects as introducing politics within the classroom . . . certainly there are key issues around continuing care, the welfare state and means testing that younger people ought to learn about in order to improve on the efforts of our own generation.'

The advocacy project: PALS (Pensioners Advocacy in Lewisham Scheme)

Citizen advocacy is a new idea which has brought tangible and indispensable support to the increasingly large numbers of isolated, vulnerable people who have nobody to represent them in their dealings with the authorities. LPF's venture into advocacy began in 1993–4. Together with the Lewisham Association of People with Disabilities and other organisations in the voluntary sector, joint finance was obtained from the health authority for a two-year pilot project. This enabled volunteers to receive advocacy training in order to provide a service to community care clients when they were being assessed for services or if they had a complaint about the service. At the end of this project experienced Forum members supported by the GLFE went on to provide training for older people who wished to act as advocates specifically for frail, elderly people who were being assessed before being discharged from Lewisham Hospital. The Forum advocates received the active support of the Elderly People's Resource Team and the hospital's social work team. The scheme works by matching an advocate to an elderly person, who wishes it, with the purpose of helping them to communicate their needs and to assert their right to be heard at a time when they are immensely frail and perhaps frightened about their future.

The Forum regarded this new burden of responsibility as a natural development of its commitment to stand up for the rights of pensioners and help them to gain the best service at a time when their needs tend to be ignored and their plight unnoticed. The Forum felt that it was important that users of the service should be involved in decisions about their care and that their progress could be monitored for some time after they had moved back to their own homes or to other accommodation. Additionally, the advocates would be able to feed back to the Forum information about the pressures on frail elderly people in hospital and raise concerns about too early discharge, inappropriate care arrangements or inadequate community care which could then be raised by Forum representatives at the relevant Council committees.

During 1995 Forum advocates took part in Citizen Advocacy conferences organised by the Centre for Policy on Ageing. The Forum received funding for the continuation of the advocacy project from the King's Fund together with small grants from the borough. The project has continued to grow and the number of advocates has increased, benefiting many vulnerable Lewisham residents. Its outstanding difference from other advocacy projects is that, in line with the Forum's policy of 'pensioners speaking up for pensioners', it is a peer advocacy project and the Forum aims to retain this unique characteristic.

Lewisham Pensioners' Forum and the European pensioners' movement

Les had grave doubts about Britain's entry into the European Union and more recently about the adoption of the euro.

Although in the period of Harold Wilson's government there was a great deal of activity in setting up anti-EU committees in the London boroughs, the views of 'left-wing' people now are more fragmented – there are differences of opinion and a minority on the left think that the euro should be adopted. Still there are concerns about the effects on employment since labour is cheaper in Britain than in some countries and it is feared that Britain is changing from being a manufacturing nation to simply an assembly line for large international global corporations.

While Les was therefore healthily sceptical and almost certainly dubious about the benefits of European economic union, he was a pragmatist and where the issue of pensions and pensioners was concerned he was keen to establish close ties with the European pensioners' movement. Thus we find that the beginning of the Forum's involvement in Europe was in 1989 when three members of the Management Committee attended a pensioners' rally in Brussels.

Further progress took place in 1993 when, following an approach to the Forum from the borough's Equalities Unit, a European Women's Project was established whose aim was to exchange life experience between elderly women in Lewisham, Dublin and Perugia in Italy and to discuss their main achievements and concerns. Rose Kerrigan was an active member of this project, representing it at conferences in various parts of England and Scotland.

Following the first Seniors' Parliament hosted by the European Socialist Parties in 1991, the first European Pensioners' Parliament was held in Luxembourg in November 1993. This was designed to reflect the political representation of the 12 European countries and every MEP was responsible for nominating a delegate from her or his constituency. Les attended as representative of Richard Balfe's constituency of Lambeth, Lewisham and Southwark. 518 pensioners were present, including 18 from the former German Democratic Republic. Discussions took place in workshops and the issues raised were: opposition to means testing of the state pension; equal opportunities; protecting occupational pensions from fraud and mismanagement; transport; integration and participation of elderly people in all aspects of policy making in order that they should be able to influence policy. Proposals were made for the setting up of a National Seniors' Parliament in every member state. George Goodfellow, also a representative at this parliament, has vivid recollections of the way Les's speech was received: 'Les spoke so well and he held the attention of our European pensioner colleagues. They applauded all the British contributors' speeches but the longest applause was for Les's speech. He was outstanding. Since that time many of those present have asked what had happened to Les and the French, in particular, kept asking about him!'

The British delegation proposed that local authorities and municipal councils should set up structures for consultation of elderly people at local level and Les spoke about Lewisham's unique Pensioners' Committee and the co-option of Forum representatives on a range of the Council's subcommittees.

Subsequently proposals for a National Seniors' Parliament in Britain went to the borough's Pensioners' Committee and the Chairperson, Councillor John O'Shea, moved a resolution in support of this aim at the Council's main committee. The British Pensioners' Parliament is now established and is held on an annual basis.

[16]

Time with the Family

How was it possible for a man who, throughout his life, spent most of his non-working hours in trade union and other political activities to have a family life? Did he even have one? The paradox is that, although Les expended so much energy in the political struggle, his intense campaigning spirit was matched by an equally deep attachment to his family. He always sought to devote time to both his public and his private life. He specialised in burning both ends of the candle! This did not mean that he was at home every evening – he very rarely was, at least on weekdays – but he recognised only too well and greatly valued the quiet support which he knew he could rely on when he came home, in the same way that other people came to place their reliance on him. It will never be known to what extent, if any, Les experienced any guilt at not spending more time with his family – it is possible that, though nothing was ever said, he knew Gladys and Lesley understood what was taking him out of the home, that burning drive to work on behalf of the poor and voiceless people who did not know how to operate in the political arena. It was his recognition of their lack of knowledge of how the system works which inspired Les to emphasise the importance of a sound education. He recognised that this was ultimately the way that people would be empowered to fight political battles in the way he had learned to do.

Les married late in life compared with many men of his generation. Little is known about his romantic liaisons before his marriage – except that at the age of 29 he fell in love with and was engaged for about eight months to a woman ten years younger than himself. The age difference, however, worked against this relationship because while Les was ready to marry and start a family the young girl (who describes herself as quite a determined and wilful young thing) was not yet inclined to settle down in marriage. She had stayed at school till she was 18 and was now enjoying her career and the life of a single girl. For some months Les hoped that she would change her mind but it was not to be and before long he began to prepare to stand in the 1949 Council elections, possibly channelling all his energies and his passion into fighting for what he passionately believed in – a socialist society.

It was as a consequence of the World War II evacuation programme that Les was to meet his wife Gladys (née Croot). A young woman called Jean Carter, the daughter of Les's friend and CP and ETU colleague Archie Carter, had been evacuated to Torquay during the war. She met and later married Gladys's brother Bob. At some stage Gladys came to London for a visit and to see her brother. One day, in Lesley's words, 'Dad was there, visiting Archie, and he met Mum for the first time – perhaps he had heard she was going to be there! Mum had just washed her hair and was looking ladylike and pretty and he invited her to go to the pictures with him.' Their courtship took place entirely in Gladys's home environment so Les must have made a lot of train journeys!

Les and Gladys were married on 29 March 1956 at Newton Abbot Registry Office when Les was 36 and Gladys seven years his junior. They both wanted a registry office wedding and to be just on their own – not because there was any dissent in the family; so it was a very quiet event and the honeymoon was spent at a hotel in Paignton. Gladys remembers that it was an extremely cold spring.

Married life started at 3 Rutt's Terrace where the extended family now consisted of Les's father and his grandmother. It remained the central home for the grown-up sons so that after he was married and living in 'dog-walking' distance Stan kept his keys to the house and, later, to the Elmira Street house which was to become Les's and Gladys's home after Charlie's death. Gladys was soon to take on the role of carer, just as Elmira herself had done many years before, but Charlie Stannard also did his share and was often to be seen taking Elmira out in her wheelchair.

Lesley was born on 30 April 1957 to the joy and delight of her parents and particularly to Les's great relief as Gladys had had to spend a considerable time in hospital. He was an unusually good father by the standards of the time when men tended not to get involved with the practical care of babies. 'She was a small baby but he cared for her so well,' says Gladys. 'He would leave me to sleep through the night and would come in in the morning and say "I've done everything for her, Glad," and that meant everything, including feeding and changing. Yes, I agree, in those days fathers never did much – but he did!'

Grandmother Elmira died in 1962 at the age of 87 when Lesley was nearly five. Mother and daughter have never forgotten all that she had done for the family over the years. In the last months a bed was brought down to the dining room for her, just as she had arranged for her daughter Edie in 1940. 'My image of her is quite hazy,' says Lesley, and both she and her mother remember her as a big old lady who had now become more serious and strict –'She certainly would not want you to go to sit on the end of her bed!' says Lesley. Elmira's death had a great impact on her three grandsons since she had been both mother and grandmother to them and had been part of the family for as long as they could remember.

The last member of the original Rutt's Terrace family, Charlie Stannard, died on 17 June 1967. The Stannards and the Bryetts before them had been living in the terrace for more than 70 years, since before Edie was born at number 14 in 1897. The move to Elmira Street came in 1970 and Gladys still lives there. Apart from the war years Les had only two addresses in his entire life. A street which bore his grandmother's name must have seemed like a good omen.

The bonds in this family were remarkably strong. Gladys had come to respect and to cherish her father-in-law so much that his death distressed her almost more than her own father's had done. This was because of all he had done to help her with the care of the ageing Elmira. Les, in his turn, forged a deep and affectionate relationship with Gladys's mother, Vera Croot, who said, 'He looked after me so well, always came to meet me at Paddington Station when I came to visit and insisted on paying my fare.'

From the earliest days of the marriage the pattern of Les's life outside the home was set. He was out in the evenings, not just occasionally but most of the time, and he was fortunate that Gladys was a self-sufficient person who was prepared to spend time alone and to provide for him a calm and quiet haven at the end of each long day. This is how she expressed it in her gentle, quiet voice: 'I wouldn't change him – it was what he wanted.' She must have realised that this pattern was never going to change, even after Les's retirement. There was not much conversation when Les came home – no talk of politics of any kind, nor of pensioners' issues even after they both became pensioners. He must have been too tired to talk and wanted to come home to something completely different and to keep the two lives apart. Gladys co-operated in this and led her own life within the home. Every member of the family and their close friends now pay tribute to Gladys for the part she played in enabling Les to live life the way he wanted to or knew he had to. 'Gladys was quiet and private, so different from the effervescent Les,' says John Griffiths, 'yet he knew, as we all knew, that she was the rock behind him; they were a team of opposites.'

Yet Lesley has vivid memories of her childhood and of the frequent and regular visits to London in the company of her father. 'These trips were like an education and a treat mixed together!' He showed Lesley all the important sights and taught her so much about the great city and she now continues the pattern by taking her own two sons on the same kinds of trips. Later she graduated to accompanying him to Millwall with her cousin Michael. Lesley describes Les as a model father who never missed parents' evenings at school; when she was much older he never imposed his own ideas on her about her future career (and he must have had them) but accepted her own decisions about the course she wanted to follow.

'We were a really close family,' says Lesley and this is echoed by his two nephews, Michael and Kevin, who tell of how happy and comfortable Les always was in their company. He was determined that the extended family must hold together and he gave the young ones his example by regular visits, with Lesley, to the elderly Bryett and Stannard relatives, some of whom lived in the almshouses at Nunhead – an unusual commitment in a middle-aged man. There were also visits to the family graves, always bearing flowers, and every family funeral was attended. 'I wish he could have enjoyed the world of nature more,' Lesley goes on, 'because he loved it though he could never give much time to the garden and on family holidays in Devon he used to love relaxing in the sun on Babbacombe Downs.' However, his mother-in-law has other memories of those 'holidays' – he would always bring work with him and often went to meetings instead of resting. There were always papers to be worked on and in the evenings he would go for long walks, in the dark, alone, returning late to watch a little television and to do more work.

Back at Elmira Street there were plenty of visitors and the telephone was always ringing and political discussion went on. After his retirement from Express Newspapers and before he became immersed in the pensioners' movement Lesley recalls his passion for crosswords, maths and logic puzzles – he had an outstanding mathematical brain and there was never a word he did not know in the crossword. The standard of education at Brockley Central was high and those of us who worked with him 60 years later could not fail to compare his exceptional writing skills and clear handwriting with that of many school leavers today. The family gatherings at Elmira Street were very special. Kevin and Michael remember their uncle as especially kind and always great fun to be with, in Kevin's words, 'a quiet, kind and very self-contained man'. He remembered them at every birthday and Christmas with cards and presents throughout his life, even when Michael was travelling abroad for five years. This was exceptional for a man of his generation or of any generation. He also took on the responsibility of writing all the Christmas cards. It was just the same Les who managed to get a card to the Bacons on their first wedding anniversary when Les was already in the war zone. 'Les always found a way,' Harry says proudly, remembering his old friend.

Both nephews and Les's son-in-law John Griffiths share identical impressions of Les's extreme tolerance and understanding of people who held different political views. Kevin writes, 'Despite his own strong left-wing convictions he never once belittled me when, as a teenager, I decided I wanted to support the Liberal Party.'

Michael says that they all knew about his interest in politics and committee work, and 'whenever we visited there were always papers around the house and he was always doing something, but the over-riding quality was his modesty. We would sit together as a family and we knew he had much more knowledge than the rest of us put together; so as we all discussed the current political crisis Les wouldn't come in on the conversation. He just took a back seat and did not speak unless someone asked him a question. If I made a political statement he would never say that I was wrong. He just listened, never tried to influence us, never told us we were talking rubbish!'

When young Lesley began to go to watch football at White Hart Lane instead of the Den Les recognised that something serious must be going on between his daughter and John Griffiths. 'I'll never forget how warmly he welcomed me,' says John. The wedding day approached and John remains moved to this day at the thought of Les's speech as father of the bride. 'He was so emotionally charged and that speech was superb! I had to get up to speak after him and cursed him for that! Yes, he was a very emotional man and Lesley had to keep tugging at his cuffs to keep him going when the tears began to flow.'

Lesley and John gave Gladys and Les two fine grandsons, Matthew and Owen, and with their arrival the Stannards were once again a three-generation family, Les and Gladys replacing Elmira and George Bryett as the loving grandparents, determined to play their part in supporting Lesley in the raising of the two boys. This statement is no flight of fancy – we know that Les wanted very much to continue the tradition of parents and grandparents supporting one another, because he made sure to mention it in the speech he made on the day when the London Borough of Lewisham gave him the first Community Award.

[17]

The Last Months

The beginning of the end of this remarkable pioneering socialist's life came in the early spring of 1996. Gladys began to show signs of poor health and her husband became anxious at her refusal to eat. This was a new experience for him since Gladys had always prepared all his meals and he had never had to think about food or about whether anyone else was eating properly. Alison Purshouse remembers how hard he tried to entice Gladys to eat with a variety of tempting foods. She was admitted to hospital on 28 April and remained there till 9 September, spending four weeks in intensive care because, in addition to her own grave illness, she was also one of the first patients known to have contracted MRSA while in hospital. Les was typically unstinting in his generous praise for the staff and for the nursing care she received throughout. He visited her not just daily, but at every opportunity. 'He was there all day every day,' remembers Bert Gramston. 'We would invite him to come out for a drink but he would not leave her bedside.'

Before long, the family and friends and colleagues who had, for some years, been trying to persuade him to reduce his workload, became increasingly concerned. This was sometimes expressed in a critical way so that Les then took on an additional emotional burden – that of trying to keep everyone happy while, at the same time, continuing to keep up all his commitments, irrespective of the assurances he was giving. Such was his sense of personal responsibility to his family and to his work that he continued to neglect his own faltering health. 'It was no use telling him to slow down,' comments his old friend Sadie Attfield. 'He would reply, "I can't, how can I?"' Accustomed always to find his meals prepared for him, like most married men of his generation, he now began to miss meals, only occasionally having something to eat at the Town Hall cafeteria. To anyone who had ever doubted the degree and the strength of his love and devotion to his family it was now there for all to see. His commitment to work, however, did not diminish. Alison Purshouse remembers him now beginning to struggle up those dreadful steep stairs, arriving breathless and perspiring, with an alarming skin colour. 'He would then "have a go" at himself – in the same way as he used to when he mislaid his glasses or his bus pass. He would stand in the doorway and scratch his head and say, "It's about time I had a haircut to let some oxygen get to my brain!" It was the same Les but you could not smile at his antics now as he was obviously very ill.' Alarm bells also rang for Sue Mead who worked with Asquith Gibbes at the LREC and had known him from the earliest days of the Forum. 'I knew how ill he must have been feeling when he telephoned me one day to ask whether I could go round to get a prescription for him. I had always offered my help but this was the first time he had ever taken me up on it. This was immensely significant for me.' Jim Mallory too remembers that with all the stress and pressure he was under during those months Les missed only one meeting of the Pensioners' Liaison Committee.

He was admitted to the same ward as Gladys on 14 August but he remained for only three days. A friend who had not seen him for some time called at the house with a cake knowing that he was on his own. She was alarmed at the change in him and at the way he collapsed into tears when he saw her, thanking her profusely for her small gift. At some stage his brother Ron and nephew Michael came to visit Gladys. This was the occasion when Michael told Les he was beginning to work on a family tree and, to Michael's surprise, Les was unable to speak for emotion when asked about his own mother. None of them were to know that Ron – the youngest of the three brothers – was soon to die and when this happened it was a further blow to Les's own desperately weak state of health. Ron died on 26 August 1996 when Gladys was still in hospital. One night Les rang his daughter to ask whether she could pick him up and take him to her home for the night. He told her he was feeling very low. 'That was the first time dad ever asked me for anything. He never asked before this – he always waited to be asked.'

Gladys came home on 9 September and she and Les had a little more than a month together before he was admitted to hospital for the last time on 10 October. It was during this last month that a painfully thin and clearly very sick Les spoke to his own Lewisham pensioners for the last time – delivering the kind of fiery and rousing speech he himself would have heard from Kath Duncan in the streets of Deptford almost 60 years before. Despite his illness and all the trauma of the past five months Les was as clear and direct as he had always been.

For the next two months Les continued to receive treatment with occasional spells of improvement followed by further relapses. Lesley was called to the hospital on three occasions when he was in a critical condition. After that he was in a constantly critical condition. His mind was still active and he was constantly thinking about the Forum's programme and who would be attending meetings in his absence. He also wanted so much to be home with Gladys again and he asked his daughter, 'I will come home for Christmas, won't I?' Lesley remembers that her father had made it quite clear, during her mother's illness, that he would never allow her to go into a residential or nursing home and that he would see to it that she would be cared for at home. After Les's third relapse the doctors warned Lesley that her father might have to be moved to a 'home'. 'I never had to make the decision,' says Lesley, 'but I know I could never have done it – it would have destroyed us all.' Towards the end he was very low – 'I think he was ready to die,' says Lesley. 'He had been through so much. I went to him very late one night and found him wrapped in one of those silver blankets because of his body temperature. He asked me why I had come and I had to say it was because he was not at all well. He asked me about the boys. I stayed till 7 a.m. but he said I was to go home because it was Matthew's birthday.' That may have been the night that Lesley said to him, 'I really love you dad,' and he replied, 'Thank you so much for saying that.' Lesley says, 'For me that summed up the man. He never asked for anything and was so grateful that I had said that to him.' On the same night father and daughter both observed that there were only two nurses on this large ward. People kept calling out for help. 'It's frightening, isn't it?' said Les. 'There are not enough staff to go round.'

A friend called one evening when the curtains were drawn round his bed and when the doctors came out she said to them, 'Do you realise who you have there?' She wanted them to know that the sick man had spent the past ten or more years fighting for the retention of the NHS at a time when the government was cutting resources. Had Les been well and visiting one of his friends in hospital (something he frequently did) he would have been the first to say that the nurses and other staff were doing wonderful work under extremely difficult conditions and with greatly reduced resources. He would have been troubled by the fact that meals were being placed next to the patients' beds when a number of them were too sick and weak to reach out a hand to feed themselves and that there was no one there to help feed them. He would, however, have known that such a desperate situation would have to be raised urgently with the appropriate authorities at every level. He would have known that patients were not receiving the care and attention they needed to aid their recovery, but now Les himself was the helpless patient. Only two months before, on Pensioners' Day, he had praised the hospital staff for all they had done for his wife. What an irony that this same man should die in hospital so quietly and bravely in the way that he did!

Days before Les died, a young man in the bed opposite, who had suffered a stroke, was about to return home. Les was aware of the difficulties he and his family would have to contend with. He told Lesley, 'We'll have to see to arranging things for when he returns home. Get on to Alison and tell her,' and he gave full instructions about who were the responsible people to contact to ensure that all the support services would be made available.

The following account comes from Moya McKay: 'Three days before he died I was there, reading him the *Morning Star*. He was very ill. There was a huge bouquet of flowers close to his bed. At about 8 p.m. I heard on the radio, "So and so 0, Millwall 2." Les heard it. I banged on the floor and sang, "We are the Champions," and the Caribbean family visiting their relative in the next bed joined in the laughter and celebration. Les removed his oxygen mask and smiled. I looked at the flowers and the card said, "To Les, from Millwall".'

'Dad never spoke about death and illness,' says Lesley. 'He never spoke his wishes but after he died we found a paper which said, simply, that if anything happened to him we were to make sure that Father Owen conducted the service.' This is confirmed by Father Owen who remembers standing by his bedside and Les saying, 'I want you to take my funeral.' It may surprise some of Les's old friends. This is not to suggest or imply that Les had undergone a sudden conversion. Humanity and human beings were what mattered to him. He had known Father Owen for some time through the Millwall Football Club and when Owen was the Mayor's Chaplain.

They were friends and they valued each other's commitment in the work they had been doing together over the years, so it must have seemed sensible to Les that his old friend, who happened to be a priest, should conduct his funeral. Father Owen had this to say, 'I would love to think that he respected me first as a friend because that would mean far more to me coming from Les.'

[18]

The Best MP Lewisham and Deptford Never Had

'The inscription on the headstone of Christopher Wren reads: "If you want to see my memorial look around you." In the same way, Les left his influence on people for us to see. He had a burning sense of justice and a hatred of injustice. He was a civilised and democratic individual.'

Jim Dowd MP

The enthusiasm and sheer passion with which scores of people who knew and worked with Les Stannard offered their recollections of what he meant to them and what they have learned from him is truly astonishing. When the Management Committee of Lewisham Pensioners' Forum took the decision to prepare his biography the members knew of the clear legacy he had left them, but even they were surprised by just how deep and pervasive that influence had been on people who knew him in other spheres of his life and in earlier days. It has been a monumental task to try to do justice to the views and opinions of all his old friends and colleagues by bringing together those talents and qualities, all those superlatives, which they used to describe him.

What was it about this elderly man, with his shock of white hair, his unaffected accent, his cloth cap and not a tooth in his head, which so captivated and inspired so many men and women? A few of his friends knew Les also from his young days. Alf Stockwell spoke to me about him, not long before he himself died, remembering his wavy brown hair and a very quick and agile manner, standing and holding on to that old pram, with its wobbly loudspeaker, in the weeks leading up to the 1950 election; he seemed genuinely surprised, Alf added, when he did not win that election! Mike Power, who was just a child at the time, has the same intriguing sight fixed in his mind. Another old friend remembers the three brothers as all very lean – not a bit of fat on them. Les in his young days had wonderful dark hair and eyes, and altogether a very interesting and attractive face. 'My mother used to say he had the most beautiful back of the neck she had ever seen!' Tom Bell said, 'He always looked the same, with that twinkle in his eye – he looked quite old when he was young and eventually caught up with himself so that, as he got older, he seemed to look younger!' John Rampling, remembering how indefatigable Les was in pursuit of his vision to push *you* further in the direction *he* was aiming for, remarks again on that tousled hair and disarming manner which made you want to help. 'I bumped into him on a train once and he asked me where I was going. "Wherever you're going," was my immediate response; that is the effect he had on one. It was like being up against an avalanche!' This might seem like a contradiction since Les was known to be gently persuasive and never forceful. The reason people felt so drawn to support him was based in the way he inspired people to react to him. Some women have remarked on his beautiful face, drawing attention to his expression which clearly revealed the nature of the man. A wicked sense of humour lay side by side with an inability to hold back the tears on the many occasions when he was moved by anger, sadness or compassion, by a small act of kindness or simply by a memory. 'Because the personal and the political were merged in him he became irresistible,' in the words of one former Lewisham councillor (a woman) who notes that he always took knocks personally and one therefore never wanted to offend him. Yet the man who could speak so brilliantly in the public arena never went into the realm of personal feelings and was even known to blush! Jean Kysow remembers how he kept her laughing all the way from London to Blackpool telling stories of his trade union days and Abe Oppel says that, in the midst of his inspirational and unswerving commitment to the noble causes of pensioners and the evils of racism, with that infectious sense of urgency which always surrounded him, one could also glimpse a quintessentially English, almost Monty Pythonesque sense of humour. 'All this combined with a humility and generosity that can only reside in a good person.' Perhaps, as Moya McKay makes clear, what made him most lovable was that Les made no concessions to gentrification and never lost that Deptford accent.

The legacy of a good revolutionary

> 'Philosophers have only interpreted the world in different ways – the point, however, is to change it.' Karl Marx[1]

> 'They are very good at writing history but you and me are very good at making it.' Les Stannard to Victor Henning, speaking about contemporary historians.

> 'If I had to tell someone how to go about getting things done for their community, I really couldn't do better than to tell them to do it the way Les did; and one of the things I was always conscious of was that he really understood

[1] Theses on Feuerbach: Brussels Spring 1845 (from Engels, F., *Feuerbach. The Roots of Socialist Philosophy*, 1903, Chicago, Charles H. Kerr and Company.)

how things could actually be changed.' Steve Bullock, Former Leader of Lewisham Council

Les's motivation and his objectives were quite clear – they stemmed from his vision about achieving lasting change. He wanted always to change things and, in particular, to change, radically and permanently, the circumstances of working-class people and the political system which places them in those circumstances. He aimed, therefore, to bring about change in the laws and policies which affected people's economic, political and social circumstances, not only locally, but nationally and internationally. He was not a professional politician, in the sense that he never earned his living from politics, but in all his work on behalf of other people (during his working years as a trade unionist and after his so-called retirement) he was a truly accomplished politician and, as many have remarked, a formidable colleague or opponent, according to which side of the negotiating table one was at. One could say he was the best MP Deptford and Lewisham never had.

During the last ten years of his life when he devoted his energy mainly (but not exclusively) to the pensioners' movement, he addressed every aspect of their lives – starting with the state pension and the means test right through to transport, housing, safety, education and leisure and everything in between – to see what changes needed to be made at both local and national level. Sean Geraghty puts it like this: 'He was genuinely concerned, long before he became a pensioner, that people should not be thrown on the scrap heap – he was politically aware of what would become the plight of many pensioners and hoped that politically they would become a force to reckon with.' Les's vision was never knocked off course by disappointments (though there were many disappointments). It would be true to say that he always displayed the opposite of apathy, that all too common affliction of citizens of democracies. When others would sit back and say, 'Things can't change' or 'They' (meaning MPs, councillors, the Prime Minister, members of the Cabinet) 'don't care – we can't influence them,' Les believed, quite simply, that people can bring change. He was a true class warrior who knew what he wanted to achieve and went for it; but, as Jack Dunn points out, he also recognised that it was the collective effort and strength of workers which can change things. Another aspect of bringing change, therefore, meant that people needed to be made aware of what they could do and that, as Les well knew, was where education and raising awareness came in. His knowledge of who had influence and how and where decisions were taken made him a formidable campaigner.

Les never gave up when he saw how he could have an influence – the example of the setting up of the anti-racism committee at Millwall shows his tenacity. For a long time he hammered away alone about the racist fans and how something had to be done about the effect they were having. The phenomenal growth and continuing work of that committee is one of the greatest tributes to him. John Rampling says that Les was indefatigable in the pursuit of his vision. On another occasion he described Les's Management Committee colleagues as 'like little candles to his wide searchlight'. Another colleague, former Chair of the Greater London Forum, Tony Carter, draws attention to how much it meant to him when even relatively small successes were achieved. 'For Les the campaign was never enough – he ached for results. When he told me that LPF had just heard that it had secured the right to nominate the inspection team for the borough's residential homes he was as excited as he would have been by a massive pension increase.'

There is yet another aspect to the question of achieving change. Mel Wright (former senior manager of the Elderly People's Resource Team) saw how Les's influence on his own generation offered an alternative to the hitherto paternalistic charitable organisations which represent older people.

Doreen Scott, Secretary of the BPTUAA, adds that it is because of Les and others like him that pensioners, instead of being told what was best for them by the authorities, are now able to say what they want and to give their views on social issues. 'Now that is happening even in Tory Surrey!'

Professionalism and knowledge

There are thousands of quiet heroes, all over the country, working tirelessly and selflessly in support of the unvalued and disenfranchised members of our society, people who choose to give up their time year after year, during evenings and weekends. What made Les and others like him particularly effective? He recognised that in the dynamic between civil servants (who advise) and our elected representatives (who take the decisions) there was an important role to be played by the non-statutory organisations and individuals who were the consultants on particular policies. He also knew that this role would be ineffective if it was not backed up by sound knowledge of the system and the relevance of past legislative history – hence the importance of reading the official papers before each meeting, of knowing the link between the present situation and the legislation which came before it. Pat Greenwood, senior reporter on the *SE London and Kent Mercury*, says, 'He could not tolerate people who did not read their morning paper and he would expect you to know, as he did, what happened in the past, which was relevant to the events of today – for example the 1908 Pensions Act in relation to what was taking place when Mrs Thatcher severed the link with earnings. He saw it as a parent would – it was up to you to educate yourself, to find out for yourself. I respected him highly because he made me think for myself.'

Compromise, tolerance, respect and dignity

> 'His respect for people was such that he never traduced anyone.' Andy Hawkins

Les was reasoned, well read and well informed. He was also blessed with a prodigious memory. There were other factors related to his understanding of the system and how to operate within in. He was the clearest of tacticians who, as Mike Power puts it, could always see the relevance of what could be achieved now and thus never confused tactics with strategy. Steve Bullock said almost the identical thing: 'He campaigned for achievable things as well as more fundamental change and this ability meant he was respected and taken seriously by members and officers. He also understood that we, in the Council (those of us who shared his views and concerns) could not always do everything as quickly as he was proposing. This did not stop him being critical but one always felt that it was the sort of criticism that friends are entitled to make.' Les really understood pragmatism and the need to push step by step. There were times when, in the opinion of some, Les was 'not political enough' – he would draw back from an argument and sometimes did not push his views when he could have done. This might seem puzzling in someone with his determination and powers of persuasion but Alison Purshouse thinks that there were occasions when Les recognised that things could backfire and the right tactic then would be not to pursue an argument any further.

Les's son-in-law John Griffiths commented most perceptively on another factor which no one else had highlighted or, perhaps, which people found too embarrassing to raise because it is fundamentally a class issue: the fact that so many people tend not to associate a gruff voice and a working-class accent with intelligence or academic ability. There is a tendency (sometimes unconscious) to make value judgements, to categorise people, and even to dismiss them. It did not take long for John to realise the strength of the intellect which lay beneath his father-in-law's down-to-earth exterior. How many senior politicians in those harsh days of the Thatcher government may have closed their minds, at first, to that south-east London accent and the cloth cap (to say nothing of the man's age). Fortunately not everyone was so prejudiced. Over the years Andy Hawkins came to appreciate not only the power of Les's intellect but his capability in cutting through verbiage right through to the heart of an argument. Mike Power describes him as an intellectual of the working class – a man who learned from the Communist party training as a young man but whose intellect grew phenomenally by the end of his life. An old friend who knew him in his twenties said, 'He was very quick and practical and would often put an end to a discussion by saying "That's it and all about it."' How different from the mature man whose best-remembered catchphrase came to be 'That would be very helpful' – something he would often say in order to consolidate even a small measure of agreement between opposing points of view. Many have commented on his astuteness, his sagacity and his gentle persistence. It was most revealing to me when I met people who knew Les (but who did not know one another) to hear that precisely the same qualities stood out in their minds. One which was repeated over and over again was that he never pushed his own political beliefs on anyone. Another of his skills was mentioned by Jeremy Corbyn MP who remembers clearly how, unlike so many others who visit him at the House of Commons, Les was not only polite and very well informed but brilliant in his ability to present his case in a clear and precise way on behalf of the particular organisation he was representing. The case itself would no doubt have been presented by others but where Les was concerned it was refreshingly different and so much more persuasive. 'It was not so much lobbying,' Corbyn adds, 'but more like a seminar: I always learned from him. He could give a clear class analysis, pointing out that working-class people had worked for the establishment of the welfare state and for the state pension – they were, clearly, the best people to defend it. What is more, he predicted exactly how the diminution of the welfare state would bring the arrival of private pensions.'

'Everything he said was worth hearing,' says Moya McKay who noticed that when she spoke to other groups of people – many of whom were often aggressive – they would always stop and listen whenever she quoted Les, 'because they all knew that he would have done his research'. As a born communicator Les displayed another unusual quality; unlike many able speakers, he showed enormous respect for others by genuinely listening to them. He got the best from people in Andrew Spencer's view because he valued the contributions made by others, particularly when colleagues round the table had stopped listening. Spencer also remembered how Les instinctively defused tension and conflict, and he echoes the sentiments of Tom Mellish about his keenness that people, particularly those who were younger and less experienced, should participate and contribute.

Linked to his understanding of the need for pragmatism was his talent for compromise. Jack Dunn put it like this: 'It was not easy to do what Les did, as a Marxist – knowing how to work with people of different principles and beliefs, people who hated you for your Communism. Les was able to adapt to all of them. He knew we have to live with people and work with them because that is what society is – you, me and everyone else. Les would work diplomatically and if he could not persuade people to agree all the way, he would go as far as he could get them to go.' How did Les do it? Quite simply it was because his respect for human beings knew no bounds. It did not stop at those whose own views on what constitutes humanity were diametrically opposed to his own. In his mind you could not be selective in your respect for your fellow humans. For Tony Carter this quality stands out in one particular memory which illuminates Les's great loyalty to pensioners. There was an occasion when they were discussing some current issue. 'I remember saying, "That's interesting, Les, but why is it something which should interest the Greater London Forum?" He looked at me in a particular way he had when someone was being obtuse and said, "It's about dignity, Tony."'

Yet Les could be quite fearless, as Roy Martin also recalled. 'If he was certain he was right he was quite uncompromising, but always in a way that did not offend other people.' An example of this comes from Ron Cowell, describing one particular meeting at Express Newspapers. Following a discussion Les, the Chairman, made a ruling on the item. An individual in the front row who prided himself on being a great Chairman spoke up: 'Mr Chairman, I don't think your ruling conforms with Lord Citrine's book on chairmanship' – this was the committee bible. Quick as a flash Les responded, 'It may not conform to Citrine but it conforms to Les Stannard's book on chairmanship!' 'He went immediately to the next subject,' recalls Cowell. 'Without being vindictive or unpleasant he demolished the opposition and proceeded.'

Modesty

> 'He was one of the few genuinely modest people I've known in politics – most of us aren't modest at all!'
> Richard Balfe MEP

Les's modesty is one of the qualities most frequently mentioned. 'He was never self-important and would never say "Mention my name",' is how his old friend Eileen Day puts it, and Andy Hawkins remarks that he had no illusions about himself or anyone else. Jeremy Corbyn told of how clear it was to him that, unlike many others who are in it for themselves, there was no doubt with Les that he was doing it for others. His nephew Kevin said it was 'a reflection of the nature of the man that . . . he tended modestly to keep his achievements and endeavours in the wider sphere fairly separate from his family life and, despite having been involved in some of the fighting during the war, he was very reticent and unwilling to discuss it'.

Yet perhaps modesty is not quite the right word, since it is often used to describe people who have a not very high opinion of themselves. It is true that Les did not care at all about his own image and never wanted attention drawn to himself; he thought very carefully before accepting the Community Award for example. When I remarked to Gladys that she must have been very proud of him at that time she well remembered that he did not want a lot of fuss and did not say much. 'Of course I was proud of him but I did not let on.' When asked why this was she replied, 'Oh no! He's not like that is he?'

It was not so much that Les was humble (for he was forthright and proud of his beliefs) but rather that he never had time to think about himself since his mind was always fully occupied with the myriad things which had to be done. Whether it meant staying up most of the night to prepare a paper, or putting out the chairs and preparing the teacups before a meeting, or helping to sort out the papers in the office, Les would always be there, ready to give support when others considered themselves too important to carry out such mundane tasks. It never occurred to him to think about himself. Sadly this became only too obvious when he would not give up, even when his health was failing. Paradoxically, there are those who did notice a kind of humility. Alison Purshouse could detect a lack of confidence on occasions and when he seemed to need reassurance – often, after he had given a speech, he would come up and ask, 'Do you think that was all right?'

Leaflets and petitions and carrier bags

The image which has been painted so far has been one of a near perfect man, but nobody who knew Les, and certainly not Les himself, would recognise this as a true picture! Those who knew him in the early days seemed to have little to record about the negative side of his character, except for Mike Power who as a child once asked him to mend his Ever Ready train set. This was in the 1950s, possibly during the period of the guerrilla strikes which must have been some of the most active years in Les's life. Sadly, despite Mike's frequent visits to his house to remind him, the train set was never mended and Mike brought it home and renamed it the Never Ready train set!

Like many people who set high standards for themselves Les would also unwittingly set similar standards for others and would show disappointment if people did not attain what he had hoped they would or if they were not prepared to give up as much time as he did. John Rampling considers that Les never took people for granted but added, 'Some of us let him down at times.' He was so determined to push the Pensioners' Forum into deeper involvement in all local issues that he set up several sub-committees (focus groups in New Labour language) to concentrate on and even to shadow the Council's committees on specific issues like health, community care, education and transport, but members of the fully stretched Management Committee found it hard to take on more commitments. He constantly appealed for more people, and, particularly, younger pensioners, to put themselves forward for nomination, since he recognised that the most active members (himself especially) were over-burdened and inevitably many began to withdraw from active commitment because of illness.

Les had the kind of boundless physical energy and enthusiasm which left people half his age standing speechless, and one consequence of this was that he never had time to keep his own papers in order and sometimes made it difficult for his staff to work to deadlines! The Forum office maintained an excellent recording system but it was hard to keep up with the volume of paper Les managed to amass. Had the thin plastic carrier bag not come into existence in the second half of the 20th century Les would, no doubt, have had to invent it. In time, however, those useful bags began to cause problems! It must be realised that wherever he went, particularly in those last ten years, there were always papers, journals, leaflets and petitions to be distributed and collected and, while the contents of each day's harvest of papers were clear in his mind on that particular day (and much of it did get distributed as was intended), over time the carrier bags multiplied so that no one knew which bag contained which set of papers. The intention was always good, for part of the process of arousing people's awareness in the days before 'dot.coms' and emails involved the printed word and Les made a point of giving out leaflets and an on-the-spot analysis of what the current issue was all about. He was so carried away with wanting people to know what was important and what they could do, he even began to give out leaflets at the end of one old friend's funeral. This caused some surprise but Les had a 'no-nonsense' side to him; he meant no disrespect, arguing that his departed old chum would have gone along with whatever it was he wanted to draw attention to that day!

Another side to his enthusiasm was, in the opinion of some, a tendency to talk for too long at committee meetings – this was probably because he wanted to make certain that all he had learned at other committees should be fully passed on and shared. 'I must go back to my members' was a phrase he repeatedly used. Conversely, when he delivered his passionate and fiery Pensioners' Day speeches many would have liked them to go on for longer. Joan Ruddock says, 'His arguments were presented in a passionate way and you could depend on it that no matter how well you had spoken, Les would speak better!'

Other words that frequently cropped up in memories of Les were 'highly principled' and 'incorruptible' and more than one old colleague told how much he was valued for his determination and integrity by even his most bitter opponents. Even more remarkable was the way he kept himself always 'above' – in the sense of never descending to nastiness or to personality campaigns, an attitude which invited reciprocation from those whose policies differed from his.

Many references were made to Les's dry and somewhat unusual sense of humour, and also to the warmth he brought to his friendships. 'He was always open to other people and it was a real and genuine meeting of two people when you met him,' remembers Elizabeth Sclater. Father Owen says, 'Had I known him at a distance I would have thought of him exclusively as a great man but he was, principally, my friend and I co-existed with him at all times in everyday conversation. He was a lovely person to be with and naturally fun. You have to have a sense of humour anyway if you want to watch Millwall.' Other friends marvelled at how he managed to balance his forceful campaigning with being such a warm and approachable human being. There were those who talked about that quality of 'omnipresence' as another of Les's trademarks, saying how you bumped into Les here, there and everywhere, always ready to engage you in conversation. For Maura Rafferty he was 'the only person that anybody knew who could be in any number of places at one time. People would come in and say they were at a demonstration in Central London and Les was there; later on the same day he was seen somewhere else and, again on the same day, at yet another meeting. He played a central part and a proper role in each of those places, even if he did not stop very long. He would have been in perhaps five or more places in a day and evening, always with his carrier bags and his papers – at some stage he would leave in order to go somewhere else. He was like a cat, slinking about, always with that unassuming manner.' Les was important in so many things yet never claimed credit for anything. Maura again: 'What he did was because he believed in things; he just supported everything that was right in life.'

The Communist co-operator

We know that Les became a Communist at a very young age and, despite the enormous and cataclysmic changes in the world-wide movement and within the Communist party in Britain, his belief in and courageous adherence to the original principles never changed. So many of those who have contributed to this work have said, 'He was not a typical Communist.' It is interesting to go more deeply into the meaning of that statement and why so many people used it.

Les was also steeped in the culture of Co-operation from an even earlier age and it seems plausible to claim that this culture, and the conflicts within it, was woven into his Communism. The effect that the Communist training had on Les's personality should not be discounted. It made him absolutely reliable and committed to whatever he considered was important. Joan Ruddock MP did not use the word 'Communist' but spoke of the sound philosophy from which his whole life stemmed and his deep roots in political theory.

Many Communists had ceased to be members of the Communist Party of Great Britain after the Hungarian Revolution (1956). Serious divisions then began to emerge at the 35th Congress in 1977; they centred round the drafting of the British Road to Socialism and also the content, style and management of the *Morning Star*. A special Congress called in April 1988 led to the closure of the CPGB and the re-establishment of the party (now renamed the Communist Party of Britain) on the basis of its existing rules, principles and programme. In every essential respect the CPB adheres to the continuation of the original party, including the association with the *Morning Star*, which embraces the broad left movement. The 'revisionists' in the old CPGB went on to form the Democratic Left and abandoned the British Road to Socialism. It changed its name to the New Times Network in 1999, and currently has a membership of a few hundred. The break-up of the original party – and the way different groups of the membership subsequently evolved – caused, and still causes, great anguish amongst members of the CPB (current membership now about 2000) and those who quietly withdrew their membership.

Mike Power (Campaigns Officer at the TUC) worked closely with Les in the CPGB in the early 1970s when they both belonged to the Lewisham and Borough committee and later (in the 1980s) to the Deptford Branch. (Branch membership was based on the area where members lived or could be determined by the industrial branch in which they worked.) At this time each borough had its own committee and secretariat and several branches and both men attended the fortnightly meetings. Les held a number of posts; he was, for example, responsible for membership for a while. Towards the end of the seventies and in the early eighties when the party was beginning to collapse, Les held the whole branch together – looking after the membership, and working as a kind of joint secretary. He was very heavily committed and had a strong belief in the principle of democratic centralism and, in Power's view, did not seem to appreciate or want to engage in arguments about policy. The decisions of Congress were what mattered to him. Others were now openly discussing policy between meetings and conferences and did not consider it rational simply to continue holding to existing policies whilst change was noticeably taking place around them. Yet Power does not believe the term 'hard-liner' applied to Les, rather that he displayed utter loyalty to the organisation. The impression given at Les's memorial service of a 'hard-line hero' was not in his view correct. Les was a much more complicated and sensitive person with a broader understanding of the kind of objectives which the original CPGB had set itself in the British Road to Socialism. Perhaps this is why he kept his own counsel and did not share his views with others at a time when the process of irrevocable change had begun during the late eighties and early nineties when considerable differences were emerging within the movement.

Les Stannard was not a secretive person, but where his Communism was concerned he was a very private person. As many of his friends have said, he lived by his Communist beliefs and saw no need to explain them, still less to persuade anyone to adopt them. During the process of research the question which had to be asked was whether it would be best to respect this privacy and not to delve into the position Les adopted after the 1988 Congress. On the other hand it seemed that an account of his life would not be lacking in respect if it examined the decisions he made at that troubled time. A few of his former colleagues were able to share their knowledge. The late Wally Barnes said he remembered that Les would go to meetings of the emerging Democratic Left in order to present the case for the original party under the new title (CPB). Another former colleague recollects Les's unease about developments which took place in 1982. The editor of the *Morning Star* was gravely concerned about what was taking place in the CPGB. An article in *Marxism Today* attacked the trade unions and made accusations of corruption, on the eve of the 1982 TUC Conference. Leading trade unionists responded and the *Morning Star* carried a front page attack on *Marxism Today*; schisms developed between the *Morning Star's* Executive and the workers which, in turn, led to a wide gap between the *Morning Star* and the CPGB Executive. These schisms caused a great deal of distress to people like Les and Rose Kerrigan who had always regarded the party and the *Morning Star* as one and the same. It needs to be understood that the *Morning Star* was, for them, the daily expression of the party and, whereas *Marxism Today* was the voice of the CPGB, the *Morning Star* was owned by the worker shareholders who were part of the wider labour movement and not just CPGB members.

During this time many comrades were also becoming uneasy about some of the positions the party was taking, regarding the Soviet Union's internal and foreign policies. The whole period became extremely traumatic and had a range of outcomes for members. The majority remained in the party and accepted the party line. Another group continued to support both the party and the *Morning Star*. A third group of members, though unhappy with the situation, kept quiet but did not renew their membership. A fourth group, equally unhappy, openly ceased to be members and eventually formed the Democratic Left. There seems to be little doubt that Les belonged to the third group – it was in his character to keep very quiet and slowly to ease out and this has been confirmed by the CPB who say there is no record of his membership having been renewed after 1988. A spokesperson for the party says that it is safe to assume that Les ceased to be a member from that time.

Interesting light is shed on Les's position by a former CPB member who knew Les and his involvement with the Lewisham Branch. This branch was a strong and determined one and despite the disagreements and divisions within the wider movement and the decisions taken by individual members, she said that they all continued to work together on the basis of their fundamental training and beliefs and no better example of this can be shown than that of Les who literally threw himself into the pensioners' movement.

At the end of Les's life it could be said that he did not leave the Communist Party but that the Communist Party left him. So strong was his commitment that perhaps he did not feel it necessary to speak about what it meant to him, even to his closest friends and colleagues, much less to try to persuade anyone by promoting the party line. Yet he was always open about his Communist membership. He lived his life by his Communist beliefs and in all his activities he sought to persuade by logical yet impassioned argument rather than by spouting dogma. Alison Purshouse sees him as a 'natural Communist' who communicated in a natural way – 'Nothing he said was hard to grasp and although he was highly intelligent and aware of all the nuances he could employ he always got his message across simply and left you to interpret it in your own way.'

For the greater part of his working life Les and others like him were persecuted for their Communism. One of his old friends draws a parallel between the persecution of Communists and that of Catholics – both belonged to organisations which were highly organised from above and demanded unconditional and unquestioning allegiance. Did Les perhaps recognise these features in the Catholics he encountered in RACS during the 1950s and during the long years when Communists were banned from holding office in the EETPU and the Trades Councils, and when they also suffered discrimination by employers?

'New Left' politics is an all-embracing term for the leftist movements which succeeded the changes which befell the former Communist Party in the late 1980s and early 1990s. Michael Kenny (pp. 206–7) believes there is no simple dichotomy between those in New Left movements and former Communists, indeed that the emergence of the New Left shows how former Communists' political allegiances were determined by new organisations and traditions. He adds that, for even the most coherent and virulent opponents of Stalinism, aspects of the Communist heritage continued to shape political choices and preferences – however profound their break from Communism appeared. It is not clear from what is known about Les whether this comes close to the position he took when he quietly decided not to renew his membership, or whether the conflict between his party and the trade unions was the determining factor.

Some of Les's friends and colleagues believe that he partly

shared the outlook of the Democratic Left and some have speculated about what might have been his response to 'the Third Way' – a phrase which was already being used in his lifetime. Dave Sullivan thinks it all depends on the views people hold of the Communist Party – some think of it as an extreme left-wing organisation while others see it as a 'thinking' one which is what Sullivan believes it grew into – a critical voice to the Labour Party. Sullivan concludes that Les might have shared some of the 'Third Way' views but that he would most certainly have hated some of the New Labour attitudes and relationships with the trade unions. He would have resisted many of the policy changes (such as those affecting pensioners) but as a thinker he would have seen the need and the reasons for change. 'Les was a much more complicated person than many people thought. He was a thinker, an activist and an advocate – not just one of those things but all of them,' says Sullivan, 'so he would have seen a lot of sense in some of the Third Way arguments,' but, at another level, Sullivan recognised that he would have rejected them.

Jeremy Corbyn put it quite differently and talked about 'this silly Third Way nonsense'. He sees that Les would now be called old-fashioned. 'He certainly was an old-fashioned socialist and co-operator, an old-fashioned trade unionist and supporter of community groups and an old-fashioned activist in civic life.' Corbyn, who questions the actual meaning of the word 'modern' by New Labour, considers that far from being old-fashioned Les was a totally modern, democratic and forward-looking person who was quite clear in his mind that if we want a decent society we have to pay people a just wage, we have to educate all the children, look after all members of our society and guarantee security in retirement. Failure to do so, Les knew, would result in a split society which is what we now have in Britain.

We know for certain that Les never did join the Democratic Left and John Esterson says, categorically, that Les was always a Communist whether he carried a card or not. Mick O'Connor says, 'We shared common ground – Les was a die-hard of the old school and he would never waver. Those of the old school stand by their principles, still believing they will be vindicated in the end, no matter how many battles are lost, and especially when they are vilified by the media.' Richard Kavanagh stresses the importance of the world movement of the working class as a determining factor in Les's beliefs.

Balfe sheds interesting light on the question of the 'typical Communist'. He remembers Les as a great conciliator, 'capable of minimising difference where people had things in common. In fact many people never realised he was a Communist, thinking that he must be a member of the Labour Party because he was such a conciliatory sort of figure.' Rafferty and Wakefield recognised the same quality – that of bringing opposing arguments and drawing out an agreement. Both women, so much younger than Les, were often thrilled and inspired by the history and colour he brought to the Trades Council meetings – his experiences of working to support the cause of the International Brigade in the Spanish Civil War, the vivid memories of Cable Street and the blackshirts and – over and over again – the shining image of Kath Duncan. Trudi Coutinho makes another observation: 'People in the CP, just as in every other sphere of life, sometimes did things for ulterior motives. In such instances, when Les became aware of a colleague's wrong behaviour he would deal with the matter and speak to the person in a way that was always so gentle.'

Andy Hawkins brought to mind Les's position on the issue of the full participation of the working class had there ever been a workers' revolution in Britain. There was a Socialist Forum which used to meet regularly in Lewisham at the time of the Prague Spring in 1968. It was open to anyone on the left but there was discomfort in the minds of some Labour Party participants who were being warned off by the local hierarchy about people 'like Les' taking part. There were voices in this Forum (now prominent Labour Party establishment figures) expressing the view that strict control of 'the workers' would have to be taken. Les's impassioned reaction to these suggestions gives us a clue to the kind of Marxist he was. He brought to mind the way events had developed in the Soviet Union in the early part of the 20th century, arguing that a revolution would have to have the support of everybody, describing what the consequences of suppression might be. As John Lloyd explains (p. 395), in the context of trade union activity, Lenin demanded a small, coherent, disciplined political party and wanted to deny the possibility of working-class progress through democratic change in Parliament, based on a mass working-class political party. Lenin wanted the vanguard of the working class to 'debate' issues – but once the decision was taken by the appropriate committee, dissent and continuing argument would not be tolerated. In Lenin's view, 'party members would not be tainted, in their iron discipline, with the soppiness and toleration expected of mainstream democratic parties like the Labour Party'.

Thus, Les, who appeared at times to be a staunch democratic centralist, did not believe in control of the workers by an inner circle. This is an apparent contradiction which only strengthens the views of those who have drawn attention to the complexities in his character.

Asquith Gibbes knew Les both in the CP and when he joined the Executive Committee of LREC. Les had come to the Executive through the Co-op, rather than the party, perhaps because people were squeamish about having a Communist there. He recalls that Les was a unique person whose concern for issues transcended everything, and who gave equal weight to pensioners, race, women or equal rights. 'Perhaps I would not call it an obsession,' says Asquith, 'but he was possessed by these issues – they had a hold on him and he was able to give his time, his energy, his thought and commitment to each one of them in an equal way.' Mike

Power recognised the same qualities, adding that Les's strong anti-racism stemmed from his realisation that racism was divisive of the working class. Les also had a keen interest and a genuine understanding of cultural diversity. Furthermore his determination to fight racism was also influenced by the fact that his beloved Deptford was one of the places to which Caribbean immigrants had come to live in the mid-fifties. Gibbes goes on to remark that he has mixed with many Communists but what distinguished Les's Communism was that he did not deal with issues on the periphery as so many of them did but worked directly with people. On the issue of racism, for example, the Communists were slow at putting their own house in order and were slow to involve black people in the party. They certainly knew about colonialism and neo-colonialism but they tended to operate at a distance. Les, on the other hand, was always conscious of the individual person and how she or he was affected. In this way he stood out from others in both the CP and the Labour Party. 'He was an unusual Communist – his Communism was not necessarily visible, but his commitment was.' When asked whether Les would ever have supported a bloody revolution Gibbes said an emphatic 'no' but they both recognised that this is how many people regarded Communists – that Communists carry with them something so disgusting that others rejected them. Power also notes that, unlike many Communists, Les had a genuine humanistic streak. His commitment to ALCARAF, to pensioners, to the tenants' association was not so much a Communist commitment but stemmed from the fact that he cared about the issues in each case. He was not there to promote the party but because he was genuinely anti-racist, genuinely concerned about his neighbours and about the plight of pensioners.

Les's life has been described as schizophrenic, in that his political life was quite separate from his life at home. Yet unlike so many Communists who talk endlessly about their love of the masses but have little time for people around them, Les showed a real commitment to and love of his family and friends – evident in the number of former comrades' funerals that he attended. In the case of his own family there are those who believe that Les went out of his way to protect them from his political activities to such an extent that his two lives were completely separate from each other.

Father Owen Beament knew Les chiefly through his work with the Borough Council and with Millwall. He may be regarded as someone who works outside the political arena, never getting involved with political parties, least of all the Communist Party – yet his contact with Les over many years gave him a different slant on Communism. 'I have often suggested that the first Communist Manifesto is The Magnificat for in the house of God we are all equal, not that some are more equal than others – and that was characteristic of Les, wasn't it? Whoever he was speaking to – you were you – whether you were the Queen of England or an unknown person in the street.'

Staunch Communists would say that it was Les's Communism which motivated him and gave him his caring, compromising nature and the determination to fight inequality wherever he encountered it. Others seem to want to believe that his personality and his approach must have come from some other influences in his life, or that he 'inherited' them. I suspect that, as a true Communist himself, Les would not have given much credence to inheritance as a determiner of people's beliefs, perspectives and attitudes. My own knowledge of the man convinces me that he would almost certainly have been entirely in support of Marx's dictum, 'Man's consciousness does not determine his being but it is his social being which determines his consciousness.'[1] His own life experiences give abundant evidence that it was his observation of and involvement in family and outside events during

[1] Marx, Karl, *A Contribution to the Critique of Political Economy*, London, 1971, Lawrence and Wishart.

his growing years, as well as his Communist training, which jointly contributed to the young man who grew into the mature Les Stannard – described by his old friend and Pensioners' Forum colleague, Stan Tulloch, as 'a colossal man'.

A famous biographer once said, 'To the dead we owe the truth,' but how can we know the truth about a person when so much is inevitably hidden? What is more, most thinking people struggle with conflicts and hide much from themselves. Les was surely no exception. This account cannot, in all truth, reveal everything that is thought to have been known about him and there is much that will continue to intrigue us about his character and, in particular, about how he lived out those retirement years. Some have asked how he saw himself and, indeed, whether he stopped to see himself at all as he lived that punishing life of self-denial, of frenetic daily activity, contrasted with the quiet at home. It is clear that he was passionately moved by a sense of outrage about society's injustice to pensioners and other disenfranchised groups, but were there other reasons for the way he drove himself so mercilessly, especially in those last ten years?

Les was an outgoing, gregarious person whose identity grew and developed in the many relationships he made. He responded and adapted enthusiastically to everyone he met, no matter how little he may have appeared to have had in common with them initially, so that all his friends and colleagues gained immeasurably from having known him. They will, undoubtedly, continue to ask questions about the contrast between his public and his private life. I have taken the decision not to attempt to answer them but hope that this account of his life and work will enable readers, as well as his family, friends and colleagues, to form and to treasure their own views and memories.

The Memorial Meeting

A Memorial Meeting to celebrate the life and pay tribute to the work of Les Stannard was held on 14 March 1997 at the TUC, Congress House, Great Russell Street, London WC1 at 1.30 p.m.

The hall was full and representatives of every organisation with which Les was involved from the recent and distant past joined the guests of honour – Les's daughter Lesley Griffiths, other close family members and friends and members of Lewisham Pensioners' Forum – in a moving celebration which sought to emphasise the life of Les as a man of vision, a true socialist and tireless political activist.

The opening address was given by the late Margaret Witham, an old friend and colleague and President of the Greater London Pensioners' Association. She spoke of Les as a tireless fighter for pensioners' rights and champion of all those working for a better life with decency and dignity in old age, and spoke for the entire pensioners' movement when she said, 'His memory will live on in the work that *we* do to try to ensure this.'

Jack Jones, President of the National Pensioners' Convention, made the following address: 'The pensioners' movement and the trade union movement have both lost a fervent spokesman, advocate and champion. Les was a fearless advocate of the pensioners' cause and devoted his energy and time to the interests of elderly people. In the process he united women with men and black people with white in defence of the Welfare State. What stands out in his history is that he was first and foremost a trade union man. He believed in the principle of solidarity. His experience in the TU movement gave him the necessary abilities when he turned his attention to the pensioners' movement. I pay tribute and salute his memory on behalf of the National Pensioners' Convention. With Les's efforts Lewisham became a beacon of light on behalf of the pensioners' movement.'

Sadly, a full record of all the addresses was not kept. Speakers represented the following organisations: Lewisham Pensioners' Forum, the National Pensioners' Convention, the British Trade Union Action Association, the London Borough of Lewisham, the Greater London Pensioners' Association, the Greater London Forum, the Lewisham and Deptford Trades Council, Age Concern (London), the London Committee on Accessible Transport, the former Electrical Trades Union, the Daily Express Chapel and the Press Branch and the Kent Miners.

A touching tribute was paid by Les's oldest friend, Harry Bacon, Chairman of Lewisham Pensioners' Forum, who spoke of their colourful experiences as young lads before the war and of Les's concern for elderly people when he was only in his twenties. He ended by mentioning Les's brilliant last speech at the Forum's ten-year celebrations, so soon after he had come out of hospital and only weeks before his death.

Ida Hackett, Secretary of the East Midlands Region of the BPTUAA, recalling the support that Les had given during the miners' strike in the Nottinghamshire coal fields, spoke of his total dedication to ordinary people. 'Our grateful thanks go to Les's family for sharing him with us. Les was a "gentle giant". He lived a rich and varied life but his first and total dedication was to the interests of ordinary people. This dedication won him tremendous respect. He had no personal ambition except to serve the movement. He could have got on, as the phrase goes, but instead of that he stayed with the grass roots. His adherence to principle was incorruptible. He was a man with such a broad vision of life, who worked to bring together peoples of all races and creeds, encouraging them to fight for their rights. He saw the pensioners' movement as carrying forward his job in the trade union movement. He showed solidarity with people in all spheres and he was a true internationalist. He opposed discrimination. To say he will be sorely missed is a gross understatement. He is one of the very few people who cannot be replaced.'

The following words were spoken by Jeremy Corbyn MP: 'We all know people through different routes and it is only at times like this that all the strands of someone's life are brought together and we see the breadth of purpose. Les had always fought for a pensioners' organisation to bring all together in one campaign; he was brilliant at bringing people together and uniting them around an objective and he was aware of all the wider issues. He understood the need for an overriding principle, that of caring for everybody on the planet.'

Jim Mallory, Leader of Lewisham Council, said that 'Les was one of the people of whom you could say "This person is Lewisham" . . . He has put Lewisham on the national map, giving the Council a great sense of pride. He was our most precious asset.'

Two specially written poems were read out and a final tribute was paid by Harry Crompton, representing the British Pensioners and Trade Union Action Association, who presented a gold medal to Lesley Griffiths. The medal had been struck as a surprise gift to her father in recognition of his work for pensioners.

Ida Hackett then recited this poem, *Mourn Not the Dead* by Ralph Chaplin which, she felt, was a fitting epitaph:

Mourn not the dead that in the cool earth lie –
Dust into dust –
The calm, sweet earth that mothers all who die
As all men must;

Mourn not your captive comrades who must dwell –
Too strong to strive –
Within each steel-bound coffin of a cell,
Buried alive;

But rather mourn the apathetic throng –
The cowed and the meek –
Who see the world's great anguish and its wrong
And dare not speak!

Her final words were: 'All his life Les dared to speak out against the wrongs in the world. I am sure that if he could speak to us now he would say, "Don't mourn, comrades, organise and fight." This is the finest tribute we can make to Les as we lower our banners and say, "Farewell, Mr Lewisham."'

APPENDIX I

The Community Award – 26 January 1993

'Tonight, the Worshipful the Mayor, Councillor John O'Shea, is presenting Les Stannard with the first Mayor's Community Award certificate. The Council motion that: "This Council recognises the tireless activity of Les Stannard in the community over many years in giving voice to Lewisham pensioners' needs and aspirations whenever possible" will be proposed by the Leader of the Council, Councillor Steve Bullock, and seconded by the Chair of the Pensioners' Committee, Councillor Dolly Hyne.'

Les Stannard's acceptance speech

Mr Mayor, Madam Mayoress, comrades and friends. When I first received the letter from the Mayor I was quite embarrassed. There are a lot more deserving people in Lewisham than me, particularly the carers who are looking after their loved ones day in and day out, very often under extremely difficult conditions and without the support that the Social Services Committee can give. However, to say that I was more than pleased to accept this is totally inadequate to express my feelings at the moment.

Mr Mayor, may I thank you for the honour that has been bestowed upon me and the pensioners' movement in Lewisham.

Forty-three years ago, after the first post-war general election, I, together with other candidates, went to Lewisham and to the New Cross Cinema to talk to our supporters and our opponents and, on that occasion, when I had to address the audience, I told them that I would still be fighting for working people in Deptford long after they had been forgotten. The tribute that you are paying me tonight, Mr Mayor, makes me feel that I have honoured that pledge and may I thank all those, my friends in the meeting hall tonight, who have helped me meet that obligation and made me the person that I am today.

It is the European Year of Older People and I want to say that I hope for solidarity between the generations – and may I reflect on some of the events of the past. I hope the Education Department, particularly in this year, will use the benefit of my generation before we pass on, in order to enable us to talk about living history. Today, especially today, when prominent historians question the role of Churchill in World War II and ask whether he did the right thing in opposing Hitler and Mussolini, they, the historians, can't understand what Thatcherism or Nazism mean. It is too late for those people who laid down their lives in the war, and for the civilians who were bombed out in the air raids over London, to convince them otherwise; but I am pleased with those of you who will allow my generation, while it still exists, to talk to young people about those things that future historians will confuse children about.

Already politicians have failed to solve the economic conundrums. Neo-Nazi groups are re-emerging in Germany and France; Yugoslavia is tearing itself apart. Perhaps the younger generation can learn from us tonight about the mistakes we once made. Perhaps you will allow me, at this meeting, to comment on what the older generation did for me when I was young. It might put the idea of solidarity between the generations into perspective.

I would like to thank my grandmother and grandfather who were of great assistance to my mother and father in the trying days of the twenties and thirties. Many people who can't pay their mortgages now might think again about whether they can look after grandparents or grandchildren in order to let other people go to work. My grandparents kept my family's head above water with what they did for us.

I would also like to thank two of your predecessors, Councillors Chisnall and Wild, who in the 1930s persuaded the Deptford Labour Party and the old Deptford Borough Council to put street lighting into every street in Deptford. It gave quite a considerable number of young people, including myself and Harry Bacon (down there), a chance to be trained electricians and gave us an opportunity to earn a living for over fifty years both in civilian life and in the services.

I learned a lot from two people in the South-East Branch of the Electrical Trade Union (the ETU as it then was) – Bill Benson and Bill Smith, who said to me, as a teenager, that good trade unionism and job organisation are essential if working people were going to improve their lives.

May I thank two ladies, very active in Deptford politics until their deaths – my old friend Kath Duncan and Nora Sheedy, who taught me that socialism wasn't a pipe dream, but something that had to be worked for if working people were to have control over their lives and the economic facilities and the freedom to exercise it.

One of your former colleagues, Jack Waldron, Secretary of the Deptford Trades Council, with his colleague Bill Trop, soon showed me that the revolution was not around the corner and that much hard work had to take place between Trades Council meetings. All these people have played an important part in my development and have encouraged me to speak up and join the debate – often against policies that have been operated by the present majority party and their trade union colleagues, particularly when they thought that workers should pay for the economic problems and operated a wage freeze policy.

May I thank my wife Gladys and my daughter Lesley, for their toleration in putting up with consequences that arose from events over the last forty years and, above all, may I thank my former workmates who are here tonight, who often encouraged the employers to give me work with electrical contractors when my name was mud.

Like the old Deptford Council, with its electric light, in Lewisham, in this past decade, we have developed important projects which will be equally important in the history of Lewisham. I'd like to thank the former leader Dave Sullivan and the present leader Steve Bullock, and all of you councillors for making those decisions.

May I go on to refer to Millwall Football Club and the Millwall in the Community Scheme – not only has it taken the lead, not only has it been a lead for other football clubs and local authorities throughout Britain, it has weaned many young people away from becoming football hooligans and, more importantly, it is stopping the young people of today from becoming the next century's neo-Fascists. All races live in harmony in Lewisham today and I hope they will for years to come.

Now, may I speak about the real issue of the meeting. In setting up the Pensioners' Forum, Lewisham Council not only extended democracy to an important section of the population – those people who have been paid off (!) – but by setting up the Lewisham Pensioners' Committee within the Council's structure, they have set up a formula which pensioners' groups and local authorities in other parts of Britain are aiming to achieve; later generations will thank you for your foresight.

May I thank the original co-ordinator, Helen Tomkins, for the work she has done in helping develop the Forum and its organisation, and the present co-ordinator Alison Purshouse for continuing her work. May I thank Waheeda Malick and Elizabeth Sclater from the Central Policies Unit and the Equal Opportunities Unit of the Council for the support they have given. Not to forget the other Council workers who we need to do business with from time to time. May I thank the organisations which offer a service to pensioners, like Age Concern and Pensioners Link, which works alongside it.

May I thank Asquith Gibbes and Sue Mead at the Lewisham Racial Equality Council – without them we would not have maintained our existence. The Forum today is involved in a wide spectrum of issues, far more extensive than we ever imagined. Without the Management Committee, and the support from the members of the Lewisham Pensioners' Action Group, who are the motor of the pensioners' movement and numerous other pensioners' groups in Lewisham, we would be unable to maintain the commitment we need to present the pensioners' case.

The policies that have been discussed at Lewisham Pensioners' Forum have been debated in the movement also in London, Britain and Europe. 1993 has been proclaimed the Year of Older People and pensioners will use it as a year to establish pensioners' rights as they are laid down in the British Pensioners Charter and the Declaration of Intent.

We will maintain our fight for universal benefits, irrespective of what the present government and the Tory 'No Turning Back' Group says, and all those people in the majority party who think that the Social Justice Committee is going to enable party members who have adopted Tory ideas to introduce means-testing by the back door – well, may I say, you've set up the very organisation in the Pensioners' Forum that's going to argue tooth and nail with those kinds of people!

In the next few weeks, due to government financial restrictions, you will be making hard decisions about elderly people. We live in trying times and I hope that when contemplating your decisions, you might come along to us and say that we ought to gee up the Treasury in order to make a few more bob available to look after the people of Lewisham. I refer particularly to community care where everybody knows that there's not going to be enough money coming over. Unfortunately, when I looked at the television I saw a reference to Marden Court. I don't know what's happened there but, originally, when the Kent homes were on TV we came to the first or second meeting of the Pensioners' Committee and said that we did not want the same thing to happen in Lewisham. Now, with the development of our residential homes panel we have been able to see that people are being looked after properly and I hope that you are going to be able to make the money available for that to continue.

Friends, in order to proclaim equality the European Commission has decided that men and women should retire at the same age. I hope they say they are going to have the same pension and I hope this government is not going to force women to work till 65 if they don't want to . . .

May I thank you most sincerely, Mr Mayor, for the honour that you've given me tonight. There's comrades here from the Greater London Forum for the Elderly. The Assistant General Secretary of the British Pensioners Movement (the BPTUAA) is here. I hope we've done you justice in the Pensioners' Forum. Men like Jack Jones and Fred Baker are synonymous with the pensioners' movement and today, because of the tools you have given us, Lewisham Pensioners' Forum is as well and I thank you for it. I thank you.

APPENDIX II

Les Stannard's last speech on the tenth anniversary of Lewisham Pensioners' Forum, 25 September 1996

Madam Mayor, may I express how pleased I am to speak at this Tenth Anniversary Rally – the first step I hope in resuming some of my activities as one of Britain's campaigning pensioners. During the trauma I personally have faced in recent months there were times when I thought my activities would be strictly limited.

May I thank you, Madam Mayor, and your partner, for your personal support and for visiting me in Lewisham Hospital. May I thank the countless Lewisham and London pensioners for the support and good wishes they expressed to me and my family in the nineteen weeks which Gladys spent in hospital.

In the ten years of its existence Lewisham Pensioners' Forum has campaigned vigorously for the National Health Service. We have supported nurses and other NHS workers in their campaigns for better wages. We have campaigned against hospital closures – particularly against the closure of Guy's Hospital. Lewisham pensioners collected thousands of signatures in support of the Guy's campaign against closures. We are pleased that Lewisham Council campaigned with us – and placed petitions in libraries and other public offices. We are pleased that the South East London Health Commission listened and agreed that Guy's should remain open until the turn of the century.

We have supported the National Health Support Federation since it came into existence and Lewisham pensioners have been well represented at the conferences held in the Westminster Conference Centre and University College, London.

We have campaigned against Tomlinson and his policy on London hospital closures and thousands of Lewisham people signed our petition for one Health Authority for London.

May I thank the Lewisham MPs who have made Committee Rooms available at the House of Commons so that our supporters could express their views about the health services and community care. With your support we will continue to campaign in the coming months – even during the General Election – to ensure that all parties and their candidates support our position that more resources are made available for the National Health Service. Television and the south London press have both reported on the £19 million deficit in Lambeth, Southwark and Lewisham. We hope that this will not lead to a deterioration in services.

May I now talk about the Basic State Pension – it will be the subject of much discussion in the coming weeks when the Labour Party and Conservative Party Conferences take place. We are still supporters of the National Pensioners' Convention policy of universal benefits and a state pension one-third of average earnings for a single pensioner. We need, immediately, to restore the link between the pension and average earnings so that Britain's elderly people can enjoy part of the new wealth created by society. Since Mrs Thatcher's government broke the link with earnings in 1980 a single pensioner has lost £21 a week and a married couple £34 a week, yet some MPs who voted to rob pensioners then voted to give themselves a 26% rise in Parliament on 10 July 1996.

As Vice-President of the National Pensioners Convention I have accompanied Jack Jones and Jack Thain at meetings with Tony Blair, Paddy Ashdown and the Tory minister responsible for pensions. We have expressed our deep concern to Mr Blair about the policy advocated by the Borrie Commission that there should be a 'top-up' payment for pensioners now on Income Support. This policy is now advocated by Harriet Harman MP for Camberwell and Peckham – as Shadow Minister for Social Security. It is a policy pinched from Lilley and Portillo when they were members of the Tory 'no turning back group'. The top-up payment will be no good for them as they will not qualify. 88 years ago when the first basic state pension was paid, campaigners, churchmen, social workers and ordinary people wanted it paid to everybody over 70. In August 1945 in the first post-war election, people voted for Beveridge's universal benefits from the cradle to the grave.

In 1996 and into the next century there is no reason why this should not continue. There are arguments that the country can't afford it – yet we are still the seventh richest nation in the world. Some people say we must not pay too much income tax. We should remind the nation that our generation paid 33% income tax in post-war Britain to help pay for the nationalised industries that were taken under state control. If we worked over-time on Saturday afternoons to help rebuild Britain our tax went up to 40% – the rate now paid by millionaires and chairmen of former state industries!

May we say to all present, that our generation learned what 'means testing' meant in pre-World War II Britain. Our mothers, fathers and grandparents hated a 'top-up' pension whichever party operated it. To those who would extend 'means testing' we say we do not want it.

Last year we celebrated 50 years after the end of World War II – politicians from all parties patted our generation on the back for our efforts on behalf of Britain. Now, 12 months later, leading to the General Election, none of them are giving specific commitments to elderly people, except a kick in the teeth. What is clear is that we cannot put up with another government continuing the policies that have robbed us over the years. To those who say we are only looking after ourselves, we refute this: a decent state pension will be as necessary to our grandchildren as it is to us!

In 1938 Chamberlain and the Tory Party might have done a deal with Hitler – Britain's people stopped it happening. After a long struggle Fascism was defeated. In 1997–98 and the years leading to the millennium we need to draw a lesson. What our parents and our generation voted for in 1945 has not been achieved, but the younger generation can use our experience to build a people's Britain where life might be better in years to come.

In the last ten years pensioner power has become a force – make sure you give it your support to make it grow stronger.

APPENDIX III

The Les Stannard Memorial Fund

Within days, if not hours, of the announcement that Les Stannard had died in Lewisham Hospital on 8 December 1996 his colleagues vowed to set up a memorial fund in his name – a fund which would benefit the efforts and activities of pensioners' groups in Lewisham and, thus, the lives of the borough's pensioners. A board of trustees manages the fund and for the first four years the following groups which submitted the most innovative applications received a sizeable award: Lewisham Pensioners Action Group, Millwall Over 50s Club, Friends of Broadoak and Downham Elderly Health Project.

It is now intended that the remaining funds be devoted to the setting up of a permanent memorial – perhaps a library in the new Elderly People's Resource Centre which is planned for the Borough.

On 6 June 1999, a permanent bollard was unveiled in the small seating area surrounding Lewisham Clock Tower, close to where Les and his colleagues used to stand collecting signatures for petitions before they moved to their current position within the shopping centre. The stonemason's inscription on the bollard has this wording: 'Les Stannard. Pensioners' Champion and Friend of the People'.

Every year on Pensioners' Day in September a prominent speaker delivers the Les Stannard Memorial Address not only to keep Les's memory alive but also to inspire the current generation of active pensioners to continue the fight for justice. The greatest tribute that could be paid to Les and to his many pensioner colleagues who worked tirelessly during their retirement years, is that the campaign for the restoration of the earnings link has finally gained national prominence. Many of those pioneers are sadly not alive to witness the vast change in the public attitude towards the older generation and the serious attention of politicians of all parties, such that the pensioners' lobby of Parliament held in Westminster Hall on 7 November 2000 was one of the largest and most effective lobbies ever held there. While the restoration of the link with earnings has still not been achieved, the Chancellor of the Exchequer in his pre-budget speech on 8 November announced the biggest increase in the non-means-tested state pension since 1980.

BIBLIOGRAPHY

Anim-Addo. 1995. in *Longest Journey. A History of Black Lewisham*. London. Deptford Forum Publishing

Attfield, J. 1981. *With Light of Knowledge*. London and West Nyack. RACS/Journeyman Press

Baker, B. 1981. *The Far Left. An Exposé of the Extreme Left in Britain*. London. Weidenfeld and Nicolson

Bonner, A. 1961. *British Co-operation*. Manchester. Co-operative Union

Branson, N. 1985. 'Myths from Right and Left' in Fyrth (ed) *Britain, Fascism and the Popular Front*. London. Lawrence and Wishart

Branson, N. 1997. *History of the Communist Party of Great Britain*. Volumes 1–4. (1941–51) London. Lawrence and Wishart

Briggs, R. 1998. *Ethel and Ernest*. London. Jonathan Cape

Chadwick, O. 1992. *The Christian Church in the Cold War*. London. Allen Lane

Chaplin R. 'Mourn Not the Dead' (1964) in J. L. Kornbluh (ed) *Rebel Voices* (Industrial Workers of the World Anthology). Ann Arbor. University of Michigan Press

Communist Party of Britain (Pamphlet) *70 Years of Struggle – Britain's Communist Party 1920–1990*. CPB London. 1991

Co-operative Women's Guild. 1903. *The Co-operative*

Wholesale Society from the Standpoint of the Women's Co-operative Guild. Report to Annual Congress, Lincoln. 1908

Co-operative Youth (n.d.). *The Organ of the British Federation of Co-operative Youth*. Vol 1.1.No 108

Copeman, F. 1948. *Reason in Revolt*. London. Blandford Press

Davies, Margaret Llewelyn. 1904. *The Women's Co-operative Guild 1883–1904*. Women's Co-operative Guild

Dismantling the Health Service: A Reply to 'Patients First'. 1980. Communist Party of Great Britain: Social Services Advisory Committee

Docklands Action News. September 1984. *Bulletin of the Campaign to Restore Democracy in Docklands*

Dromey, J. and Taylor, G. 1978. *Grunwick: The Workers' Story*. London. Lawrence and Wishart

Electrical Trades Union. *Report on the Proceedings for Policy Conferences*. 1948–56

Electrical Trades Union London District Committee in conjunction with the Labour Research Department. 1938. *The Film Strike: The Projectionists' Case*. London

Electrical Trades Union. *Minutes of the London S. E. Branch*. May 1946 to March 1947

Electrical Trades Union. *Light and Liberty. Souvenir of 50 Years of the ETU 1889–1939*. Foreword J. Rowan. Hayes. ETU Publications

End The Ban (n.d.) Published by Communist Party Members of the EETPU

Fishman, Nina. 1995. *The British Communist Party and the Trade Unions 1933–45*. London. Scolar Press

Fyrth J. 1985. *Britain, Fascism and the Popular Front*. London. Lawrence and Wishart

Gaffin J. and Thoms, D. 1993. *Caring and Sharing: The Centenary History of the Co-operative Women's Guild*. Manchester. Holyoake Books. 2nd Edition

Glazebrook, George. 1989. *Where No Flowers Grow – A Child's Eye View of Deptford 1921–31*

Goodman, G. 1985. *The Miners' Strike*. London. Pluto Press

Halley J. L. 1988. *Squadrons of the RAF and Commonwealth 1918–1988*. Air-Britain Historians Ltd. Tonbridge

Hanson, Eric O. 1987. *The Catholic Church in World Politics*. New Jersey. Princeton University Press

Heller, F., Wilders, M., Abell, P. and Warner, M. (n.d.) *What do the British Want from Participation and Industrial Democracy?* Anglo-German Foundation for the Study of Industrial Society. Bonn and London.

High Courts of Justice, Queen's Bench Division. *Proceedings of the 1960 Court Case B No 1846*

Jacobson, D. 1992. *The Evidence of Love*. London. Allison and Busby

Jedin, H. (ed). 1981. 'The Church in the Modern Age' in *History of the Church*. Volume X. London. Burns and Oates

Joint Industry Board for the Electrical Contracting Industry. (n.d.) *Handbook*

Jones, J. 1986. *Union Man – an Autobiography*. London. Collins

Kenny, M. 1995. 'Communism and the New Left' in Andrews, Fishman and Morgan (ed) *Opening the Books – Essays on the Social and Cultural History of British Communism*. London. Pluto Press

Kershaw, R. and Pearsall, M. 2000. *Immigrants and Aliens*. Kew. Public Records Office

L'Estrange, Ewan C. 1947. *Early Surnames of Devonshire, from the Exchequer Subsidy Roll 1332*. Self-published. Paignton, Devon

Lewisham Pensioners' Forum. *Annual Reports 1988 to 1999*

Lightbown, C. (n.d.). *Millwall in the Community* (with photographs by Chris Schwarz). London. Millwall Football Club

Lloyd, J. 1990. *Light and Liberty – History of the Electrical,*

Electronic Telecommunication and Plumbing Union (EETPU). London. Weidenfeld and Nicolson

London Borough of Lewisham. Minutes and Agenda Papers of the Pensioners' Committee 1986 to 1996

Lynes, T. 1985. *Maintaining the Value of Benefits*. Family Income Support Part 7. No 638. Policy Studies Institute

National Pensioners' Convention. 1998. *Pensions – not Poor Relief*. London. NPC

National Pensioners' Convention. Research Committee 1999. *Pensions – Who Pays?* London. NPC

National Pensioners' Convention. 1999. *The Unwanted Generation – A Response by the National Pensioners' Convention to the Government's Green Paper 'A New Contract for Welfare – Partnership in Pensions'*

Peck J. (ed) 1992. *The Chomsky Reader*. London. Serpent's Tail

Pope Pius XII. 1949. *Selected Letters and Addresses*. London. Catholic Truth Society

Public Records Office. AIR 25 Pieces 795–804 (RAF 202 Group); AIR 26 Ref. 358 (RAF 256 Wing); AIR 27 (24, 112 and 148 Squadron); AIR 29 Ref 776 (RAF Unit 136 Mobile Aircraft Depot (MAD) – later named Advanced Aircraft Depot)

Reaney, P. H. 1967. *The Origin of English Surnames*. London. Routledge

Reaney, P. H. and Wilson, R. M. 3rd Edition 1991. *A Dictionary of English Surnames*. London. Routledge

Rhodes, R. 1998. *An Arsenal for Labour*. Manchester. Holyoake Books

Rolph, C. H. 1962. *All Those in Favour: The ETU Trail*. London. Andre Deutsch

Royal Arsenal Co-operative Society Education Department. *Comradeship and Wheatsheaf*. Co-operators' Monthly Journal (1934 edition)

Royal Arsenal Co-operative Society. Minutes of the Political Purposes Committee. 1922–86. British Library

Sanders, J. 1989. *Across Frontiers*. London. Canary Press

Schaffer, G. 1949. *Light and Liberty – 60 Years of the ETU*. With an introduction by W. C. Stevens. Hayes. ETU Publications

Steele, J. 1993. *Turning the Tide – The History of Everyday Deptford*. London. Deptford Forum Publishing

Stevens, W.C. (foreword). 1952. *Light and Liberty. Official History of the ETU*. Hayes. ETU Publications

Towers, B., Cox, D. and Chell, E. September 1981. 'Do Worker Directors Work?' in *Employment Gazette* No 384

University of Warwick. Modern Records Centre. TUC Records of Deptford Trades Council and of Lewisham and Deptford Trades Council correspondence. (79/D/2 and 79/D/2/8 and 79/L 3 and 4)

Webb, C. 1927. *The Woman with the Basket – the History of the Women's Co-operative Guild, 1883–1927*. Manchester. Co-operative Wholesale Society

Woddis, R. 1978. 'Ethics for Everyman' in *The Woddis Collection*. London. Barrie and Jenkins

Wyatt, W. 1956. *The Peril in Our Midst*. London. Phoenix House

Wyatt, W. 1985. *Confessions of an Optimist*. London. Collins

INDEX

INDEX